As For Me —

MY PRAYER

AS FOR ME —

MY PRAYER

A COMMENTARY ON THE DAILY PRAYERS

by

NISSAN MINDEL

SIXTH PRINTING

Published by

Merkos L'Inyonei Chinuch, Inc.
770 Eastern Parkway
Brooklyn, N.Y. 11213 (718) 774-4000
5745 ● 1984

Printed in the United States of America
BOOK-MART PRESS, Inc.
N. Bergen, N.J. 07047

As for me, may my prayer unto You, O G-d,
Be in a time of grace,
O G-d, in the abundance of Your mercy,
Answer me in the truth of Your Salvation.

PSALM 69:14

ACKNOWLEDGMENTS

To my colleague, Dr. Gershon Kranzler, for helpful cooperation.

To my wife, Nettie Mindel, for editorial assistance and proofreading.

To my daughter, Frida Schapiro, for preparing the Indexes.

TABLE OF CONTENTS

vii

viii

SONG OF THE DAY   שיר של יום

AFTERNOON PRAYER — תפלת מנחה

EVENING PRAYER — תפלת ערבית

GRACE AFTER MEALS — ברכת המזון

קריאת שמע שעל המטה
PRAYER BEFORE RETIRING TO BED

INDEXES — מפתחות

PREFACE

The present volume is not a translation of the *Siddur*, but rather a commentary and an exposition. Quotations and excerpts from the prayers, in their English rendition, are presented primarily for the purpose of spotlighting the main themes, ideas, and concepts contained in the prayers. In such instances the author frequently chose to render his own translation where he felt that his version would more accurately reflect the thoughts behind the text.

Our daily prayers consist almost entirely of selections and readings from our sacred literature, the T'NaCh (our Holy Bible) and the Talmud. The selection and order (hence, "Siddur") of these prayers are the creation of our Divinely inspired Prophets and Sages. Thus our prayers echo the eternal and infinite word of G-d. We address ourselves to G-d in *His own words,* inasmuch as human language is too poor and too limited to convey the sublime outpouring of our Divine soul—for this is the essential meaning of *Tefilah,* "service of the heart," as explained more fully in the Introduction.

In arranging the structure of our daily prayers, our Prophets and Sages of old were mindful to select Biblical and Talmudic passages which would evoke our deepest religious feelings and inspire our soulful attachment to our Father in Heaven. But, at the same time, they were equally mindful to include texts which contain the basic truths and tenets of our faith, from elementary moral and ethical values to the highest concept of pure Mono-theism which we proclaim in the *Shema.* They clearly intended the Siddur to be both inspirational and instructive. To put it in another way, our Siddur was designed to be not only the vehicle for the "service of the heart" but also to be a vehicle for the "service of the mind." This is where *kavanah*—attunement of both the heart and the mind—comes in. Indeed, it has been said that *kavanah* is the very soul of prayer, and that "prayer without *kavanah* is like a body without a soul."

Unfortunately, human nature is such that the repetition of the prayers day after day, some sections of it three times daily, tends to reduce what should be a profound daily experience to an absent-minded recitation. To be sure, even a superficial recital of the daily prayers has value, since it cannot be devoid of an awareness of G-d and of a sense of dependence on Him. However, in order that our prayers should impress themselves upon our heart and mind, a basic knowledge, at least, of their *inner* meaning and content is indispensable.

This, then, is the main purpose of the present commentary: To bring out and expound the deeper content of our daily prayers.

Hopefully, the reader who takes time out to read through the following pages will find his knowledge of our daily prayers enriched in some measure, and his appreciation of the Siddur deepened in some degree. If so, his effort, and the author's, will be amply rewarded.

NISSAN MINDEL

Nissan, 5732
Long Beach, N. Y.

INTRODUCTION

As for me, may my prayer unto You, O G-d, be in an acceptable time; O G-d, in the abundance of Your mercy, answer me in the truth of Your salvation.

PSALMS 69:14

I

THE MEANING OF PRAYER

The Hebrew word תפלה (*Tefilah*) is generally translated into English by the word "prayer." But this is not an accurate translation, for to *pray* means to beg, beseech, implore, and the like, for which we have a number of Hebrew words which more accurately convey this meaning. Our daily prayers are not simply requests addressed to G-d to give us our daily needs, and nothing more. Of course, such requests are also included in our prayers, but by and large our prayers are much more than that, as we shall see presently.

WHY DO WE PRAY?

Prayer is a commandment of G-d;[1] G-d has commanded us to pray to Him, and to Him alone. In times of distress, we must turn to G-d for help; in times of comfort, we must express our gratitude to G-d; and when all goes well with us, we must still pray to G-d daily that He continue to show us His mercies and grant us our daily needs.

---

[1] Rambam Code, Hil. Tefilah 1:1-2.

1

In our prayers to G-d we often address Him as our Merciful Father, or as our Father in Heaven, for G-d regards us, and we regard ourselves, as His children.[2] The question may be asked, Why do we have to pray to our Father in Heaven for our daily needs? Does not G-d know our needs even better than we ourselves? Is not G-d, by His very nature, good and kind, and always willing to do us good? After all, children do not "pray" to their loving parents to feed them, and clothe them, and protect them; why should we pray to our Heavenly Father for these things?

The answer to these questions is not hard to find after a little reflection. In fact it has been amply explained to us by our great Sages, including our great Teacher and Guide Rabbi Moshe ben Maimon (Maimonides):

> *We are told to offer up prayers to G-d, in order to establish firmly the true principle that G-d takes notice of our ways, that He can make them successful if we serve Him, or disastrous if we disobey Him; that success and failure are not the result of chance or accident.*[3]

Like all other commandments which G-d has commanded us to do, not for *His* sake but for *ours*, He has commanded us to pray to Him for *our* sake. G-d does not need our prayer; He can do without our prayers, but *we* cannot do without our prayers. It is good for *us* to acknowledge our dependence on G-d for our very life, our health, our daily bread, and our general welfare. And we should do so every day, and many times a day. We must often remind ourselves that our life and happiness are a gift from our Merciful Creator, for we should then try to be worthy of G-d's kindnesses and favors to us. G-d does not owe us anything; yet He gives us everything. We should try to be the same way

---

2 Deut. 14:1.
3 Guide, III, ch. 36; see also chs. 44 and 51.

towards our fellow-men and grant favors freely. We should express our gratitude to G-d not merely in words, but in *deeds*: by obeying His commands and living our daily life the way G-d wants us to do, especially as it is all for our own good.

Knowing that G-d is good and that nothing is impossible for Him to do, we can go about our life with a deep sense of confidence and security. Even in times of distress we will not despair, knowing that in some way (best known to G-d) whatever happens to us is for our good, a blessing in disguise. We do not like to suffer, so we pray to G-d to help us out of our distress, and grant us the good that is not hidden or disguised, but the good that is *obviously* good, obvious even to our fleshy eyes and limited understanding. We gain strength, courage and hope in our trust in G-d. Our daily prayers strengthen our trust in G-d. *In G-d We Trust* has been our Jewish motto since we first became a people.[4] Its adoption by the American people when it became a "nation under G-d," commendable though it is, is, of course, not original.

A Time of Self-Judgment

Our Sages declare that the ladder which our father Jacob saw in his dream, with angels of G-d "going up and coming down on it," was also the symbol of prayer.[4a] By showing the ladder to Jacob in his dream, a ladder which "stood on the earth and reached into the heaven,"[5] our Sages explain, G-d showed Jacob that prayer is like a ladder which connects the earth with the heaven, man with G-d. The meaningful words of prayer, the good resolutions which prayer brings forth, are transformed into angels which go up to G-d, and G-d sends down angels with blessings in return. That is why Jacob saw in his dream that angels were "going up and coming down," although one would

---

[4] Exod. 14:31.
[4a] Zohar I, 149b; Torah Or, 88a; Likutei Torah, Beshallach 2ʰ
[5] Gen. 28:12.

have expected angels to come down first and then go up again.

Thus, what we said about prayer in answer to the question: "Why do we pray?" is but the first step on the "ladder" of prayer. On a higher level prayer has to do with things that are higher than the daily material needs, namely spiritual things.

The Hebrew word *tefilah* [תפלה] comes from the verb *pallel* [פלל], "to judge."[6] We use the reflexive verb *lehitpallel* ("to pray"), which also means "to judge oneself." Thus, the time of prayer is the time of self-judgment and self-evaluation. When a person addresses himself to G-d and prays for His blessings, he must inevitably search his heart and examine himself whether he measures up to the standards of daily conduct which G-d had prescribed for man to follow. If he is not one who fools himself, he will be filled with humility, realizing that he hardly merits the blessings and favors for which he is asking. This is why we stress in our prayers G-d's infinite goodness and mercies, and pray to G-d to grant us our heart's desires not because we merit them, but even though we do not deserve them. This is also why our prayers, on week-days, contain a confession of sins which we may have committed knowingly or unknowingly. We pray for G-d's forgiveness, and resolve to better ourselves. Prayers help us to lead a better life in every respect, by living more fully the way of the Torah and Mitzvoth which G-d commanded us.

AVODAH — SERVICE

On a still higher level, prayer becomes *avodah*, "service." The Torah commands us "to serve G-d with our hearts,"[7] and our Sages say: "What kind of service is 'service of the heart?'—it is prayer."[8] In this sense, prayer is meant to purify our hearts and our nature.

---

6 E.g. Ps. 106:30.
7 Deut. 11:13.
8 Taanith 2a.

The plain meaning of *avodah* is "work." We work with a raw material and convert it into a refined and finished product. In the process, we remove the impurities, or roughness, of the raw material, whether it be a piece of wood or a rough diamond, and make it into a thing of usefulness or beauty. The tanner, for example, takes raw hide and by various processes converts it into a fine leather. The parchment on which a Sefer-Torah is written, or a Mezuzah, or Tefillin, is made of the hide of a kosher animal. So is raw wool full of grease and other impurities, but through various stages of "work" it is made into a fine wool, from which we can make not only fine woolens for our clothes, but also a Tallith, or Tzitzith.

The Jewish people have been likened in the Torah to soil and earth, and have been called G-d's "land of desire."[9] The saintly Baal Shem Tov, the founder of Chasiduth, explained it this way: The earth is full of treasures, but the treasures are often buried deep. It is necessary to dig for them; and when you discover them, you still have to clear away the impurities, refine them or polish them, as in the case of gold, or a diamond, and the like. So is every Jew full of wonderful treasures of character—modesty, kindness and other natural traits, but sometimes they are buried deep and covered up by "soil" and "dust," which have to be cleared away.

We speak of a person of good character as a "refined" person, or a person of "refined" character. It entails an effort, and very often a hard effort, to overcome such things as pride, anger, jealousy and similar bad traits, which may be quite "natural" but still unbecoming for a human being, least of all for a Jew.

Tefilah, in the sense of *avodah,* is the "refinery" where the impurities of character are done away with. These bad character traits stem from the "animal" soul in man, and are "natural" to it. But we are endowed with a "Divine" soul, which is a spark of

---

9 Malachi 3:12.

G-dliness itself,[10] and the treasury of all the wonderful qualities which make a man superior to an animal. During prayer, our Divine soul speaks to G-d, and even the animal soul is filled with holiness. We realize that we stand before the Holy One, blessed be He, and the whole material world with all its pains and pleasures seems to melt away. We become aware of the *real* things that really matter and are truly important, and even as we pray for life, health and sustenance, we think of these things in their deeper sense: a life that is worthy to be called "living"; health not only physical, but above all spiritual; sustenance—the things that truly sustain us in this world and in the world to come, namely the Torah and Mitzvoth.

We feel cleansed and purified by such "service," and when we return to our daily routine, the feeling of purity and holiness lingers on and raises our daily conduct to a level which is fitting for a member of the people called a "kingdom of priests and a holy nation."[11]

TEFILAH — ATTACHMENT

The highest level on the "ladder" of prayer is reached when we are so inspired as to want nothing but the feeling of attachment with G-d. On this level *Tefilah* is related to the verb (used in Mishnaic Hebrew) *tofel,* to "attach," or "join," or "bind together," as two pieces of a broken vessel are pieced together to make it whole again.[12]

Our soul is "truly a part of G-dliness," and it therefore longs to be reunited with, and reabsorbed in, G-dliness; just as a small flame when it is put close to a larger flame is absorbed into the larger flame. We may not be aware of this longing, but it is there

---

10 Tanya, beg. ch. 2.

11 Exod. 19:6.

12 Tos. Pesachim 5:9.

nevertheless. Our soul has, in fact, been called the "candle of G-d."[13] The flame of a candle is restless, striving upwards, to break away, as it were, from the wick and body of the candle; for such is the nature of fire—to strive upwards. Our soul, too, strives upwards, like the flame of the candle. Such is its nature, whether we are conscious of it, or not. This is also one of the reasons why a Jew naturally sways while praying. For prayer is the means whereby we attach ourselves to G-d, with a soulful attachment of "spirit to spirit," and in doing so our soul, as it were, flutters and soars upward, to be united with G-d.[14]

Let us consider this idea a little closer.

Every Mitzvah which G-d has commanded us to do, and which we perform as a sacred commandment, attaches us to G-d. The word *Mitzvah* is related to the (Aramaic) word *tzavta*, "together-ness," or "company." In English, too, we have the word to "enjoin," which means to "command," for the commandment is the bond that joins together the person commanded with the person commanding, no matter how far apart the commander and the commanded may be in distance, rank or position. When a king commands a most humble servant to do something, this immediately establishes a bond between the two. The humble servant feels greatly honored that the king has taken notice of him and has given him something to do, and that he, an insignificant person, can do something to please the great king. It makes him eager to be worthy of the king's attention and favor.

If this is so in the case of every Mitzvah, it is even more so in the case of prayer. For nothing brings man closer to G-d than prayer, when prayer is truly the outpouring of the soul and, therefore, makes for an "attachment of spirit to spirit," as mentioned earlier. If any Mitzvah brings us closer to G-d, prayer

---

13 Prov. 20:27.
14 Tanya, chs. 19, 46.

(on the level of which we are speaking) is like being embraced by G-d. It gives us a wonderful spiritual uplift and blissfulness, than which there is no greater pleasure and fulfillment.

Prayer, we said, is like a "ladder" of many rungs. To get to the top of it, we must start at the bottom and steadily rise upwards. In order to be able to do so, our prayers have been composed prophetically by our saintly prophets and sages of old, and have been ordered also like a "ladder," steadily leading us to greater and greater inspiration. We must, therefore, become familiar with our prayers: first of all their plain meaning, then their deeper meaning, and finally, with the whole "order" of our service.

II

THE THREE DAILY PRAYERS

Jewish Law makes it our duty to pray three times daily: in the morning, in the afternoon and at nightfall. These prayers are called *shacharith* (morning prayer), *minchah* (afternoon prayer) and *arvith*, or *ma'ariv* (evening prayer).

Our Sages tell us that the custom of praying three times a day was originally introduced by our Patriarchs, Abraham, Isaac and Jacob. Abraham introduced prayer in the morning, Isaac—in the afternoon, and Jacob added one at night.[15]

In the *Zohar*[16] (where the inner meaning of the Torah is revealed) and in Chabad[16a] it is explained further that each of the three Patriarchs represented a particular quality which they introduced into the service of G-d. Abraham served G-d with *love;* Isaac—with *awe;* Jacob—with *mercy.* Not that each lacked the

---

15 Berachoth 26b; Ber. Rabba ch. 68.

16 Zohar I, 96a, and frequently.

16a Torah Or, 17a, f., 23d f., etc.

qualities of the others, but each had a particular quality which was more in evidence. Thus Abraham distinguished himself especially in the quality of *kindness* (חסד) and *love* (אהבה), while Isaac excelled especially in the quality of strict *justice* (דין) and *reverence* (יראה), while Jacob inherited both these qualities, bringing out a new quality which combined the first two into the well-balanced and lasting quality of *truth* (אמת) and *mercy* (רחמים). We, the children of Abraham, Isaac and Jacob, have inherited all these three great qualities of our Patriarchs, and this enables us to serve G-d and pray to Him with love and fear (awe)˙ and mercy. The quality of mercy comes in when we realize that our soul is a part of G-dliness, and we feel pity for it because it is so often distracted from G-d by the material aspects of the daily life.

When the Torah was given to us at Mount Sinai, our way of life was set out for us by G-d. *Torah* means "teaching," "instruction," "guidance"; for the Torah teaches us our way of life in every detail of our daily life. The Torah contains 613 commandments. Among them is the command to "serve G-d with all our heart and all our soul."[17] How do we serve G-d with our heart? By praying to Him. In doing so, we fulfill not only the commandment of praying to G-d, but also other commandments, such as to love G-d and to fear Him, which are separate commandments.

During the first one thousand years, or so, since the time of Mosheh Rabbenu, there was no set order of prayer. Each individual was duty-bound to pray to G-d every day, but the form of prayer and how many times a day to pray was left to the individual.[18]

There was, however, a set order of service in the Beth-Hamikdash in connection with the daily sacrifices, *morning* and *evening,*

---

[17] Deut. 11:13.
[18] Rambam, Hil. Tefilah 1:3.

while the evening sacrifice extended into the *night*. On special days, such as Shabbos, Rosh-Chodesh and Festivals, there were also "additional" (*musaf*) sacrifices. Accordingly, it was perhaps not unusual for some Jews to pray three times a day, morning, evening and night, in their own way. King David, for example, declared that he prayed·three times daily,[19] and Daniel (in Babylon) prayed three times daily facing in the direction of Jerusalem.[20] There is evidence that there were, even during the time of the first Beth Hamikdash, public places of prayer, called *Beth-Ha'am*,[21] which the Chaldeans (Babylonians) destroyed when they destroyed Jerusalem and the Beth-Hamikdash.

After the Beth-Hamikdash was destroyed and the Jews were led into captivity in Babylon, Jews continued to gather and pray in congregation. The places of prayer became like "small sanctuaries"—*Beth-Mikdash-me'at*.[22] But during the years of exile, the children who were born and brought up in Babylon lacked adequate knowledge of the Holy Tongue (Hebrew) and spoke a mixed language. Therefore, when the Jews returned to their homeland after the seventy years' exile was over, Ezra the Scribe together with the Men of the Great Assembly (consisting of prophets and sages, 120 members in all) fixed the text of the daily prayer (*Shemone Esrei*—the "Eighteen Benedictions"), and made it a permanent institution and duty in Jewish life to recite this prayer three times daily. Ever since then it became part of Jewish Law (*Halachah*) for each and every Jew to pray this ordained and fixed order of prayer three times daily, corresponding to the daily sacrifices in the Beth-Hamikdash, with additional (*musaf*) prayers on Shabbos, Rosh-Chodesh and Festivals, and a special "closing" prayer (*Ne'ilah*) on Yom Kippur.

---

19 Ps. 55:18.
20 Daniel 6:11.
21 Jeremiah 39:8.
22 Ezra 11:16.

Thus, the main parts of the daily prayers were formulated by our Sages. These included the *Shema* and *Shemone Esrei,* which still are the main parts of our morning and evening prayers, while the *Shemone Esrei* is the main part of the *Minchah* service also. The daily Psalm (from *Tehillim*) which used to be sung by the *Leviim* (Levites) in the Beth-Hamikdash, became part of the morning prayer. Other Psalms of David were included in the morning prayer, and special benedictions before and after the *Shema* were added. By the time the *Mishnah* was recorded by Rabbi Judah the Prince (about the year 3910—some 500 years after Ezra), and especially by the time the Talmud was completed (some 300 years later, or about 1500 years ago), the basic order of our prayers, as we know them now, had been formulated.

THE SIDDUR

The *Siddur* is our traditional prayerbook, containing the three daily prayers; also the prayers for Shabbos, Rosh-Chodesh and the festivals. "Siddur" means "order," for in the Siddur we find our prayers in their proper and fixed order. Sometimes, for the sake of convenience, the Shabbos and Rosh-Chodesh prayers may be printed in a separate volume. The prayers for Rosh Hashanah and Yom Kippur are usually printed in separate volumes, called *machzor* ("cycle"). Sometimes the prayers for the Three Festivals (*Shalosh Regalim*) — Pesach, Shavuoth and Succoth — are also printed in separate volumes.

The oldest Siddur that has come down to us is the Siddur of Rav Amram Gaon, Head of the Yeshiva of Sura, in Babylon, about 1100 years ago. He had prepared it at the request of the Jews of Barcelona, Spain. It contains the arrangements of the prayers for the entire year, including also some laws concerning prayer and customs. It was copied and used not only by the Jews of Spain, but also by the Jews of France and Germany, and was in fact the standard prayer-book for all Jewish communities.

Seder Rav Amram Gaon remained in handwritten form for about 1000 years, until it was printed for the first time in Warsaw in 1865.

Rav Saadia Gaon, who was head of the Sura Yeshiva less than 100 years after Rav Amram Gaon, arranged a Siddur for the Jews in Arab countries, with explanations and instructions in Arabic. The Rambam (Rabbi Mosheh ben Maimon, also known as Maimonides), in his famous Code of Jewish Law, also prepared the order of the prayers for the whole year (including the *Haggadah* of Pesach), following the section dealing with the Laws of Prayer. One more of the old Siddurim to be mentioned is the *Machzor Vitri,* composed by Rabbi Simcha Vitri, a disciple of the great Rashi, and completed in the year 1208.

THE NUSACH

Nusach means "text" or "form," and is sometimes referred to also as *Minhag,* which means "custom" or "rite." When we pick up a Siddur, there will be an indication on the front page what *Nusach* or *Minhag* the Siddur belongs to, such as *Nusach Sfard* (Spanish), *Nusach Ashkenaz* (German), *Nusach Polin* (Polish), *Nusach Ari* (arranged according to the saintly Rabbi Yitzchak Luria), etc.

It should be understood that in all these various Siddurim the main body of the prayers is the same, but there are certain differences in the order of some prayers, minor changes also in the text of some, additions of *piyyutim* (poetical hymns composed by saintly authors).

According to the explanation of the Maggid of Mezeritch,[23] there are as many as 13 *Nuschaoth* of prayer or *Minhagim*. Each *Nusach* represents a tribe or "gate," and the Ari composed a *"General Nusach-Gate"* through which any Jew can enter into the presence of G-d.

---

[23] Disciple and successor to the Baal Shem Tov.

We have already mentioned that the *Seder Rav Amram Gaon* served as the standard *Siddur* for most Jewish communities dispersed throughout the world, inasmuch as it was based on the Talmud and Tradition. But in certain communities there were local *Minhagim* (customs), including certain *piyyutim,* which in time became standard for *those* communities. The main *Nuschaoth* were those of *Sfard and Ashkenaz,* as well as of the Italian Jews. The first printed Siddur was that of *Minhag Romi* (Roman, or Italian, Jews). It was printed in Soncino (Italy) in 1486. The first *Nusach Ashkenaz* Siddur was printed in Prague in 1513 (part 2 in 1516), and the first *Nusach Sfard* was printed in Venice in 1524. In due course many other Siddurim were printed according to the customs of Polish, Rumanian, Balkan, and other countries where the *Nusach* differed. When the saintly Rabbi Yitzchak Luria arranged the Siddur according to the Kabbalah, many communities adopted it, and a new series of *Nusach Ari* Siddurim were printed. Printers were not always careful in the printing, and errors were not uncommon. Finally, the great Rabbi Schneur Zalman of Liadi, who was both a great Talmudist and Kabbalist sifted some 60 different Siddurim and arranged the *Nusach* in accordance with the original *Nusach Ari* which became known as *Nusach Chabad.*

But whatever traditional *Nusach* one follows, it is sacred and acceptable to G-d. The important thing is to pray with devotion, with love, reverence, and mercy, as explained earlier.

THE LADDER

Whatever *Nusach* is yours, you will find the structure of the prayers basically the same. The Morning prayers begin with the *Morning Blessings,* continue with *Pesukei d'Zimra* (Psalms and sections from the T'NaCh, introduced by a benediction and concluded by a benediction), followed by the *Shema* (which is also introduced and concluded by a benediction), and then comes the main prayer, the *Shemone Esrei* ("Eighteen"—actually, nineteen benedictions), known also as the *Amidah* ("standing," because it must be recited in a standing position). Then follow a series of other prayers, concluding with *Aleinu.*

We have already mentioned that our Sages declared that the ladder which our Patriarch Jacob saw in his dream, and which "stood on the earth but reached into the heaven," was also symbolic of prayer. Indeed, our prayers are so arranged that they lead us step by step higher and closer to G-d. This will become more evident as we get better acquainted with the plain and inner meaning of the blessings and prayers.

תפלת שחרית

∘

MORNING PRAYER

ברכות השחר

MORNING BLESSINGS

מודה אני

*"I give thanks unto You, O living and eternal King,
for having restored within me my soul, with mercy;
great is Your trust."*

The first thing we become aware of when we awake from our
sleep in the morning is that we are awake and alive. When we
went to bed the night before, we were tired and exhausted, "dead-
tired"; we wake up refreshed, in both body and soul, as if we
were reborn again. It is only right that we should thank G-d for it.

Our Sages have told us that every night when we go to sleep,
our Divine soul returns to its heavenly abode and gives an account
of the good deeds and bad which the soul, in partnership with
the body, had done during the day. Indeed, in the prayer before
going to bed we say, "Into Your Hand I pledge my soul; You
have redeemed me, O G-d, G-d of truth."[1] A pledge is something
that the debtor gives to the creditor as security that the debt
would be paid, and usually the creditor will not return the pledge
as long as the debtor still owes him money. But G-d is very
merciful, and although every day we are indebted to Him, He
returns our soul to us.

Furthermore, our Sages declare: When a person gives a pledge,
even if it is a new thing, it becomes old and stained by the time

---

[1] Ps. 31:6.

17

it is returned. But G-d returns our "pledge" new and polished, even though it had been "used," and so it is written, "They are new every morning; great is Your trust."[2] How grateful we must be to G-d![2a]

Incidentally, the fact that we go to bed "dead tired" and wake up refreshed, returning from the unconscious world of slumber, is something like a "revival of the dead." It strengthens our conviction of the "Resurrection of the Dead" (תחית המתים), and this adds further meaning to the words "great is Your trust," for we have absolute trust in G-d, not only that He will return our soul in the morning, but also will return our soul into our body at the end of days, when all the righteous dead will rise from their "sleep." (We affirm this clearly in the second blessing of the *Shemone Esrei*—ונאמן אתה להחיות מתים—"You are trustworthy to revive the dead.")

Modeh ani is said immediately upon our awakening, even before we have washed our hands, because G-d's proper Name is not mentioned in this prayer, but only "King."

על נטילת ידים

"Blessed are You, O G-d our L-rd, King of the universe, Who has sanctified us with His commandments, and commanded us concerning the washing of the hands."

This is the very first blessing we make in the morning, and we recite it after we have washed our hands in the proper manner, before drying them.

Let us consider the meaning of a blessing in general.

Generally speaking, there are two main kinds of blessings:

---

2 Eichah 3:23.
2a Midrash Tehillim on Ps. 31:6, Eichah Rabbathi on 3:23.

Blessings which we have to make before eating or drinking anything (*Birechoth Hanehenin*), and the blessings which we have
to make before performing the Mitzvoth.

A blessing before eating or drinking anything is an expression
of gratitude to G-d for having given us all the good things to eat
and drink. If we ate or drank anything without making a blessing
first, it would be like enjoying a party without thanking the host
for his kindness.

As to the blessing we make before performing a Mitzvah,
such as, putting on Tzitzith or Tefillin, eating in the Succah, performing the Mitzvah of the Lulav, and so on, it is also an expression of gratitude but in a different sense. In this blessing we add
the words, "Who has sanctified us by His commandments and
commanded us to . . ." Here we thank G-d for having given us
the privilege of serving Him and fulfilling His commands, for
through this service we become attached to G-dliness and share
in G-d's holiness and perfection, as has been noted above in
explaining the term *Mitzvah*.[2b]

We should note at once the structure of the blessing, which is
the same in all similar blessings, which we make before performing any Mitzvah: We begin in the *second* person ("Blessed are
You") and end up by using the form of the *third person* ("Who
has . . ."). One of the reasons for this is as follows: We begin
with the second person, because we are speaking to G-d, in His
very Presence, feeling very close to *our* G-d. But G-d is also the
"King of the Universe,"—the infinitely great and majestic King,
Who has created the universe and rules it with a knowledge and
power beyond our understanding, as if He were hidden from us.
Thus, G-d is both present and "absent," revealed and hidden.
We can see some of G-d's power and wisdom as it is manifested
in the world around us, but His essential Nature is unknown

[2b] See p. 7.

to us. This is expressed in our Holy Tongue by using both forms: *You* (Thou) and *Who* (He).

When we speak of G-d as "blessed" (ברוך), we mean that G-d is the *source* of all blessings, just as when we say that G-d is "wise," or "strong," or "good," and so on, we mean that G-d is the source of wisdom, strength, goodness, etc.

Similarly, G-d is *holy*, in the sense that He is exalted over and above this material world, and though He is present in this world He is also separate from it. Some of this quality of holiness He has bestowed upon us by giving us His commandments. For, by fulfilling His Will we are attaching ourselves to Him. In this way we, too, raise ourselves above our material life, and at the same time bring holiness into everything we do and into the world around us. This is the meaning of "Who has sanctified us [made us *holy*] by His commandments."

Having, immediately upon awakening, thanked the Living and Eternal King for restoring our soul to us, we realize that we must submit ourselves to His Will and obey His commands. And the washing of our hands is the first expression of our obedience, and this brings us into a closer relationship with G-d, Whom we may now call *our* G-d.

There are several reasons why we are commanded to wash our hands in the morning. We are ready to begin a new day of *service to G-d*. The *Kohanim* (priests), before they began their service in the Beth-Hamikdash, were commanded to wash their hands (and also feet). We, Jews, are called a "kingdom of priests and a holy nation,"[3] and the washing of our hands reminds us about it.

Another reason is that during our sleep, when our Divine soul departs, an "unclean" spirit takes over (sometimes giving rise to unclean thoughts or dreams). We therefore wash our hands of

---

[3] Exod. 19:6.

that unclean spirit, to restore the purity and cleanliness to our body and mind.

The proper way to wash our hands in the morning is by taking the pitcher or glass of water in our right hand, passing it to our left, pouring water over the right hand, then changing hands and pouring water over the left, then again on the right and left, and a third time.

There is a simple word in Hebrew for "washing" (רחץ), but this word is not used in the text of the blessing. Instead the words נטילת ידים are used, because the word נטל also means to "raise" and "uplift." This is, again, symbolic of the sacred nature of this washing of the hands, to indicate that we are lifting up and dedicating our hands, as well as the work of our hands, to G-d, our G-d, King and Master.

אשר יצר

"Blessed are You, O G-d, our L-rd, King of the Universe, Who has formed man in wisdom, and created within him many openings and passages. It is revealed and known before the Throne of Your Glory that if one of these be closed {when it should be open}, or one of these be opened {when it should be closed}, it would be imposible to exist and stand before You even for one moment. Blessed are You, O G-d, the Healer of all flesh, Who works wondrously."

As we see from the text of this blessing, it is a blessing of thanksgiving, the first of many we shall say during the morning prayer and throughout the day.

Having returned from the unconscious world of slumber, we become aware of one of the greatest miracles of this universe: our physical body, with all its fine and delicately constructed organs and vessels. The daily rebirth of our physical powers moves us to sing G-d's praises long before we realize the greatness of the Creator through the wonders of nature in the world around us.

The feeling of being healthy, refreshed, and possessing the strength and ability to live a healthy physical life calls forth our gratitude to our Creator. The "simple" processes of respiration, digestion and all other normal functions of our body are miracles of Divine wisdom; we hardly think of them, unless, G-d forbid, anything goes wrong. We would be ingrates if we were to take these blessings for granted and not thank G-d every morning for His care, as the "Healer of all flesh."

This Blessing (which is said also upon washing the hands after leaving the toilet room) is characteristic of our Jewish view that our human body is something to be kept clean and sacred. It reminds us that not merely the highest organs of the human body, but even the lowest, fulfill vital functions, upon which our wellbeing and very existence depend.

Our Sages of old marvelled at the wonders of the human body and expressed their wonderment in words similar to the above Blessing. Thus, according to the Targum, the Prophet Ezekiel rebukes the mighty king of Tyre, who had boasted of his power and wealth, by reminding him that his body was a vessel conceived with great Divine wisdom and made of passages and openings sustained miraculously by G-d, and that had he considered his own body and its delicate balances, he would not be proud, but humble and grateful.[4]

In a similar vein, another Sage, Rabbi Tanhuma,[4a] declared: A blown-up balloon, if it have a hole the size of a needle-point, would lose all its air; but the human body is full of openings, yet does not lose the breath of life.

---

[4] Ezekiel 28:12-13.
[4a] Ber. Rabba, ch. 1.

We can only thank our Creator for His "wondrous deeds" in granting us a healthy and well-functioning body, and this we do in this Blessing of "Asher Yatzar."

א־להי, נשמה

"O, my G-d, the soul which You gave me is pure: You created it, You formed it, You breathed it into me, and You will take it from me, but will restore it unto me in the future to come. So long as the soul is within me, I give thanks unto You, O L-rd my G-d, and G-d of my fathers, Master of all works, L-rd of all souls. Blessed are You, O G-d, Who restores the souls unto dead bodies."

In the blessing of *Asher Yatzar* we thanked G-d for the wonders of our body and physical health. In the present blessing, our thoughts are turned from our body to our soul, and we thank G-d for the daily miracle of the restoration of our soul to our body, as we already mentioned briefly in *Modeh ani.*

"The soul which You gave me is pure." Unlike certain other faiths which hold that man is born with a sinful soul, the Jewish faith holds that every Jew, without exception, is born with a pure soul, free from sin or any blemish. Moreover, our soul is Divine; it is a "part of G-dliness." It is created apart from the body, and survives the body. Only during our lifetime, our soul is connected with, and lives in, our body; but the soul is eternal, having existed before it came to live in the body, and continuing to exist after the body dies. The purpose of the soul's coming down to live in the body is to be able to fulfill the Divine commandments in the daily life, commandments which by and large, can only be fulfilled with the aid of the body and the bodily organs. This is why we have 248 positive commandments ("Do's") and 365 prohibi-

tions ("Don'ts"), which, our Sages declare, correspond to the
248 organs and the 365 blood vessels of our physical body.[5]
The fulfillment of the 613 Divine commandments thus purifies
the body. At the same time, most commandments are connected
with some physical object, such as wool for Tzitzith, leather for
Tefillin, wood for Succah, wax or oil for candles, and so on;
while our body is sustained by physical food, over which we make
a blessing, before and after eating or drinking anything. In this
way, we purify and make holy, not only our body, but also
Nature around us. All this we accomplish by means of our soul,
through the agency of our body. But the soul itself is pure and
holy when it comes to dwell in our body, and requires no purifi-
cation for itself.[6] Of course, the soul, too, is enriched through its
experience during its "temporary" residence in the body, and in
many respects becomes wiser and more understanding of G-dliness.

"You breathed it into me." Our Sages say that just as when
one breathes out with force, the breath comes from "within," so,
in a manner of speaking, our soul is G-d's own "deep breath."
In this way, our Sages emphasize the G-dly quality of our soul.[7]
Of this, we are, of course, told in the Torah. In the first chapter
of Genesis we are told that all living things were created alive,
their body and life coming at the same time. Man, on the other
hand, was created in the "image" of G-d, endowed with a G-dly
soul. In the second chapter of Genesis we are told that G-d first
formed man's body from the earth and "breathed into his nostrils"
a living soul. Man is therefore not just a more advanced "animal," in the "animal kingdom," but a *different* creature, a world
by himself.

"You preserve it within me." Being part of G-dliness, our soul
has a natural desire to be with G-d always, and to return to its

---

[5] Tanhuma Hakadum, Tetze; Makkoth 24a. See *The Commandments*, by Nissan
Mindel (KPS, Brooklyn, N.Y. 6th ed. 1966.).

[6] Tanya, chs. 37, 38.

[7] Zohar, quoted in Tanya, ch. 2, beg.

heavenly home, where it came from. It has no interest in material things and material pleasures, for it is pure spirit and delights only in spiritual things. Were it not for G-d Who preserves it within our body, it would fly out of our body and return to heaven. But the soul has a mission to fulfill on this earth, and G-d orders her to stay for its allotted time. Therefore, so long as the soul is within our body, we must serve G-d and fulfill His commandments, for He is our Lord and Master.

At the end of our life on this earth, our soul returns to its Creator, in the World of the Souls, where it is held to account for all that it has accomplished, or failed to accomplish, during our lifetime. When the time of the Resurrection (Revival) of the Dead will come, G-d will bring back to life the righteous dead, and the soul will return to a purified body, to enjoy everlasting life.

Thus, our sleep and our awakening are a daily reminder of our soul's eternal life. Sleep is but a sixtieth part of death, our Sages say.[8] We must always remember that our soul is pure, and we must do our best to keep it pure.

הנותן לשכוי בינה

Blessed are You, O G-d . . . Who gives the cock understanding to distinguish between day and night.

The crowing of the cock is one of the wonders which G-d implanted in Nature. By some hidden peculiar sense, the cock knows the time when the darkness of night is about to lift and give its place to the light of day.

We Jews, who see G-d's hand in every one of the innumerable wonders of Nature, praise G-d for giving the cock the understanding to sense the breaking of dawn.

---

[8] Berachoth 57b.

Normally we should have to make this blessing only when we actually hear the cock crow, just as we make similar blessings when we see or hear any natural phenomenon, such as thunder, lightning, a rainbow, or any similar natural occurrence, in all of which we Jews recognize the manifestation of G-d's power and creation. Why, then, do we make the above blessing every morning, even though we do not hear the cock crow?

The answer is that this blessing, as also the others that follow, has a deeper meaning. Day and night, light and darkness, are synonymous with good and bad, knowledge and ignorance, happiness and misery. People who live in the "dark" are those who have no knowledge of G-d. Terrible experiences are referred to as "nightmares." We speak of the "dawn" as the beginning of a new and hopeful era, after the "night" of a series of misfortunes.

Bearing this in mind, and considering that *Sechvi* ("cock") also means "heart," we can see the other and deeper meaning of this blessing. The heart is the seat of feeling and understanding. That is why we find in the Torah such expressions as a "wise heart," or an "understanding heart." Now, while G-d has given the cock a special sense to distinguish between day and night, He has given man a special sense to distinguish between good and bad. For G-d has endowed man with a Divine soul which enables him to think and to feel what is right and what is wrong.

Indeed, the famous Talmudist and Codifier Rabbenu Osher ben Yechiel, known as the ROSH (about 5010-5087; 1250-1327), tells us that this blessing does not essentially refer to the crowing of the cock, but to the ability of man to distinguish between good and bad. For this reason, Jewish Law requires us to say this blessing even if we have never heard the crowing of the cock. However, since the crowing of the cock occurs at dawn, the blessing has properly been inserted among the first morning blessings.

The logical sequence of the first morning prayers now becomes clear. First, we thank the Supreme King, the Giver of Life, for

returning our soul to our body when we awake in the morning
(*Modeh ani*). Next, we thank our Creator, the Healer of All
Flesh, for keeping our very delicate and intricate body in good
working order (*Asher Yatzar*). We continue by taking·notice of
our pure soul which G-d has given us, and which we must
endeavor to keep pure in order that we merit eternal life (*Elokai,
Neshamah*). Then we come to a series of blessings, the first of
which is the expression of our gratitude to G-d for having given
us intelligence to enable us to distinguish between bad and good.

פוקח עורים

*Blessed are You, O G-d . . . Who opens the eyes of
the blind.*

This blessing, as also several of the blessings following, reflects
the process of our changing from the state of sleeping to that
of wakefulness.

When we sleep our eyes do not function. Even if we sleep
with our eyes open, we do not see. During our sleep we are like
blind, sightless people. Therefore, when we wake up and see
again, we thank G-d for restoring to us the power of sight.

But, as we have already noted in connection with the preceding
blessing, there is a deeper meaning in the words "Who opens the
eyes of the blind." G-d has given us the gift of seeing more than
"meets the eye." We "see" not only with our eyes of flesh, but
also with our "eyes" of reason: We "see" the truth; we "see" the
hand of G-d in everything that is around us. There are people
who have perfectly good eyesight, yet they are "blind" to spiritual
matters; they cannot "see" the benevolent Divine Providence that
guides the destinies of everything and everyone; they are like
sightless people groping in the dark.

We have a commandment in our holy Torah, "You shall not

curse the deaf, nor put a stumbling block before the blind; but you shall fear your G-d."[9] Here we are commanded not to curse, or defame, anyone who cannot "hear." It does not matter whether that person is actually deaf, or is not within hearing; in either case he cannot defend himself, or clear himself. Similarly, when we are warned against tripping up a sightless man, we must not merely guard against causing physical injury to a physically blind man, but also against "tripping up" the spiritually "blind" or weak person, by leading him astray, or by showing a bad example to children, and the like. We are reminded that though the "deaf" man does not hear our words, and the "blind" man does not see the stumbling block which we place in his path, G-d does hear and see everything. We must fear G-d and beware of doing anything so wicked.

In a like manner, when we wake up in the morning, and thank G-d "Who opens the eyes of the blind," we thank Him not only for giving us *physical* eyesight, but also spiritual *insight*. We thank G-d for enabling us to understand something of His greatness and His mercy, and in doing so we must resolve to emulate His ways.

מתיר אסורים

Blessed are You, O G-d . . . Who releases the bound.

This blessing reflects the second stage in the process of awakening. During our sleep we are not in control of our movements. We are like people who are bound with ropes. But when we wake up, we feel "released"; we are again in control of our movements, and can get out of bed.

In a deeper sense, there are people who are "tied hand and foot" in a variety of ways. One may find oneself enmeshed in economic difficulties, bound by financial obligations; one may find

---

[9] Leviticus 19:14.

oneself a "prisoner" of circumstances. Worse still, a person may be a captive of his own habits and inclination, and so loses control of his actions. In all such cases, one can only turn to G-d "Who releases the bound" to help him break the chains, whatever they may be. We have this also in mind, when we say this blessing.

זוקף כפופים

Blessed are You, O G-d . . . Who raises up them that are bowed down.

King David, in the Book of Psalms,[9a] praised G-d with the words "G-d supports all the fallen, and raises up all those who are bowed down." This verse is also the origin of the above blessing. It is recited in the morning, for the same reason that the previous blessings are recited; the reason being that these blessings reflect the various stages of awakening and getting up. So with this blessing. When we get up, we stand and walk upright, and we thank G-d for "raising us up," since all our movements are possible only thanks to G-d, just as we owe our very life to G-d.

At the same time, we think of these words in the sense that King David wrote them, namely, that G-d raises up those who are "bowed down" under various burdens, economic or spiritual, or are "weighed down" by worry and anxiety. For G-d knows everybody's burdens, and He is kind and merciful in helping everyone carry one's burden, or lifting the burden altogether.

We also think of those who are "bowed down" in the sense of being humble and subservient to G-d. Humility and obedience are qualities which G-d holds in high esteem, and He "raises up" those who cultivate these fine qualities.

9a Ps. 145:14; 146:8.

Finally, this blessing provides food for further thought:

The human being is unique in that he always walks erect, in the erect posture which characterizes the human being, as distinct from the four-legged animals. There are certain creatures in the animal kingdom that *sometimes* walk erect, or that may be taught the trick of walking erect on their hind legs; but that is unusual and "unnatural" for the four-legged animals. That is why we call them *quadrupeds* ("four-legged"). The human being alone has two *legs* for walking and two *hands* for doing.

There is a deeper significance in the *upright* human form. To "walk upright" has come to mean *good conduct,* as befits a human being. The human form, and the animal (four-legged) form, represent, in a visible way, the difference between the nature and purpose of a human being and those of the dumb animals.

In the four-legged creature, the head and the tail, and the various organs of the body between the head and the tail (the breathing organs, the heart, the digestive organs, etc.) are all, more or less, on the *same level.* They all have purely *natural* functions; for the animal is a creature of the earth, so that even its head is inclined towards the earth, and is hardly higher than the tail.

In the human being, however, the head is the uppermost part of the body. It reaches out towards heaven. For the head is the seat of the intellect and Divine soul.

The intellect produces thoughts and ideas. In the human being who does not live like an animal, the thoughts and ideas are of a sublime nature; he thinks of G-d; he distinguishes between good and bad. These thoughts and ideas are expressed in *speech.* Man is called the "speaking creature." He prays to G-d, studies G-d's Torah, and worships G-d with every breath of his mouth. And so we find the breathing organs (*lungs*) directly below the brain and intellect which are in the head.

Thoughts and ideas also produce the proper feelings and attitudes, which are located in the *heart.* And so we find the human heart directly below and between the lungs. The organs of digestion are next in line, since these are connected with the lower functions, which are common to both man and animal in all respects.

Thus, the organs of the human body, contrary to those in the animal body, are placed in a significant order due to the erect *human form*, as distinguished from the animal form.

Now, when a person sleeps, and the mind is at rest, he lies prostrate in bed. In this position the head and the legs, with all other organs in between, are on the same level, as in an animal. For when the human being is inactive, not doing anything which is superior to the lower animals, he is to all intents and purposes the same as they. But when he awakes, jumps out of bed, ready to serve his Creator, he is *man* again, standing on his two feet on earth, but his head reaching out to heaven. His human stature at once marks him for the man that he is.

We, Jews, take note of the human stature every morning, and have a special blessing—זוֹקֵף כְּפוּפִים, whereby we thank G-d, our Creator, for our erect posture, symbolic of our special station in the scheme of creation. It remains up to us to "walk upright," not only physically, but also *spiritually,* in our daily conduct as human beings, and not as beasts in human form.

מַלְבִּישׁ עֲרֻמִּים

Blessed are You, O G-d . . . Who clothes the naked.

Getting dressed in the morning is, of course, one of the most natural things. But it is characteristic of the Jewish way of life that even such a simple and natural thing as putting our clothes on in the morning is an occasion for a blessing. We bless G-d Who clothes the naked.

This blessing has its origin in the narrative of the Torah, where it is stated that G-d made clothes of skins for Adam and Eve and clothed them.[10] Inasmuch as nothing in the Torah is in vain, or superfluous, and the purpose of the Torah is to instruct us ("Torah" means "instruction"), our Sages tell us that the story of G-d's clothing Adam and Eve teaches us to follow G-d's example and to clothe the needy and the poor. This is one of the first things of which this blessing reminds us.

Again, like all the other blessings discussed earlier, this blessing, too, provides further food for thought:

Man is the only living creature that has to dress himself in clothes. All other animals and birds are born with their "clothes" on, or "grow" their own "clothes"—furs, feathers, etc., which protect them from the elements: cold, heat, rain, and the like. But human beings wear clothes not just for protection against the elements. There are climates in certain parts of the world where no clothes are necessary for protection, yet even the natives of those climates wear certain coverings. Adam and Eve, too, the Torah tells us, first walked about naked, but then G-d made clothes for them to cover their nakedness. The reason for this was that before Adam and Eve sinned by disobeying G-d, they were quite innocent and free from unworthy thoughts, so they walked about without clothes and were not ashamed.[11] However, after their disobedience to G-d, they were filled with a sense of shame, realizing how easily they can fall prey to temptation. Therefore G-d provided them with clothes.

Thus, every decent human being has an inborn sense of shame to display his nakedness; or, what comes to the same thing, a sense of inborn decency and modesty to cover his body at all times.

---

10 Gen. 3:21.
11 Gen. 2:25.
11a Tanya, ch. 5 etc.; Iggereth Hakodesh, ch. 29.

The standards of modesty insofar as clothing is concerned, differ for various people. The Jewish people have their own standard of modesty, called *Tzniuth*, laid down by Jewish Law and by the traditions hallowed over the ages. These laws include, among other things, the covering of the head by married women, avoidance of exposure of parts of the body which should be covered, and generally the utmost modesty in every way. The blessing of מלביש ערומים is thus a timely reminder every morning, to observe our Jewish standards of modesty in our daily conduct.

In a deeper sense, still, our Sages speak of "clothes" in terms of Mitzvoth and good deeds, the "garments" of the soul. The soul, like the body, requires "food" and "clothes," except that the soul's food and clothes are *spiritual*: knowledge of the Torah is the "food" of the soul; the observance of the Mitzvoth and the practice of good works in the daily life are the "garments" of the soul. Therefore, just as the blessing reminds us of our duty to feed and clothe the needy and poor, so are we reminded of our duty to "feed" and "clothe" our own souls, as well as the souls of those that are poor in spiritual matters. We must help them to acquire more knowledge of the Torah and Mitzvoth and Jewish way of life, so that they should be well-fed and well-dressed in every respect, materially as well as spiritually.

הנותן ליעף כח

Blessed ... Who gives strength to the weary.

Having opened our eyes after a good night's sleep, having stretched our limbs, straightened our back, and clothed ourselves (in the order of the blessings, discussed previously), we are now ready to begin the new day with fresh vigor. The blessing "Who gives strength to the weary" therefore follows in logical order.

The miracle of rest and renewed strength is experienced every morning, when we rise from our sleep to begin the new day with renewed energy. But, as in the case of many other wonders which we see daily, or at regular intervals, like the rising of the sun and the changing of the seasons, our attention is not usually excited by these events. Thus, our prayers and blessings remind us not to take things for granted. This is why we say the blessing "Who gives strength to the weary" in the morning, so that we should thank our Creator for His wonderful kindness and infinite wisdom and power in making it possible for His creatures to rise every morning full of strength to perform their duties.

The text of the blessing is derived from *Isaiah,* where, in a beautiful passage the prophet declares:

> The Creator of the ends of the earth faints not, neither does He become weary. . . . He gives strength to the weary, and to him who has no might He increases power. Even the youths may be faint and weary, and the young men may utterly stumble. But they that hope to G-d shall renew their strength. . . .[12]

The prophet tells us that strength is not necessarily a quality found in youth; it is, however, always found in *hope,* and in confidence. Consider: two persons, one young and the other old, walking the same road, or climbing the same mountain, with the goal far out of sight; who will reach it: the young one, starting out with full strength, but with little hope, or the old one, lacking in strength, but full of hope? The youth will soon get out of breath, and, despairing of ever attaining the goal, will give it up in frustration. But the old man will steadily forge ahead constantly renewing his strength by hope and confidence. This is what the prophet tells us: Physical strength will be of no avail, where

---

[12] Isaiah 40:28-31.

there is no hope, but "they that hope in G-d will renew their strength."

And so, when we start a new day, which may be a difficult one, it is good to bear in mind that it is G-d "Who gives strength to the weary." With hope and trust in G-d, no road is too long or too hard, and no obstacles are too difficult.

רוקע הארץ על המים

Blessed . . . Who spreads the earth over the waters.

The text of this blessing comes from Psalm 136:6, which reads "[Give praise to G-d. . . .] to Him Who spreads the earth over the waters, for His kindness endures forever."

As we are about to take our first step (which is the subject of the blessing immediately following), we remember G-d's kindness in creating the world in such a way that the earth is spread out *over* and above the waters, so that we can live on dry land. On the third day of Creation—we read in the beginning of Bereishith—G-d ordered the waters, which covered the earth, to gather into one place, so that dry land should appear. And this is how the seas and oceans were formed, covering the greater part of our globe. Large masses of water remained *under* the earth's surface, from which come the wells and springs of fresh water. Thus our earth is surrounded by water, and is "spread" *over* water. Were the land masses on the same level, or below the level, of the water, the earth would be flooded and uninhabitable. Furthermore, though earth and rocks are heavier than water, the waters below the earth's crust remain trapped and do not burst forth in a destructive flood. (It was only during the Flood at the time of Noah, that G-d opened "the springs of the great deep" to add to the torrential rains, and the whole earth was flooded).

It is by Divine grace ("for His kindness endures forever")
that we live on dry land, *above* the sea level, and this, too, deserves
our remembering it daily, and our constant gratitude to the Creator.

המכין מצעדי גבר

Blessed ... Who directs the steps of man

Who would consider "walking" a remarkable feat? When a
baby begins to walk, it is a cause of excitement for the happy
parents. But soon the baby learns not only to walk, but also to run
about and to jump, and the novelty wears off quickly. We do not
think it very remarkable that we are able to walk. Yet every step
involves an intricate operation of muscles and bones and joints
and balances. Only the Creator could create such a walking creature, which can walk with ease and comfort.

Thus, on reflection, we realize that "walking" is, after all, not
such a simple matter, and we owe our Creator a debt of gratitude
for it. But the blessing has yet a wider and deeper meaning. It
reminds us that man's movements, though they are quite free and
voluntary, have a deeper purpose connected with Divine Providence. This will become clear when we trace the text of this
blessing to its original source in *Psalms* 37:27, which reads:
"The steps of man are directed by G-d, and He (he) delights
in his (His) way." The saintly Baal Shem Tov, who gave us a
deeper insight into the meaning of Divine Providence, explained
this passage to mean that while a Jew goes about his business
visits people and places, which he thinks necessary for his personal
business, there is really a more important—*spiritual*—purpose in
his moving about from place to place, and meeting different
people. This is especially true when one goes to a new city, or
country, whether on a visit, or for a permanent change. The more
important reason, or purpose, is connected with something more

than his own good: It may be for the purpose of doing someone else a favor, materially or spiritually; or to spread a good influence; or to show a good example of conduct; or strengthen and spread Torah and Mitzvoth in his environment; or all of these combined.

Thus, when the Jew realizes that "the steps of man are directed by G-d," *he* (the man) will delight in *His* (G-d's) way, and *He* (G-d) will delight in *his* (man's) way (for the passage lends itself to interpretation both ways).

שעשה לי כל צרכי

Blessed . . . Who provided for me all my need.

In the Talmud[13] this blessing is associated with the tying of the shoestrings. Thus, this blessing follows in logical order the previous blessing "Who directs the steps of man."

The connection between this blessing and the tying up of the shoestrings is explained by the famed Abudraham[13a] in the sense that as long as a person is barefooted, he cannot go out to work, but when he puts his shoes on and ties them up, he is ready to go out and take care of his needs.

In making this blessing, we declare that all our needs are actually provided by G-d. Note that the past tense is used in this blessing ("provided"). The reason is that we express our conviction that all our needs are *already provided* by G-d, even before we start the day; for it has already been decreed by Divine Providence how much each person should earn that day. It is up to us to go out and make the necessary effort to "collect" what has been set aside for us. Our efforts provide *natural* channels to receive that which has already been decreed for us by the *supernatural* blessing of G-d. And so it is written, "And G-d, your G-d,

---

13 Berachoth 60b.
13a Rabbi David Abudraham completed his work in Seville, Spain in 1340.

will bless you in all that you do."[14] Our "doing" is the "channel" or "vessel," whereby or wherein we receive G-d's blessing.

Success or failure in business is not necessarily a measure of a person's cleverness or stupidity; nor of a person's industry or laziness. Ultimately "it is the blessing of G-d that makes one rich."[15] The person who realizes this, will make the *necessary* effort, but will not "kill" himself in trying to amass a fortune. He will rather use his excess energy to advance himself spiritually and intellectually. For, in the realm of the spirit and of knowledge, effort and success are indeed closely linked together.

The psychological effect of starting the day with the thought of this blessing firmly implanted in our mind, cannot be over-emphasized. The conviction that G-d provides—indeed, has already provided—all our material needs, leaves no room for anxiety and worry; for overexertion and undue mental strain. On the contrary, the person goes about his daily business with confidence; with a peaceful mind and joyous heart. Moreover, this kind of disposition is good not only for one's health, but also for one's business.

Incidentally, this blessing is not said on Yom Kippur and Tisha B'Av, since we are not permitted to put on (leather) shoes on those days.

אוזר ישראל בגבורה

Blessed . . . Who girds Israel with strength.

In the Talmud[16] this blessing is associated with putting on the belt.

In olden days, a sash or belt, used to be worn over a loose garment. It was worn for support and comfort. For the warrior,

---

14 Deut. 15:18.
15 Prov. 10:22.
16 Berachoth 60a.

the belt was especially important, because it held the weapon, such as sword, or knife (in later days—a pistol). The belt was therefore the symbol of strength and power.

For us, Jews, however, the belt has a *spiritual* meaning. According to the Abudraham, the belt is the symbol of *strong attachment,* because the belt is, of course, tightly attached to the body. And so it is written: "As the girdle cleaves to the loins of a man, so have I caused to cleave unto Me the whole house of Israel, and the whole house of Judah, says G-d; that they might be unto Me for a people, and for a name, and for a praise, and for glory."[17] In this sense, the blessing is to be understood to mean that G-d is closely attached to the Jewish people, and He is therefore the source of strength of the Jewish people. This strong attachment of G-d to the Jewish people, and of the Jewish people to G-d, is something special with the Jewish people. Through good times and bad, the Jewish people remained faithful to G-d and His Torah, and this is what gave them strength to weather all storms throughout their long history in exile among the nations of the world.

There is yet a deeper meaning to this blessing. Jewish Law requires that a belt be worn during prayer, in order to draw a line between the upper part of the body and the lower part, or, as our Sages expressed it, "that the heart should not see the lower nakedness."[17a] This emphasizes the necessity to attain the highest possible degree of purity of thought and heart during prayer. The spiritual qualities of the human being—thought, feeling, and speech—are all located in the upper organs of the body, while the lower physical functions (which are more or less common to all animals) are located in the lower organs of the body.[17b]

---

[17] Jeremiah 12:11.
[17a] Berachoth 25b.
[17b] See p. 30 above.

The belt (or, as is customary among pious Jews to put on a special sash, called a "gartel") separates the upper and lower parts of the body, and this serves to strengthen our purity of mind and heart. In this sense, the blessing "Who girds Israel with strength" speaks not of physical strength, but of strength of character and self-control, which is the true definition of strength, as our Sages said, "He is strong who conquers his (evil) inclination."[18]

Many are the temptations which confront a person during the day. The blessing "Who girds Israel with strength" reminds us that G-d has given us the strength to overcome all temptations. It is up to us to draw upon this strength, through our own will and determination to remain attached to, and united with, our G-d.

עוטר ישראל בתפארה

Blessed . . . Who crowns Israel With Glory

This blessing too, according to the Talmud,[19] is connected with an item of clothing, namely the headgear.

It will be noted that, as in the case of the preceding blessing, the word "Israel" (the Jewish people) is mentioned in this blessing. These are, in fact, the only two blessings in this series where the word "Israel" is mentioned. For, both the belt and the headgear (covering the head) have a special significance for the Jewish people. Insofar as non-Jews are concerned, the belt (as mentioned above) is worn for comfort and power (as the holder of a weapon), whereas for the Jews it has deeper meaning connected with attachment to G-d and moral strength. Similarly in regard to covering the head. Non-Jews cover their heads for protection against the elements: cold, rain, or a sun-stroke. But

18 Avoth 4:1.
19 Berachoth 60a.

for the Jew, the covering of the head has a deep meaning, associated with *Yirath Shamayim* ("Fear of Heaven"). The explanation of it is as follows:

The head is the uppermost part of the body, and it houses the brain and the intellect. From the intellect stem all those high qualities which distinguish the human being from the lower species, such as knowledge and wisdom, speech, human kindness and all other virtues. Above all, we recognize that there is a Creator, Who created the whole world, ourselves included, and Who takes care of all His creatures with love, and that we should therefore love G-d and respect His laws and commandments. Moreover, we realize that we are always in the presence of the Divine Majesty, no matter where we are. This knowledge and constant awareness of G-d's Presence fills our heart with awe and trembling and humility. Therefore, by covering our head we show that there is something higher than our own wisdom, something that is *above* us. The Jewish way of showing respect is thus quite the opposite to that of non-Jews. The conventional way of non-Jews is to bare their heads; they "take their hats off"; this is *their* custom. When they go into their houses of worhip, they uncover their heads. We Jews, on the other hand, cover our heads in the synagogue; but G-d is *everywhere*: in our homes, in the street, in the subway—*everywhere*. So we always cover our heads.

We wear the skull-cap, or hat, with pride and dignity, as if it were a crown of glory. It reminds us of the One Above, as our Sages said: "Know what is above you: a seeing Eye, a hearing Ear, and all your deeds are recorded in a book."[20] This helps us to be true to ourselves, as a holy people in whom G-d takes pride, and through whom G-d is glorified, as it is written, "You are My servant, O Israel, in whom I am glorified."[21]

---

[20] Avoth 2:1.
[21] Isaiah 49:3.

שלא עשני גוי

Blessed . . . Who has not made me a Gentile.

By this blessing the Jew expresses his gratitude to G-d for not
having made him a member of any other nation, or faith, in the
world.

Since Jerusalem and the Beth Hamikdash were destroyed by
the Romans nearly two thousand years ago, the Jews have been
dispersed among all the nations of the world; idol-worshippers,
Christians and Moslems. A small minority among every nation in
the world, hated and oppressed, the Jews could have escaped all
that persecution by accepting the religion of the majority. But the
Jews remained steadfast in their loyalty to G-d and His Torah.
Many a Jew marched to his martyred death chanting *Aleinu
l'shabe'ach*—"We must give praise to the Master of All . . . for
not having made us like the nations of the [various] lands" (the
hymn with which we conclude each of our three daily prayers,
which will be discussed in its proper place). Far from envying his
non-Jewish neighbor, the Jew makes a blessing every morning
in gratitude to G-d for not being a Gentile. This gratitude stems
from the realization that being a Jew means being a member of
the nation that was chosen by G-d to receive the Torah with its
613 Divine commandments, which not only ensures a high moral
and saintly life, but also unites the Jew with G-d.

The question may be asked: "Why not make the blessing in a
positive way, namely, 'Who has made me a Jew,' instead of 'Who
has not made me a Gentile'?"

The answer is as follows: The making of a Jew is not merely
an accident of birth; one has to *live* like a Jew in the daily life—
and this is up to *us!* G-d has given us the freedom to do as we
please; to obey Him, or to disobey Him; to be true to ourselves,
or to betray our heritage and trust; to live up to the Torah and

Mitzvoth, or to disregard them and live like the heathen. It is therefore up to *us* to be *truly* Jewish; that is, to be Jewish not only by birth but also in actual life and in our daily conduct. This is why we do not thank G-d for *making* us Jewish; the *making* of a Jew is a matter of the Jew's own will and determination.

שלא עשני עבד

Blessed ... Who has not made me a bondman.

When G-d brought the children of Israel out of bondage, G-d declared, "Unto Me (and none else) shall the children of Israel be bondmen."[22] G-d is our only Master, and we serve Him alone.

Slaves are first mentioned in the Torah soon after the Flood. Noah cursed Canaan, saying that the Canaanites would be slaves unto their brothers. In the time of Abraham, slaves were not uncommon. Abraham himself had slaves, but Abraham's slaves were "slaves" in name only; they were rather members of his household. Eliezer, who proudly declared, "I am a slave of Abraham,"[23] was the manager of Abraham's household[24] and he was treated almost like an equal. In fact, Abraham, when he was yet childless, thought that Eliezer would be his sole heir. When Abraham was blessed with a true son and heir, Isaac, Eliezer still hoped that his (Eliezer's) daughter would make a worthy wife for Isaac, and, as our Sages tell us,[24a] Eliezer hinted it to Abraham when the latter sent him to choose a wife for Isaac from among Abraham's kinfolk in Mesopotamia.

The children of Israel had tasted the bitter experience of bondage when they were enslaved by the Pharaohs of Egypt for

---

22 Lev. 25:55.
23 Gen. 24:34.
24 Gen. 15:2.
24a Rashi on Gen. 24:39.

several centuries. Never were they to impose such a fate on other human beings. The Torah laid down strict laws for the protection of slaves. So many obligations were imposed on the master, that the saying among Jews was: "He who acquires a slave, acquires a master over himself!"[24b] An escaped slave who came to a Jew for asylum, was not to be returned to his master, but was to receive refuge and protection, unlike any other property which a Jew would be duty-bound to restore to its rightful owner.

Theoretically speaking, there could be two types of slaves in the Land of Israel: a Canaanite and a Jew. The Canaanite was protected by the Torah against bodily harm. On his part, the slave was duty-bound to observe a limited number of the precepts of the Torah. The possibility of a Jewish slave could arise in case of theft, where the thief could not make restitution for the stolen article. The Court could then sell him into slavery; but who would want to have a thief in his household? Another possibility could be where a poor man voluntarily sells himself to work off his debt. In each of these cases, when the *Shemittah* (Sabbatical) Year came, the "slave" had to be set free. The Torah, however, grants the slave the privilege (!) to remain in bondage, if he so desires and is so attached to his master; but then he must go free on the Jubilee Year. Thus, the Torah provides that there should not be anything like a permanent class of slaves in the Jewish society, as was common *everywhere* else in the world, and still exists in some countries. Even in the United States of America slavery was abolished only in 1865 (by the 13th Amendment)!

The blessing "Who has not made me a bondman" refers to a Canaanite slave, and we say this blessing to thank G-d for our freedom to serve Him without restrictions, and to fulfill *all* of the commandments of the Torah, not merely *some* as in the case of a bondman.

24b Kiddushin 22a.

In a deeper sense, this blessing reminds us that we are *free* not only from bondage to others, but also from bondage to our own nature. For none is more slave than one who is a slave to his own passions and habits. But G-d has given us the wisdom and capacity to be truly free, and it is only a matter of our own will and determination.

שלא עשני אשה

Blessed . . . Who has not made me a woman.

Anyone who is familiar with the high esteem in which the Jewish woman is held in the Torah, and with the place which she occupies in Jewish life, will not be foolish enough to think that this blessing casts a reflection on Jewish womanhood. Suffice it to mention that during the era of prophecy, there were seven prophetesses mentioned by name in the T'NaCh. They were: Sarah, Miriam, Devorah, Hannah, Abigail, Huldah and Esther.[25] Sarah, the Torah tells us, was in some respects even superior to Abraham, for G-d told Abraham, "All that Sarah will tell you, listen to her."[25a] Moreover, our Sages of the Mishnah and Talmud frequently emphasized the moral strength and spiritual excellence of the Jewish woman. They reminded us that it was in the merit of the righteous Jewish women that the children of Israel were liberated from Egyptian bondage[26]; that at the giving of the Torah, the women were approached first; that women had no part in the Golden Calf, but at the building of the Sanctuary the women were the most generous; that they had a leading part in the miracles of Purim and Chanukah, etc., etc. History also records that throughout the long martyrology of our people in

25 Megillah 14a; Rashi.
25a Gen. 21:12.
26 Sotah 11b.

exile, Jewish women faced death with the same courage as the men, and sometimes greater, in their devotion to G-d and the Torah and the Jewish way of life.

Thus, when the Jew makes the blessing thanking G-d for not making him a woman, he does not say these words with any feeling of superiority, but quite for another reason, as will be made clear presently.

In the nature of things, the husband's task is to be the bread-winner, while the wife has to take care of the home and the children, and to manage the whole household. This is a very complicated task, requiring a great deal of skill, patience, under-standing, and many other high qualities, which Divine Providence so generously bestowed upon the women. It is doubtful whether any executive position which the husband may hold requires greater skill and is more exacting than the domestic responsibilities of the wife and mother.

In view of the above, the Divine Torah has exempted the Jewish woman from the obligation to fulfill certain Mitzvoth. She is equally with her husband duty-bound to observe *all* the prohibitions of the Torah, the "don'ts" (and these are in the majority—365 don'ts to 248 do's). However, in regard to the positive commandments, the Jewish woman is excused from the fulfillment of *some* of them (by no means all), mainly those which have a time factor or limit, out of consideration for her important wifely and motherly duties to which the Torah gives precedence.

In this respect, therefore, the Jewish woman is rather "privi-leged" than "underprivileged."

However, the male Jew, who has not been given the special privileges enjoyed by the Jewish woman, has something to com-pensate for them, namely, the opportunity to commune with G-d more frequently through the fulfillment of those Mitzvoth from which the Jewish woman is exempt. This is no small compensation, and it is for this reason—for the opportunity to serve G-d with these additional Mitzvoth—that the male Jew makes the blessing, "Who has not made me a woman."

המעביר שנה . . . הגומל חסדים טובים לעמו ישראל

Blessed . . . Who removes sleep from my eyes. . . . Who bestows benevolent kindnesses upon His people Israel.

The last of the series of benedictions which are connected with our getting up in the morning is: "Blessed . . . Who removes sleep from my eyes and slumber from my eyelids." This blessing was originally said after washing the face, for it is then that the last traces of sleep are washed away. However, we usually wash our hands and face together before commencing the whole series of the morning blessings. Incidentally, *shenah* ("sleep") refers to proper sleep, while *tenumah* ("slumber") refers to drowsiness.

This blessing ("Who removes sleep . . . eyelids") is *not* complete, and therefore no "Amen" should be said by anyone hearing it, for it continues with a beautiful prayer which concludes with the blessing: "Blessed . . . Who bestows benevolent kindnesses upon His people Israel." In other words, this is a prayer that begins and concludes with a blessing. (Such a prayer is called a "Long Blessing" in the Talmud.) The prayer itself reads as follows:

And may it be Your will, O G-d our G-d and G-d of our fathers, to make us familiar with Your Torah and to attach us to Your Commandments. Bring us not into sin, nor into transgression, nor into iniquity, nor into temptation, nor disgrace. Let not the Yetzer hara (evil inclination) have sway over us. Keep us afar from a bad person and a bad companion; attach us to the Yetzer tov (good inclination) and good deeds; subdue our inclination to be subservient to You. Grant us this day, and every day, to find grace, kindness and mercy in Your eyes, and in the eyes of all who see us; and bestow upon us benevolent kindnesses. Blessed are You, O G-d our G-d, Who bestows benevolent kindnesses upon His people Israel.

As we are about to start the day, we realize that our path is full of pitfalls and temptations. Some of the temptations come from outside (bad people, bad companions); some lie within us, because of our human nature, which is more inclined towards the pleasures of the body than the aspirations of the soul.

Therefore we pray that G-d help us to become accustomed in the way of the Torah and Mitzvoth, for these are our guides in the daily life, which keep us away from temptation and sin. By acquiring the habit of learning and thinking Torah and fulfilling the daily Mitzvoth, we develop a holy and pure nature, and so will not easily fall victim to temptation.

We mention in this prayer the *Yetzer hara*—the "evil inclination," and the *Yetzer tov*—the "good inclination." Both of them are powerful forces which reside in our mind and heart. The first one tempts us with all kinds of pleasures, and tries to distract our mind and heart from G-d, from the good and the holy. The more one indulges in the pleasures of the body, the more powerful the *Yetzer hara* becomes, so that the *Yetzer tov* becomes a "small thin voice" which can hardly be heard.

In this conflict within us between our two natures—one seeking the good and the holy; the other interested only in worldly pleasures—we ask for G-d's help. For, while all depends on our own efforts, our own will and determination, we realize that human nature is often too weak, and needs G-d's aid. Thus our Sages said, "He who sanctifies himself a *little* by his own efforts, is helped *a great deal* from On High."[27]

At first glance there seems no connection between the opening blessing of this prayer ("Who removes sleep") and the prayer itself, as well as the concluding blessing of this prayer. However, thinking a little more deeply, we can see that there is a connection. When a person is asleep, his intellect is asleep, too, and only the imagination remains awake, giving rise to all sorts of dreams and fancies. The ordinary temptations in the daily life are mostly in the imagination, which excites the feeling of anticipation of pleasure out of all proportion. The *Yetzer hara* can succeed only if it catches the intellect napping. In fact, the *Yetzer hara* tries to lull the intellect into sleep. A person in full control of his faculties will not easily fall victim to temptation. If we are really to keep "awake" and alert against the tricks of the *Yetzer hara*, we must study the Torah regularly and fulfill the daily Mitzvoth with devotion and attachment. In His abundant mercies, G-d, our Creator, has given us the power and capacity to overcome the evil inclinations. Furthermore, He has given us the Torah and Mitzvoth as our constant guides, guardians, and companions; and He has given us a *Yetzer tov* to help us further. What more could He do for us? The rest—just a little *personal effort*—is up to us.

If we consider the above prayer carefully, we will see how true is the sequence in which the prayer is arranged. The first thing necessary is to be familiar with the Torah. This will make us cleave to G-d's commandments, and turn us away from sin and transgression. Then the evil inclination will have no power over us. Then, also, will we be able to tell who is a good man and who is a wicked one. We will keep away from the path of the evil companion and, moreover, will be able to subdue our own evil

---

[27] Yoma 39a.

inclination, to the service of G-d. Thus, we will attain grace and
kindness in the eyes of G-d and in the eyes of all who see us.
In all of this, however, we must have G-d's assistance, and, as
already mentioned before, if we make a firm resolution to do
good, we will have G-d's assistance to carry it out.

יהי רצון

*May it be Your will, O G-d my G-d, G-d of my
fathers, to deliver me this day and every day from
arrogant men, and from arrogance, and from a bad
man, and from a bad companion, and from a bad
neighbor; and from any mishaps; from an evil eye,
from an evil tongue, from slander, from false testimony, from human hatred, from libel; from a pre-
mature death; from bad ailments, and bad accidents;
from the destructive adversary, from a harsh judgment, and a harsh litigant, whether he be a son of the
covenant, or not be a son of the covenant; and from
the judgment of purgatory (punishment in after-life).*

This prayer has its origin in a prayer which the saintly Rabbi
Judah used to say (in a somewhat shorter form) at the conclusion
of his prayers, as related in the Talmud.[28] It has been placed in the
early part of our Morning Prayers in order that it follow the
preceding prayer which is similar in many respects.

The prayer speaks for itself. We pray to G-d to save us from
all sorts of unhappy encounters with bad people, whether they be
Jewish ("sons of the covenant") or Gentiles. We pray to be saved
from bad companions and bad neighbors. "Bad companions" are
not necessarily "false" companions; they may be really friendly

---

28 Berachoth 16b.

and even devoted friends. Yet if their views on life and real values are not in accordance with our Torah and Divine commandments, they are likely to be a bad influence on us or our children, however well-intentioned these companions and neighbors may be. We also pray, of course, to be saved from wicked people, people who gossip and slander, who are false and treacherous, and who are filled with envy and hatred. With all our efforts to avoid such unpleasant encounters, we can never be certain that such people will not cross our path, and we pray to G-d to save us from them.

At the same time, we pray to G-d to save us from any kind of accident, sickness, etc. which are not caused by other people.

One of the meanings of an "evil eye" is this: There are people who are envious of others. A person who displays his good fortune to one who is less fortunate may easily arouse the latter's envy and ill-feeling. The envious person may well ask himself: "Why, in the name of justice, has he this and that, while I have not? Is he really more deserving than I?" This, in effect, amounts to a "complaint" addressed to the Heavenly Court. Now, our Sages say that every person is judged by the Heavenly Court each day, each hour.[29] A person's good deeds and bad may just about balance the scale, so that a good word spoken in his behalf by a neighbor may tip the scale in his favor. Conversely, any "complaint" against him, might tip the scale in the other direction. None of us considers himself so blameless and righteous as to be able to face Heavenly judgment with an easy heart. This is why we all pray to G-d to save us from an "evil eye," as we pray to be saved from an "evil tongue." However, the person who has complete faith and trust in G-d, and in His benevolent Providence, need fear no "evil eye," for G-d will not let down anyone who relies upon G-d's protection.

---

[29] Rosh Hashanah 16a.

על דברי תורה
BLESSINGS ON THE TORAH

To study the Torah is one of the most important Divine Commandments, for the Torah is our true guide in life; and as in the case of other commands, we must make a blessing before beginning to study the Torah.

Our duty to study the Torah begins first thing in the morning. That is why our Sages have made the blessing over the Torah an integral part of our Morning Prayers. They have also included three paragraphs from the Torah, to follow the blessing: One paragraph from the Chumash, (*The L-rd bless you and keep you, etc.*); one from the Mishnah, (*These are the things which have no fixed measure, etc.*); and one from the Gemara, (*These are the things whose fruits man enjoys in this world, while the capital is laid up for him in the World to Come, etc.*). Our Morning Prayers also include additional portions from the Torah (as the "Shema" for instance), and thus we learn every morning a minimum of our holy Torah.

Of course, we are commanded to study the Torah in all our free time, but the blessings over the Torah which we make in the morning suffice for the rest of the day, and we do not have to make a blessing every time we read or study something from the Torah in the course of the day or night.

The first of the blessings which we make over the Torah in the morning is,

> "Blessed are You . . . Who has sanctified us by His commandments, and commanded us concerning* the words of the Torah.

---

*In some versions: "to occupy ourselves with".

"Make pleasant, therefore, we beseech You, O G-d our G-d, the words of Your Torah in our mouth and in the mouth of all Your people, the house of Israel, so that we with our offspring and the offspring of all Your people, the house of Israel, may all know Your name and learn Your Torah for its sake. Blessed are You, O G-d, Who teaches the Torah to His people Israel."

All this is one blessing and we are, therefore, not to say "Amen" at the conclusion of the first paragraph.

According to the explanation of Rabbi Joseph Caro, author of the Shulchan Aruch (1488-1575), this blessing refers to the "Oral Law," that is, all the traditions and explanations of the "Written Law," which have been given to Mosheh on Mt. Sinai, which are contained in the Talmud. The reason for putting this blessing ahead of the other blessing (which will follow later) is that we cannot really study and understand the "Written Law" without the "Oral Law," and in fact, most of the study of Torah is centered on the study of the Talmud.

And now, let us consider carefully, every word of the blessing, in order to understand the full meaning of it.

We ask G-d to make the words of the Torah pleasant to us, that is to say, that we should be able to study the Torah willingly and find enjoyment in it. We further ask G-d that not only we ourselves be learned in the Torah, but that also our children and children's children, study the Torah *for its own sake.* These words are a timely reminder of the duty of the parent to see that his children and grandchildren get a Torah-true education and help perpetuate the Torah. We conclude the blessing with praising G-d "Who teaches the Torah to His people Israel." Here we express our gratitude to G-d for the great privilege of being the standard-bearers of the Torah, the greatest gift that G-d has given us.

אשר בחר בנו ... נותן התורה

*Blessed ... Who has chosen us from all peoples and
has given us His Torah. Blessed are You ... the Giver
of the Torah.*

We hear this blessing in the synagogue many times, for whenever the Torah is read in the synagogue and people are called up
to the Torah, each person so honored must make this blessing.

The above blessing is the second blessing over the Torah which
we say in our Morning Prayers. The *first blessing* refers to the
Oral Law (תורה שבעל פה). However, the blessing we are now
considering refers to the Written Law (תורה שבכתב). And that is
why this blessing is recited in the synagogue before the reading
of the Torah, as mentioned above.

Rav Hamnuna, an Amora who lived in Babylon about sixteen
hundred years ago, is the cited author of this blessing. As soon as
a child is able to speak, he said, his father must teach him, "The
Torah which Moses commanded us, is the inheritance of the
congregation of Jacob."[30] He believed that it was the responsibility
of the Jewish community to provide schools for the young children. Failing to do so was the reason why Jerusalem was destroyed,
Rav Hamnuna said.[31]

Even a little consideration of the meaning of the blessing will
tell us how important this blessing is. In this blessing we thank
G-d for having chosen us from among all the peoples of the earth
to give us His most precious possession—the Torah. It is indeed
a unique privilege to have been selected for this great and holy
task—to spread the knowledge of G-d among all the peoples of
the world. We can justly be proud of it, but it must not be an
empty pride, or vanity. If we cling to the Torah devotedly, if we

---

30 Deut. 33:4.
31 Sab. 119b.

observe its Divine laws and teachings, then indeed we can truly be proud of the privilege of having been chosen as the standard-bearers of the Torah.

As Rabbi Judah Halevi (12th cent.) told us in his famous book on the Jewish faith, "The Kuzari," we are not to be vain about "having been chosen to receive the Torah." To be selected as the "People of the Book" is not merely like a reward given to the best pupil. It is rather an obligation which we alone, of all the nations of the world, have taken upon ourselves. It is the obligation to be a "kingdom of priests, and a holy nation."[31a] The other nations refused, and still refuse to accept such obligations as are contained in the 613 commandments. We, however, have accepted the Torah without reservations. Throughout the ages we have clung to the Torah devotedly and selflessly. Although there are many Jews who, unfortunately, do not observe the Torah with the same devotion as others, there can be no doubt that the Jewish people as a whole has remained loyal to the Torah with all its heart and soul, and will continue to do so, forever.

We have been chosen to show by our own way of living, the right way of living. We have been chosen to proclaim the unity of G-d as the sole master of the world, and to show all the peoples of the earth how to interpret G-d's will as contained in the Torah, through the careful observance of all G-d's commandments.

Considering the words of the blessing a little further, we will note the words, "His Torah" and "The Giver of the Torah." By the words "His Torah," we proclaim daily that the Torah is given by G-d, that every word of it has come to us from G-d on Mt. Sinai. By the words "The Giver of the Torah," we again emphasize the same thought and, at the same time, reaffirm our devotion to the Torah as if we received it from the mouth of G-d *today*. That, indeed, is why we do not conclude the blessing with the words, "Who *gave* us the Torah," but "The Giver of the Torah," which

---

31a Exod. 19:5; Deut. 7:6.

also means "Who *gives* us the Torah"—(*nothein* is in the present tense).

Indeed, our Sages said that we must always consider the Torah as *new*. We must continually imagine ourselves before Mount Sinai, hearing the words of G-d, and seeing the great Divine Revelation.

יברכך

THE PRIESTLY BLESSINGS

And G-d spoke to Moses, saying: Speak unto Aaron and unto his sons, saying, Thus shall you bless the children of Israel, saying unto them:

> *G-d bless you and protect you;*
>
> *G-d make His face to shine upon you, and be gracious unto you;*
>
> *G-d lift up His face unto you, and give you peace.*

And they shall put My name upon the children of Israel; and I will bless them.[32]

We read this Scriptural passage in the morning blessings in order to follow up the blessings of the Torah with actual reading from the Torah.

The Priestly blessing is a commandment given to the Kohanim to bless the Jewish people with this "three-fold blessing."

It is the general custom of Jewish congregations outside the Holy Land that the Kohanim perform this duty during the Musaf service on festival days. In the Holy Land it is performed every morning; on weekdays, Shabbos and festivals. This Mitzvah is called *Duchenen*, from the Hebrew word *duchan* (דוכן), "raised platform."

---

[32] Num. 6:22-27.

Many are the meanings and significances contained in the letters and words, and in the combinations of letters and words, of this "three-fold blessing." This is why the Kohanim had to pronounce the exact text of this blessing in the holy tongue, without any change. We will bring here only a few of the many explanations and interpretations which have been revealed to us by our Sages.[32a]

"G-d bless you"—refers to material blessings, such as wealth and worldly possessions; and "protect you" from harm, for it often happens that wealth can be a source of danger, either the danger of turning away from the Torah and Mitzvoth, or the danger of thieves and robbers.

"G-d make His face shine upon you," etc., refers to the light of the Torah. It has been said, "The wisdom of a man illuminates his face,"[33] and true wisdom is the wisdom of the Torah. Thus we pray that G-d may open our eyes to see the light of the Torah, to illuminate our daily life.

"G-d lift up His face unto you and give you peace," refers to everlasting life in the world to come.

In pronouncing these blessings and mentioning G-d's Name each time, the Kohanim put G-d's Name upon the Jewish people, for G-d's Name is the source of all these blessings. Whereupon G-d promises that He "will bless them." "Them" has two meanings here: "them"—the Jewish people, meaning that G-d will personally "confirm" this blessing of the Kohanim; and "them" refers to the Kohanim, meaning that G-d would bless the Kohanim who bless the Jewish people.[33a]

It has also been said that the "three-fold" blessing comes to us in the merit of our three Patriarchs, Abraham, Isaac and Jacob

---

[32a] Bamidbar Rabba; Yalkut—on Num. 6:22-27.
[33] Eccl. 8:1.
[33a] Chulin 49a; Sotah 38b.

אלו דברים
THESE ARE THE THINGS

These are things which have no fixed measure: the
corner of the field, the first fruits, appearance (before
G-d at the three pilgrimage festivals), acts of benevo-
lence, and the study of Torah.[34]
These are the things of which a man enjoys the fruits
in this world, while the stock remains for him for the
world to come; they are: honoring father and mother,
acts of benevolence, diligent attendance at the house
of study morning and evening, hospitality to visitors,
visiting the sick, dowering the bride, accompanying
the dead, concentration in prayer, making peace be-
tween man and his fellow, and between husband and
wife; but the study of the Torah equals them all.[35]

The blessings for Torah learning include not only the *Torah-
She-biKthav* ("Written Torah," i.e. T'NaCh), but also the *Torah-
She-be'al-Peh* ("Oral Torah," i.e. Mishnah, Gemara, etc.). There-
fore the Scriptural passages are followed by Talmudic passages.

The Mishnah quoted here is the first of the tractate *Peah*. It
mentions such Mitzvoth as have no limit fixed by the Torah
(though the Rabbis set limits in most cases). The first Mitzvah
mentioned in this connection is that of *Peah*, "the corner" of a
field, which must be left unharvested for the needy to reap.
(Hence the name of the tractate *Peah*).

The Torah[36] commands that the owner of a field, at harvest
time, must leave a corner of his field untouched "for the poor and
the stranger." The Torah gives no definite measure as to the size

---

34 Peah 1:1.
35 Sab. 127a; Kid. 39b.
36 Lev. 23:22.

of this corner. But the more generous a person is, the more generous G-d is to him.

The "first fruits" (*Bikkurim*) of the field, vineyard and orchard had to be brought to the House of G-d as an offering.[37] They were given as gifts to the Kohanim. However, the quantity was not specified in the Torah.

"Appearance" before G-d at the three pilgrimage festivals (Pesach, Shavuoth, and Succoth), was obligatory on all Jewish adult males when the Beth Hamikdash was in existence.[38] These appearances were not to be made empty-handed,[39] and were to be accompanied by special sacrifices. However, the Torah does not specify how many appearances one was to make during any particular festival, or the value of the sacrifice which should accompany such visits.

"Acts of benevolence" include a variety of kind and charitable deeds, such as visiting the sick, giving hospitality to wayfarers, and other favors extended to friends and strangers. Again, it is left to the individual to decide how many favors and benevolent acts he wishes to extend to others.

"Study of the Torah" (*Talmud Torah*) has no limit, for we are commanded to study day and night.[40] Every Jew is commanded to study the Torah. People who are in business, or on a job, are required to study the Torah whenever they have a free moment, but, at any rate, they must set aside a time in the morning and in the evening for the study of the Torah. There is, of course, no end to the Torah, since it is the wisdom of G-d, Who is infinite, and Whose wisdom is infinite. Of the Torah it is said, "Its measure is longer than the earth, and wider than the ocean."[41] As one great Sage said, "Whatever knowledge of the Torah I have acquired

---

37 Exod. 23:19.
38 Exod. 23:17.
39 Deut. 16:16-17.
40 Joshua 1:8.
41 Job 11:9.

during my lifetime, I have barely scratched the surface of the Torah; it is like a drop from the ocean."[41a]

The Talmudic section that follows, speaks of such Mitzvoth as are rewarded both in this world and in the world to come.

Our Sages declared, "There is no reward for a Mitzvah in this world."[42] What is really meant by this statement is that there are not enough worldly goods in this world to be adequate reward even for one Mitzvah. But there are Mitzvoth, such as are enumerated in the quoted passage, the "fruits" of which a person enjoys right here in this world, while the main reward (called here the "stock") remains undiminished in the world to come. These Mitzvoth, which include a variety of "good deeds" are such that there is an *immediate* benefit to somebody, whether it be one's own parents, or helping a poor bride get married, and the like. Such good deeds, as the Rambam pointed out in his Commentary on this Mishnah, create good-will and are emulated and reciprocated, all of which makes a good society to live in. The doer of these good deeds earns the respect and affection of his fellow-men, in addition to the *Divine* reward, in this world and in the world to come. Thus the reward is both *immediate* (in this world) and everlasting (in the world to come).

Quite fittingly, this passage concludes with the words, "And the study of the Torah equals them all," since it is said here in connection with the Blessings over the Torah, which had just been recited in the Siddur.

41a Sanhedrin 68a; see also Shir Hashirim Rabba 1:20; Avoth dR. Nathan 25.
42 Kiddushin 39b.

תפלת השחר

PRELIMINARY PRAYERS
AND READINGS

מה טובו

MAH TOVU

*How goodly are your tents, O Jacob, your dwelling
places, O Israel.[1] As for me, in the abundance of Your
loving kindness I will come into Your house; I will
bow down toward Your holy Sanctuary, in fear of
You.[2] And as for me, may my prayer unto You, O G-d,
be in an acceptable time; O G-d, in the abundance of
Your loving kindness, answer me in the truth of Your
salvation.[3]*

The above selected verses introduce the second section of the
Morning Prayer (according to the order of prayer in Nusach Ari).

The first section (discussed earlier) consists of the Morning
Blessings. The second section is highlighted by the *Akedah*, the
Shema and a series of Scriptural and Mishnaic passages dealing
with the daily sacrifices and the incense, concluding with the
Beraitha of Rabbi Yishmael.

The familiar verse *Mah tovu* was first uttered by Balaam, the

---

[1] Num. 24:5.
[2] Ps. 5:8.
[3] Ps. 69:14.

61

magician and enemy of the Jews, whom Balak, king of Moab, hired to curse the Jewish people. However, before Balaam could utter any curse, G-d turned all his curses into blessings. Thus it was G-d's words that came from Balaam's mouth, when the latter showered blessings upon the Jewish people in most beautiful poetry.

The "tents" of which this verse speaks, in addition to the plain meaning of the word, also meant the houses of study.[3a] Balaam expressed admiration for the modesty and sanctity of the Jewish home, praising at the same time the "tents of Torah," where the Torah is studied.

The "dwelling places" referred to the Mishkan and Mikdash, the central sanctuaries of the Jewish people, which, since the destruction of the Beth Hamikdash have been replaced by the synagogues.

The second verse expresses the thought that it is a great Divine kindness which enables us to enter G-d's House, the synagogue, to pray to Him. G-d welcomes us to His house as we are, without any previous fasting and penitence to cleanse our soul from any possible sin. We come to the synagogue daily, but we must not take it for granted. We must be grateful to G-d for inviting us to His house every time we enter the synagogue, and we must, at the same time, be filled with awe and reverence, realizing that we are in the immediate presence of G-d.

The third verse emphasizes that the time of prayer is the time of Divine benevolence—an "acceptable time" in the sense that G-d accepts us and accepts our prayers. Our Sages[4] declare that the time when the congregation prays is especially auspicious. Thus, if an individual cannot, for some reason, attend congregational prayer and prays at home, he should try to do so at the time when the prayer is said in the congregation, so that his indi-

---

3a Sanhedrin 105b.
4 Berachoth 8a.

vidual prayer would join with the public prayer, and be answered.

The "truth" of G-d's salvation, mentioned in this verse, means that the salvation coming from G-d is a *true* salvation, in the sense that it is not only *real,* but also *constant* and never failing. A human being, however helpful he may want to be, cannot *always* be helpful; it therefore cannot be called "true." *Truth* is everlasting.

Looking further into this short prayer of *Mah tovu,* consisting of three verses, and being an "introduction" to the Morning Prayers, we can see that each verse stresses a different thing: The first stresses the "tents" and "sanctuaries"; the second stresses our feelings when we enter the synagogue; the third stresses the auspiciouness of the time of prayer. Thus, when we come to the synagogue to pray with the congregation, all three dimensions— place, person, time—meet in a favorable combination: The place is holy, the worshipper is filled with awe, and the time is particularly favorable. Praying individually at home, while it is a "must" if it is impossible to pray in the synagogue, obviously has not the same advantages as prayer with the congregation in the synagogue. It has one great advantage, however, and that is that it is often possible to concentrate more deeply whilst praying in seclusion. Needless to say, certain prayers (*Kaddish, Kedushah, Barechu,* etc.) can be said only in the presence of a "congregation" of at least ten Jews, and the Torah can also be read only if ten adult Jews (from the age of Bar Mitzvah and on) are present.

One more point about these *three* verses. The Zohar points out that the three verses allude to our three Patriarchs—Abraham, Isaac and Jacob. As was mentioned previously,[4a] our Patriarchs introduced the three daily prayers, and each emphasized a different quality: Abraham—love; Isaac—reverence; Jacob—mercy. (For this reason, in the *Nusach Ari* the *Mah tovu* prayer has only the said *three* verses, though in other Nuschaoth (rites) there may be more or less than three.)

[4a] See p. 8 f., above.

אדון עולם
ADON OLAM

One of the first prayers we say in the morning is the beautiful song of praise to G-d, "Adon Olam," (Lord of the Universe).

In this beautiful, rhythmical, and profoundly meaningful prayer, we proclaim G-d as Lord of the universe, Who created the world and all creatures, Who Was, Is, and Will be the only G-d; in Him we trust, and in His charge we entrust our soul and body, both when we sleep and when we are awake. This prayer concludes with the words, "G-d is with me, I shall not fear."

This prayer is, therefore, a proclamation of our selfless devotion to G-d, our deep consciousness of His greatness and supreme power, our overflowing confidence in Him Who controls the terrors of the night and the dangers of the day. Nothing can happen to us unless He decrees so. There is nothing that can challenge G-d's power and His care and protection of us.

Thus, this beautiful prayer contains some of the most fundamental and profound principles of our faith; expressed with extraordinary beauty and in the most enchanting rhymes.

We do not know the author of this beautiful prayer. Some ascribe it to the great Spanish Rabbi, poet and philosopher, Rabbi Solomon Ibn Gabirol (about 1021-1058). Others, to Rav Sherirah (about 900-1001) and Rav Hai Gaon (939-1038), who mention this prayer in their writings.

עקדת יצחק
THE AKEDAH

The story of the Binding of Isaac is well known.[5] It was the tenth and final test which Abraham underwent during his life-

---

[5] Gen. 22:1-19.

time. The purpose of this test was to bring out in our father Abraham the quality of the fear of G-d.[6]

It seems strange that in his declining years (Abraham was 137 years old at the time of the *Akedah*), after he had undergone nine previous tests and had proven his love and loyalty to G-d in so many ways, Abraham had yet to prove his *Yirath HaShem* (fear of G-d). This surely indicates that Divine worship cannot be perfect and complete without the quality of *Yirath HaShem*.

The essence of *Yirath HaShem* is: unquestioning obedience and unconditional submission to the Will of G-d. It is illustrated by the obedience of a servant to his master; the servant must obey his master without question and without condition. The weak point in this relationship is that, unless the servant also loves his master, he will not go beyond the call of duty.

To serve G-d out of love (*Ahavath HaShem*) is in many respects a more advanced form of worship. It expresses a more "noble" attachment to G-d. It is illustrated by the devotion of a son to his father. A loving son tries to please his father and anticipate his wishes. Yet, this love also breeds a certain "familiarity" and leaves room for taking certain "liberties," unless the love is coupled with the highest degree of respect at all times.

Thus, *Ahavath HaShem* without *Yirath HaShem* is not sufficient, since the basic requirement of the fulfillment of *all* Divine precepts is absolute *obedience*.

Obedience is a quality which is generally harder to cultivate than love. Human nature is such, that a person is inclined to rebel against an order. Even when a person recognizes that the order is a good one, he would much rather do it without being ordered to do so. Where the order is such that it is beyond the understanding of the person ordered, and consequently requiring "blind obedience," the inclination to rebel against it is all the stronger. Blind obedience is a natural quality found only in animals, whose

---

[6] Ibid., v. 12.

nature permits them to be tamed and domesticated, to obey blindly the will of their human masters.

Yet, it is precisely this kind of absolute obedience that we are required to show in the fulfillment of the Divine precepts. As a matter of plain common sense, this attitude is the only reasonable approach, for, by comparison to G-d, our Maker, we are infinitely more removed from our Master than the beast of burden is removed from its human master. Just as it is unreasonable to expect the beast to understand its master's wisdom, so, and infinitely more so, it is unreasonable for a human being to understand the wisdom of the Creator.

Now, let us consider Abraham's position for a moment. From his earliest youth Abraham *recognized* the existence of One G-d, the Creator of heaven and earth and all their hosts. Neither parents nor teachers had taught him this truth; he had discovered it after much thinking, for he had an extraordinary mind. Although surrounded by people who were idol-worshippers, he was so convinced of the truth which he had reasoned out, that he was prepared to die for it. It was after he had attained such prophetic wisdom and saintliness that G-d revealed Himself to him. He recognized G-d's qualities, especially the quality of *mercy* (*Chesed*), and practised it all his life. Then, suddenly, G-d orders him to offer his beloved son Isaac on the altar!

This Divine commandment was certainly beyond Abraham's understanding. It was contrary to all he knew and believed about G-d, for Abraham knew that the practice of human sacrifices (so common among the pagans) was abominable to G-d. It was easy for Abraham to risk his life to *save* a life; but now he was ordered, as he thought, to *take* a life, the life of the one dearest to him; dearer than his own life.

Moreover, not long before, G-d had solemnly promised Abraham that out of Isaac the Jewish people would be born. But Isaac was not even married; he had no son through whom G-d's promise could be fulfilled. Was G-d's word, G-d's promise, to be as worthless as that of a deceitful man? Was this the G-d for Whom he, Abraham, was ready to give his life?

Yet, Abraham did not question G-d's command, however unreasonable and disagreeable it seemed to him. Abraham *obeyed* without question. In doing so, he brought out, and gave *actual* expression to, the quality of *Yirath HaShem,* in its most absolute and most perfect form, a quality which he had in him, but which had not been tested and *fixed* in his nature. Now that it was actually put to the test, it proved to be of a permanent and effective quality which, together with Abraham's other qualities, became the everlasting heritage of his children, the Jewish people. Abraham showed us the true way of serving G-d: with love and reverence; for he was truly a "lover of G-d"[7] as well as a truly "G-d-fearing" man.[8]

There is yet another important point to bear in mind in connection with the *Akedah.*

Indeed, this point has been raised by the author of the *Tanya*[9] in order to emphasize a particular lesson of the *Akedah,* namely, the *speed* and *eagerness* with which Abraham carried out this Divine command. He "rose early in the morning," he himself saddled his donkey, and cleft the firewood. This *eagerness* to carry out G-d's command, setting aside all personal feeling, is the most remarkable aspect of the *Akedah,* more remarkable even than the actual fulfillment of the command itself, the author of the *Tanya* points out in his penetrating observation.

Abraham's eagerness and alacrity in doing a good deed had already been displayed on other occasions (in saving Lot; in his hospitality to wayfarers). But it is most impressive in the *Akedah.*

---

[7] Isaiah 41:8.
[8] Gen. 21:12.
[9] Iggereth Hakodesh 21.

From Abraham our Sages established the great principle, "The scrupulous do the Mitzvoth immediately."[10] It is not enough to fulfill G-d's commandments; we must do so at the *first* opportunity, with eagerness and alacrity, prompted by *Yirath HaShem* and *Ahavath HaShem.*

From the above discussion of the *Akedah* it will be clear why it has been included in our *Siddur.* As has already been pointed out in the Introduction, prayer (*Tefilah*) in its fullest sense is not merely a request for G-d's blessings, but a time for spiritual ennoblement. From this viewpoint, the *Akedah* is unsurpassed as a source of inspiration. It contains, moreover, some of the most basic teachings as to true Divine worship.

רבונו של עולם

THE AFTER-AKEDAH PRAYER

The *Akedah* is followed by a prayer, which begins as follows:

Master of the Universe! Just as our Father Abraham subdued his mercies towards his only son in order to do Your will with a full heart, so may Your mercies subdue your anger towards us; and may Your mercies invoke Your attributes, that You, O G-d, will deal with us in the attribute of kindness, and in the attri- bute of mercy. And in Your abundant goodness may Your anger be recalled from Your people, Your city, Your land and Your inheritance. And fulfill for us, O G-d our G-d, the thing which You did promise us in Your Torah, by the hands of Mosheh Your servant, as it is said: "And I shall remember My covenant with

---
[10] Yoma 28b.

*Jacob, and also My covenant with Isaac, and also My
covenant with Abraham I shall remember, and the
land shall I remember."[11]*

Then follow a number of additional passages from the Holy
Scriptures, including passages from the Prophets Isaiah, Jeremiah,
and Micah, all of which speak of G-d's promise to mercifully
remember His people in the midst of their suffering and exile,
and the assurance that G-d will eventually return the exiles to
their homeland, and restore the Beth Hamikdash in its former
place in Jerusalem.

The *Akedah* is thus linked with the eventual restoration of the
Jewish people. We are reminded that just as the *Akedah* was only
a *test* of Abraham's devotion and loyalty to G-d, so is the exile
and the suffering of our people a test of our loyalty to G-d. And
just as the *Akedah* brought forth G-d's blessings to Abraham, so
will the long exile and martyrdom of our people be richly
rewarded.

The connection between the *Akedah* and the exile, and the
special significance of our daily recital of the *Akedah,* are emphasized in the *Zohar* and similar sources. The *Zohar* declares[12]:
"Jews should recite the *Akedah* of Isaac every day, so that it
should shield them from all calamities; for a Voice comes forth
and says, 'Do not do any harm unto him!' "[13]

As already mentioned, the *Akedah* is recited daily, including
Shabbos and Yom Tov, but the prayer *following* the *Akedah*
("Master of the Universe!," etc.) is omitted on Shabbos and Yom
Tov and other days when no *Tachnun* (prayer of supplication)
is said.

---

11 Lev. 26:42.
12 Quoted in Siddur Otzar Hatefiloth, vol. I, p. 135.
13 Gen. 22:12.

שמע ישראל

THE (FIRST) SHEMA

Altogether we recite the *Shema* four times daily. The first time we recite the *Shema* is in the early part of the Morning Prayers, after the *Akedah* and before the passages about the sacrifices. However, here only the first section of the *Shema* is recited (*Shema . . . v'ahavta*). The second time we recite the *Shema* in the blessing of *Yotzer* (preceding the *Shemone Esrei*). The third time—during the Evening Service (*Maariv*), and lastly—before retiring to bed. (When *Musaf* is recited, the first verse, *Shema,* is recited also in the *Kedushah.*)

Shema is our declaration of our most fundamental principle of faith—our belief in *One G-d* (Monotheism). We shall discuss the meaning of *Shema* in greater detail when we come to the *Shema* in the blessing of *Yotzer.*

Originally, the obligation to recite the *Shema* consisted of reciting it *twice* daily, mornings and evenings, i.e., once in the Morning Prayer and once in the Evening Prayer. The two additional daily recitals mentioned above were instituted at a later period, dating back to Talmudic times, when the Jews were subjected to religious persecution and were forbidden to recite the *Shema* during public services in the synagogue. Under the rule of the Persian king Jezdegerd II (438-57), the Jews were forbidden to proclaim their belief in *one* G-d in public. The said Persian king was a fanatical believer in the Zaroastrian religon of "dualism," that is to say, the belief in two gods, one good and one evil. The king posted guards at the synagogue to enforce the prohibition of the recital of the *Shema.* The Rabbis then instituted that the *Shema* should be recited *before* the regular Morning Prayer.

There was another reason for reciting the *Shema* early, before its regular recitation in the blessing of *Yotzer.* There is a time-limit when the *Morning Shema* can be said, namely, within the first quarter of the day (reckoning *daylight* only). For example, if sunrise is at six and sunset is also at six, making it a 12-hour day, the *Shema* could be recited not later than 9 a.m.; if the sun rises at 7 and sets at 5, giving us 10 hours of daylight, a quarter of the day would be 2½ hours, and 9:30 a.m. would be the limit. It is not unusual, however, to start the morning service at 9 or 9:30 a.m. (especially on Shabbos and Yom Tov), and by the time the *Shema* in *Yotzer* is reached, the deadline would have been missed. (In such a case one would not have the Mitzvah of reciting the *Shema* in time, but only of reciting a Torah portion, which is quite a different Mitzvah, but not a substitute for *Keriath Shema* as a Torah-precept.) Hence the custom among many Jews to recite the Morning Blessings and the *Shema* at home every morning, soon after rising, with the intention that, if the second *Shema* would come after the time, the first *Shema* would stand one in good stead for the fulfillment of the Mitzvah of *Keriath Shema* in its proper time. That is why at least the first section (*v'ahavta*) should be included with the first.

The *Shema* is here introduced with a prayer which is in the form of a declaration. It begins as follows:

> *At all times a man should fear G-d (even) privately, acknowledge the truth, and speak the truth in his heart. He should rise early and say:*

> *Master of all the worlds! Not because of our righteous deeds do we lay our supplications before You, but because of Your abundant mercies. What are we? What is our life? What is our benevolence? What is our righteousness? What is our strength? What is our might? What shall we say before You, O G-d our G-d, and the G-d of our fathers? Are not all the mighty ones as naught before You? the men of re-*

*nown as though they had never been? the wise men
as though without knowledge? the men of understanding without sense? For most of their works are
confusion, and the days of their lives are vanity before
You, and the pre-eminence of man over beast is
naught; for all that—is vanity. Except for the pure
soul which is destined to give judgment and account-
ing before the Throne of Your glory. But all the
nations are like naught before You, as it is said,
"Behold the nations are as a drop from a bucket, and
are counted as the dust in the balance (scale); behold,
He takes up the isles as a very little thing."*[14]

A few explanatory notes, before we continue with the above
prayer:

"At all times . . . fear G-d." The expression *Yirath Shamayim*
("fear of Heaven") is very often used in the Talmud. We have
already discussed the quality of the "fear of G-d" to which Abraham gave expression in the trial of the *Akedah.* Thus the subject
of *Yirath HaShem* (or *Yirath Shamayim*) forms the link between
the prayer under discussion and the *Akedah* which it follows. The
"fear of G-d" has to be *at all times,* motivating *all* one's actions.
The test of it is to be found particularly in "private" affairs, for in
"public" affairs no person desires to appear arrogant, and without
any fear of G-d in his heart. This reminds us of the story related
in the Talmud,[14a] where we are told that when the great Rabban
Yochanan ben Zakkai was ill, and his disciples came to visit him,
he told them "May the fear of Heaven be upon you as the fear of
man." When the disciples asked in astonishment, "Master, no
more than this?" the Sage replied, "Would that it be so. You see,
when a person commits a sin, he tries to hide it from other people.

---

14 Isaiah 40:15.
14a Berachoth 28b.

If one's fear of G-d will match one's fear of man, no one will commit sin, since nothing can be hidden from G-d."

"Acknowledge the truth." This is a great and wonderful quality, for not only does this require complete honesty with one's self, but also a great deal of courage. It is not easy to admit that one has been wrong, especially if admitting it entails a certain sacrifice. Some people who, deep in their heart, know that they have been living their daily life the wrong way, will go to any length to "prove" they are "right," knowing full well that they are only trying to "justify" their actions in the eyes of others; or, at any rate, in the vain hope that they might pacify their own conscience. They find this way an easier alternative than changing their way of life. This is why our Sages say that "acknowledging the truth" is one of the "seven characteristics of the *wise* man."[15]

"Speak the truth in his heart" is one of the qualities mentioned by King David in the Psalms[16] which make a man worthy to "dwell in G-d's tabernacle," in close companionship with G-d. By way of illustration as to what it means to "speak the truth in his heart" our Sages mention Rav Safra. He had something for sale, and a man came to him while he was praying and offered him a certain price. Seeing that Rav Safra did not answer him, and thinking that his offer was too small, the man increased his offer. After the prayer, Rav Safra sold him the article at the *original* offer, since he had already decided to accept it, but did not wish to interrupt his prayer.[17]

This quality also includes that perfect honesty which would make it offensive to create a false impression even if quite harmless. For example, when a welcome guest drops in unexpectedly and the host says to him, "I will open a barrel of wine specially for you," whereas he had intended to open it in any case; or

---

[15] Avoth 5:9.
[16] Ps. 15:2.
[17] Makkoth 24a, Rashi.

invites him to a meal, knowing he will refuse it, etc. Not many people are careful about such "little, harmless deceptions," yet these and similar deceptions (their variety is legion) come under the category of *Gnevath daath* ("stealing of the mind"), which our Sages condemn as "theft."[18]

The same high degree of honesty which is expected of us in our relationship with fellow man is the least that should be maintained, of course, in our relationship with G-d, all the more so since G-d cannot be deceived.

Bearing in mind the said three virtues (fearing G-d, acknowledging the truth, and speaking the truth), the declaration continues:

> *Master of all the worlds! Not because of our righteous deeds do we lay our supplication before You, but because of Your abundant mercies. . . .*

This phrase is taken from the prayer of Daniel,[19] and it emphasizes the idea that we do not come before G-d with a demand to reward us for our righteousness and good deeds, but rather that we appear before G-d in all humility, conscious of our unworthiness. This idea is often underscored in the Torah.[20]

"What are we?!" In ourselves and by ourselves we are nothing. Even the men of power and fame, of wisdom and intelligence, are of no account, for most of their works are confusion and vanity. The only thing of consequence is our pure soul which is destined to answer to her Maker.

If speaking of *what* we are, we must admit that we are nothing, it is different when we speak of *who* we are. Thus we go on:

> *Yet we are Your people, the children of Your covenant; the children of Abraham, Your beloved, to*

---

18 Shavuoth 39a; Hulin 94a.
19 Daniel 9:18.
20 Gen. 18:27; 32:11, e.a., and frequently in Book of Psalms.

whom You did swear on Mount Moriah; the seed of
Isaac, his only son, who was bound upon the altar;
the congregation of Jacob, Your firstborn son, whose
name—because of Your love with which You loved
him, and the joy with which You rejoiced in him—
You called Jacob and Yeshurun.

In other words, if we have no claim upon G-d's kindness as a
reward for any good deeds on *our* part, we plead for His grace
and mercy by virtue of our being the people G-d chose as His
own, the children of Abraham, Isaac and Jacob, with whom G-d
had made an everlasting covenant.

(Jacob, the "chosen one" among the Patriarchs, whose name—
Israel—we bear as the people of Israel, is here mentioned by all
his three names: Jacob, Israel and Yeshurun. *Yeshurun*[21] comes
from the Hebrew word *Yashar,* "upright.")

Because we are fortunate to be the children of Abraham, Isaac
and Jacob, and the children of the Divine covenant, we continue:

Therefore it is our duty to thank You, praise You, and
glorify You, and to bless, and sanctify, and offer praise
and acknowledgment to Your Name. Happy are we!
how good is our portion, and how pleasant is our lot,
and how beautiful our heritage! Happy are we who,
at dawn and at twilight, evening and morning, say
twice daily:

Hear, O Israel, G-d (Who is) our G-d, G-d is One.
Blessed be the Name of His glorious Kingdom for
ever and ever.

Therefore . . . thank You—we have in this sentence seven
different expressions of thankfulness, which balance the seven

[21] Deut. 33:5; Isaiah 44:2.

expressions of self-negation mentioned in the section "Master of All the World" ("what are we . . . what shall we say"), which correspond to the "seven expressions of vanity" found in the beginning of Koheleth.

How good is our portion—lot—heritage. These refer to G-d, Israel and the Torah, inseparably linked and united together.

Good—pleasant—beautiful. These are the three basic qualities of a perfectly desirable thing: It must be *good,* that is, useful and beneficial; it must be *pleasant,* that is, enjoyable; and it must be *beautiful,* that is, colorful and harmonious, like the beauty we find in the harmony of colors, or in the symmetry of line, or in the symphony of music.

And all these three qualities are to be found in our Jewish way of life, the daily life permeated with Torah and Mitzvoth. This is why we say to G-d gratefully, "Happy are we!" And we say again "Happy are we" that we have been given the true belief in One G-d, and that we are privileged to proclaim G-d's unity every day, morning and evening, knowing that this One G-d is *our* G-d, in a personal and intimate way.

אתה הוא עד שלא נברא העולם

YOU ARE HE

You are He (the Same) ere the world was created; You are He since the world was created; You are He in this world, and You are He in the world to come. Sanctify Your Name in Your world upon the people who sanctify Your Name; and through Your salvation, O our King, may our horn be exalted and raised high, and save us soon for the sake of Your Name. Blessed is He, Who sanctifies His Name amongst the many.

This is a very old prayer which (in part, at least) is found in ancient Talmudic sources.[22] The *Yalkut* cites the following eloquent passage:

> *When the Holy One, blessed be He, looks down upon His world and sees people amusing themselves in theatres and circuses, contented and care-free, while His sanctuary is in ruins, He is ready to destroy His world. But when His people Israel enter their houses of prayer and houses of study, proclaim His unity and declare, "Hear O Israel, G-d our G-d, G-d is One," then all the ministering angels gather near the Holy One, blessed be He, and say before Him, "You are He ere the world was created; You are He since the world was created; You are He in this world, and You are He in the world to come. Sanctify Your Name upon them who sanctify Your Name." Then the Holy One, blessed be He, is pleased and satisfied, and He does not destroy His world, for the sake of Israel.[22a]*

The message of this passage is reflected in the prayers preceding the *Shema* of *Korbanoth*, wherein we find the words, "Most of their works are confusion, and the days of their lives are vanity... Except for the pure soul . . . Happy are we! how good is our portion. . . ." There we have the contrast between the general philosophy and way of life of the world around us—striving for material pleasures, and spending time in frivolous entertainment— and the Jewish way of life—where the important thing is prayer, study of the Torah, and bringing holiness into the everyday life.

Thus, the prayer "You are He" is, in a sense, a continuation of the same trend of thought which led up to the *Shema*. And at the

---

22 Otzar Hatefiloth I, p. 145.
22a Yalkut Shimoni 836, from Talmud Yerushalmi.

same time, it is also an elaboration of *Shema* itself, that is, of the concept of true *Unity,* the meaning of "One G-d."

When we declare that "G-d is One," we do not mean only that there is only one G-d and there is no other; but we mean also that there is *nothing else* but G-dliness; that G-d is one and the same before and after the world was created, and that the creation of the world has not brought about any change in G-d the Creator.

This is not an easy concept to grasp. In order to understand in some measure the true meaning of "G-d is One" (the Jewish concept of *Monotheism*), we have to turn to various sources of Jewish philosophy, particularly to Chasiduth based on the teachings of the Baal Shem Tov. A special section in the book of *Tanya* is devoted to this subject. What follows is only a very brief summary of the explanation:

When a human being makes anything, he does not create an entirely new thing; he only changes the form of things, using a raw material that is already available. Thus, a cabinet-maker who makes a piece of furniture, uses wood and glue or nails. Once the table or chair are made, they will not fall apart the moment their maker leaves them alone and steps outside.

But when G-d made heaven and earth and all that is in them, He had no "raw material" available; He *created* everything *out of nothing,* by simply saying, "Let there be!" Thus it is written, "By the word of G-d the heavens were created, and by the breath of His mouth—all their hosts."[23]

Since everything was created *out of nothing*—being out of non-being (unlike anything which is man-made, which is something out of something already existing before), the heaven and earth could not exist on their own; they exist only because G-d *constantly makes them exist.* If G-d would turn His attention away from them for a single instant, they would turn into nothing, as before they were created.

---

[23] Ps. 33:6.

The Baal Shem Tov (1698-1760) put it this way: It is written, "For ever, O G-d, Your word is fixed in heaven."[24] The "word" of G-d—'Let there be a firmament'[25]—is always there in heaven, and this is what makes the heavens exist. If G-d should withdraw His word, the heavens would be no more, for there is nothing else to keep them in existence.[26]

Our physical eye sees only physical (material) things. If our eye could see spiritual things, we would not see the things we now see—chairs, tables, trees, flowers, etc. Instead, we would only see their *real* being, namely, the "word" of G-d which creates and sustains everything from nothing. To put it in another way: Everything, even the "lifeless" things, such as sand, stone, wood, has a "soul," which is the source of the thing's existence, and this "soul" is nothing but the will of G-d that compels that thing to exist all the time, and not revert back to its former state of non-being.

If with our *physical* eye we see many, countless things, each apparently a separate thing, we can obtain quite a different view with our intellectual eye. Looking at the world with our intellectual eye, in the light of what has been said above, all the material "garments" of the things around us would be swept away, and in their place there would be revealed nothing but the will of G-d, which is one with G-d. Thus, in *reality,* there is nothing but G-d; the unity (oneness) of G-d is not affected by the creation of the world with all its multiple things.[27]

To help us understand a little how the creation of the world has not affected G-d the Creator, the author of the *Tanya* gives us the following illustration, based on the same idea that the world was created "by the word of G-d." When a person speaks a word, it does not affect any change in the person, for what is a word by

---

[24] Ps. 119:89.
[25] Gen. 1:3.
[26] Rabbi Schneur Zalman, Shaar Hayichud vehaEmunah, ch. 1, ff.
[27] Ibid., ch. 3.

comparison to the whole person? Much less does a word make a change in the person *before* it is spoken, but is still in the form of a thought, an unspoken word. Similarly, when the Torah says that everything was created by the "word" of G-d, it is to impress upon us that the whole world, the heavens with all their stars and planets, and the earth with all things on it and in it, everything that exists is like a "breath," or like a "word,"—like nothing in relation to G-d the Creator. Only to us, created beings that we are, these things appear like real things; to G-d they are like a "breath," or a "whiff," or a "word."[28]

So far, we have spoken of G-d as the Creator, Who has *revealed* Himself by creating the world. This is but one infinitesimal aspect of G-dliness, or, as we said before, merely a "word" of G-d. But G-d Himself is hidden from us, and even from the angels. It is the same G-d, however, Who is both "revealed" (in Creation, in Nature) and "hidden." And this is the meaning of "You are He." We speak in the second person, as if He were facing us ("Blessed are You"), but we must realize that even the *You* is hidden from us; how much more so the *He,* the Hidden G-d.

The rest of the Prayer of "You are He" speaks of the sanctification of G-d's Name (*Kiddush HaShem*). Usually, we speak of *Kiddush HaShem* when a Jew dies a martyr's death rather than give up his faith in the One G-d. We have already noted that the recital of the *Shema* in the early part of the Morning Prayer was originally instituted when the Jews were subjected to religious persecution under Persian rule.[29] Many Jews did sanctify G-d's Name by defying their religious oppressor, and proclaiming G-d's Unity. But we pray that G-d should sanctify His Name by rewarding the Jewsh people who sanctify G-d's Name, and punishing the enemies who defile G-d's Name. We further pray that G-d should send us a speedy salvation for the sake of His Name, and

[28] Iggereth Hakodesh ch. 25.
[29] See p. 70 above.

we conclude with "Blessed is He Who sanctifies His Name among the many (i.e. openly, in public)."[30]

אתה הוא בשמים ובארץ

YOU ARE HE . . . IN THE HEAVENS
AND ON THE EARTH

You are He Who is G-d the L-rd in the heavens and on the earth, and in the supernal heavens of the heavens. It is true that You are first and You are last, and besides You there is no G-d.

Gather the dispersions of those who hope in You, from the four corners of the earth. Then all men of the world will recognize and know that You are the L-rd, the only one, over all the kingdoms of the earth, that You made the heavens and the earth, the sea, and all that is in them, and who among all the creatures of Your hand, above or below, can say unto You, what You shall do, and how You shall act.

Our Father Who is in Heaven, Living and Eternal! Deal benevolently and graciously with us for the sake of Your Name by which we are called, and fulfill for us, O G-d our L-rd, the word which You have promised us by Your prophet Zephaniah, namely: "At that time will I bring you in, and at that time will I gather you in, for I will set you up for renown and for praise among all the peoples of the earth when I return your exiles before your eyes, said G-d."[30a]

---

[30] In some texts the prayer ends in the form of a regular blessing ("Blessed are You, O G-d, . . .").

[30a] Last verse of Zephaniah.

The above prayer is, of course, an extension of the preceding prayer. The thoughts expresed in it are the same: G-d's unity, immutability, and omnipotence; and the fervent hope that all mankind would recognize G-d's sovereignty. We pray that G-d gather in our exiles from the four corners of the earth, not for the sake of our good works, but as an act of pure benevolence, and in order to fulfill His promise which has kept our hope in G-d alive throughout the ages. Not before G-d restores our people to our former glory will G-d's own Name be recognized and glorified by all the nations of the world.

As can readily be seen by those who are familiar with the books of the Prophets and Holy Writings, the above prayer is a mosaic, so to speak, of Biblical verses, or partial verses.

קרבנות

THE KORBANOTH (Sacrifices)

The next section of the Morning Prayers is composed of a selection of readings, or studies, from the Torah and Talmud (including Mishnah), dealing with the laws of sacrifices (*Korbanoth*) and incense (*Ktoreth*). This section concludes with the *Beraitha* of Rabbi Yishmael on the thirteen principles (or methods) by which the Torah is interpreted.

There are several explanations why these selections have been inserted in the Siddur to be recited daily.

One reason is (as pointed out by the *Levush*[31]) to enable every Jew to fulfill the Mitzvah of "Talmud Torah" (study of the Torah). It is one of the basic commandments of the Torah that every Jew, without exception, study the Torah every day. The Torah consists of three main divisions—T'NaCh, Mishnah, and

---

[31] Rabbi Mordechai Jaffe (1530-1612).

Gemara. Thus, by reciting the Torah selections in the Siddur the Jew fulfills the *minimum* requirement of Torah study.

A further reason explains the particular choice of these readings, which, as can be seen, have to do with the service in the Beth Hamikdash of old. Our Sages tell us that he who studies the laws of the sacrifices is deemed as if he had actually offered them.[32] In another passage in the Talmud we find the same idea expanded further:

> Said Abraham, "Master of the World, it will be well when the Beth Hamikdash exists; what will happen when it does not exist?" Replied G-d, "I have already arranged for them the recital of the sacrifices; when they read it before Me, I will consider it as if they had actually offered them before Me, and I will forgive them their sins."[33]

Further emphasis on the importance of the recital of *Korbanoth* as a substitute for their actual offering (now that the Beth Hamikdash is not in existence) is given by our Sages in various Midrashic sources.

As a matter of fact, our daily prayers, morning and evening, are the counterpart of the daily communal sacrifices in the Beth Hamikdash, as was stated by Rabbi Joshua ben Levi.[34] This view is also reaffirmed by our Sages in other Talmudic and Midrashic sources. In other words, just as the purpose of the sacrifices was to bring the individual, and our people as a whole, *closer* to G-d (the word *korban* is derived from the Hebrew verb meaning "approach"), so is the purpose of prayer. This is also the reason why on Shabbos, Rosh Chodesh, and the Festivals we have the "Additional Service" (*Musaf*), namely, because of the additional

---

[32] Menachoth 110a.
[33] Megillah 31a; Taanith 27b.
[34] Berachoth 26b.

sacrifices that were offered in the Beth Hamikdash on those days.

The sacrifices, whether communal (offered for the whole people) or individual, were the means of achieving "atonement," that is, of serving as a tangible expression of repentance, in order to reestablish the unity, or the state of "at-oneness," with G-d, which had been disrupted by sin. For, whenever a sin is committed, a "wall" or partition, comes into being, which separates the sinner from G-d. The sacrifice removes that partition. How? Certainly not by "magic." The offering of sacrifices was called *avodah,* service. This service included *viduy* (confession of the sin committed), and mental concentration and contemplation. In addition, just before the animal was killed in the prescribed way, the owner of it had to press his two hands on the head of the animal, as if placing the animal in his own stead. This is to bring home to the repenter that all that is being done to the animal should really have been done to him for having transgressed the Will of G-d. However, G-d, in His mercy, permitted him to offer an animal as a substitute in his place. Therefore, the least that he, the sinner, can do is to purify his *thoughts, speech,* and *acts* which had participated in the commission of the sin, and to consecrate them again to G-d alone. This is symbolized by the abovementioned three things which must accompany the sacrifice, namely, *kavanah* (*mental* concentration), *viduy* (*oral* confession of the sin) and *semichah* (resting the *hands* on the head of the *korban*).

In a deeper sense, the *korban* assumes new dimensions. The animal sacrifice symbolizes the "animal" soul in man, which has, temporarily at least (during the commission of the sin), taken the upper hand over the Divine soul in man. The Divine soul is always dedicated to G-d. But the animal soul is sometimes moved by temptations and passions which lead man into sin. By sacrificing the animal as a *korban* to G-d, the repenter is visibly and forcefully reminded that it is the animal soul in him which needs to be offered to G-d. This message is further emphasized by the fact that all the *fat* and *blood* of the animal had to be offered to G-d.

The *fat* symbolized excessive indulgence and unused energy, and the *blood*—the passions and very life, all of which should be consecrated to G-d. Similarly are all the other details connected with the laws of *korbanoth* profoundly symbolic and instructive, each detail containing a lesson how better to serve G-d and how closer to become attached to Him (as explained at length in the holy books of the Kabbalah and Chasiduth).[35]

And while we do not have any actual *korbanoth* now, and especially because of it, our *study* of the meaning and significance of the *korbanoth,* and our *prayers* which substitute for the service in the Beth Hamikdash of old, have the same purpose—to bring us closer to G-d.

קטורת

KETORETH

The Torah readings about the *Korbanoth* (Sacrifices) are followed by the reading of the portion of *Ketoreth*—Incense.[36] It is preceded in the Siddur by the following introductory lines:

> *You are He, O G-d our G-d, before Whom our ances- tors offered the incense of the spices at the time when the Beth Hamikdash was in existence, as You have commanded them through Mosheh Your prophet, as it is written in Your Torah — —*

The Biblical reading is followed by a reading from the Talmud, namely, a Beraitha (of Tannaic origin), found (with variations) in the Babylonian Talmud[37] and Talmud Yerushalmi,[38] which deals with the actual blending of the Incense (*Pitum haKetoreth*).

---

35 Lik. Torah, Vayyikra 2b, and Index, under "Korbanoth".
36 Exod. 30:34-38.
37 Kerithoth 6a.
38 Yoma 4:4.

Our Sages of the Talmud tell us that Mosheh Rabbenu was told at Mount Sinai to use eleven kinds of spices, in certain proportions, to be blended together into *Ketoreth*. (In the Torah only several of the main ingredients are mentioned explicitly, with an allusion to a composition of eleven, as the Sages explain.) The eleven spices that went into the Ketoreth were: balm, onycha, galbanum and frankincense (70 "maneh" of each); myrrh, cassia, spikenard and saffron (16 "maneh" of each); costus (12); aromatic bark (3) and cinnamon (9)—for a total of 368 "manehs." In addition, certain other ingredients were added to improve the appearance and strengthen the odor. These included lye of Carsina, Cyprus wine (or other strong wine), salt of Sodom, and a small quantity of herb which caused the smoke to go up.

The said quantity (368 manehs) constituted a year's supply: 365 manehs, corresponding to the days of the year, half a maneh being offered in the morning and the other half towards evening. The remaining 3 manehs were offered by the Kohen Gadol on Yom Kippur, in the Holy of Holies.

The Ketoreth was offered twice daily (as already mentioned), on the Golden Altar, also called the Inner Altar, and the Altar of Incense.

The offering of the Ketoreth in the Sanctuary was one of the great mysteries of the Divine service in the Beth Hamikdash of old. The extraordinary holiness and significance of Ketoreth is emphasized in the Torah by the penalty of כרת (death) for making an identical composition as a perfume for personal use. The death penalty was incurred also if any one of its eleven ingredients were omitted. Several events in the early history of our people further emphasized the mystery of Ketoreth. On the eighth (and last) day of the Dedication of the first Sanctuary in the Wilderness (in the second year since the Exodus from Egypt), Nadav and Avihu, Aaron's two elder sons, died mysteriously in the Sanctuary when they offered Ketoreth not in the prescribed manner.[39] Later, during the rebellion of Korah, 250 of his followers died a similar death when they offered Ketoreth in a test of authority.[40] On the other hand, when, to punish the rebellious people, a widespread plague broke out immediately after the Korah rebellion, Aaron stopped the plague with an offering of Ketoreth.[41]

However, *all* Divine commandments are shrouded in mystery (the Infinite Wisdom of G-d Who commanded them), yet they also have some revealed aspects in terms of instruction and inspiration towards a holy life in the daily life and conduct of the Jew. So is the case with Ketoreth. Thus, our Sages tell us that the offering of Ketoreth brought atonement for "evil tongue."[42] It served as a daily reminder to the people, that, just as there was life and death in Ketoreth, so there was "life and death in the power of the tongue."[43]

The Midrash *Tanhuma*[44] states that the Hebrew word *Ketoreth* forms an acrostic of the initial letters of the four Hebrew words: K—*kedushah* (holiness), T—*taharah* (purity), R—*rachamim* (mercy) and T—*tikvah* (hope).

In the holy *Zohar* we find many passages on the importance of the daily recital of Ketoreth (now that it cannot actually be offered). One passage reads: "The person who recites the portion of Ketoreth with devotion every day, will be spared any manner of sorrow or hurt all that day."[45] It is followed by the declaration: "If mortal man would realize how the Holy One, blessed be He, cherishes the portion of Ketoreth, he would take each and every letter of it and put it upon his head as a golden crown."

---

39 Lev. 10:1-5.
40 Num. 16:35.
41 Num. 17:6-15.
42 Yoma 44a.
43 Prov. 18:21.
44 Tanhuma, Tetzave 14.
45 Zohar I, 218.

In Chasidic (particularly Chabad) literature, the various details connected with Ketoreth are expounded, and some of its mysteries are revealed. For example, it is explained that "Ketoreth" means "binding" (in Aramaic translation). If *Korbanoth,* as we have already noted, have to do with the idea of *approaching* G-d, *Ketoreth* symbolizes a closer attachment and *unity* with G-d. This unity of the finite world with the Infinite is achieved through the Torah, which is itself a blend of the Infinite with the finite.[46]

Furthermore, the rising smoke of the Ketoreth, which rose in a straight column upwards, symbolized the soul's yearning to soar heavenward, a yearning that can be fulfilled only through the fulfillment of the Divine commandments; man's turning to G-d.[47]

Again, Ketoreth is associated with the sense of smell, the most "spiritual" of all the human senses. Smell is regarded as something which gratifies the spirit, not the body. (That is why it is permitted to use smelling salts, and the like, on Yom Kippur, while the consumption of any food or drink is strictly forbidden.) Ketoreth is therefore said to symbolize the highest and purest form of spiritual communion with G-d. This is further emphasized by the fact that the Ketoreth had to be offered on the "Inner Altar," symbolic of the "inner heart."[48] In other words, the offering of Ketoreth expressed the inner impulse inherent deep in the heart of every Jew to bind himself to G-d through the Torah and Mitzvoth.

Commenting on the verse, "Let my prayer be set forth before You as Ketoreth,"[49] our Sages say that there was nothing King David desired more than to be able to offer Ketoreth to G-d in the Beth Hamikdash. While this wish was not granted to him, his request was granted that prayer could substitute for Ketoreth, as in the case of the Korbanoth, during the time when the Beth

---

46 Lik. Torah, Vayyikra 6d.
47 Ibid., Nasso 22d.
48 Ibid., 29a.
49 Ps. 141:2.

Hamikdash is not in existence. It is necessary to recite the portion of Ketoreth, and the prayers in general, with true devotion, as the saintly *Zohar* emphasized it.

The section of Ketoreth in the Siddur is followed (according to the Nusach Ari) by three verses from the Psalms of David, repeated three times each, and one verse from the Prophet Malachi. They are:

> G-d of Hosts (*i.e., hosts of heaven, and hosts of Israel*) *is with us, G-d of Jacob is our high refuge.*[50]
> G-d of Hosts, happy the man who trusts in You.[51]
>
> Save, O G-d; answer us, O king, on the day we call.[52]
> May the offering of Judah and Jerusalem be pleasant to G-d as in the days of yore and the years of old.[53]

אביי הוה מסדר סדר המערכה
ORDER OF THE DAILY SERVICE IN THE BETH HAMIKDASH

Having read the Biblical portions dealing with the daily Korbanoth and the Ketoreth, we now read in the Siddur (Nusach Ari) a section from the Talmud,[54] in which the Amora Abaye presents an outline of the entire order of the daily service (*Avodah*) in the Beth Hamikdash, as he taught it to the disciples of his academy, on the authority of Abba Shaul.

The order of the service was as follows:

1. First thing in the morning, a "major arrangement" of pieces of wood, stacked in the form of a miniature "house" with a "win-

---

50 Ps. 46:8.
51 Ps. 84:13.
52 Ps. 20:10.
53 Malachi 3:4.
54 Yoma 33a.

dow," was placed on the south-eastern corner of the *Mizbe'ach*
(Altar). Firewood was then placed in the "window" to set the
wood on fire. On this fire all the daily Korbanoth were eventually
burnt.

2. A second firewood arrangement, similar to the first, was
then placed on the western side of the Altar. The glowing coals
from this fire were to serve for the burning of the Ketoreth
(Incense) on the Golden Altar in the Inner Sanctuary. The coals
were carried in a golden pan.

3. Next, two pieces of wood, each one cubit long, were placed
on the burning wood arrangement.

4. This was followed by the "removal of the ashes" from the
"Inner Altar" (or Golden Altar, or Incense Altar), upon which
the Ketoreth had been offered on the previous day. A golden
vessel was used for the removal of the ashes.

5. Next came the "dressing of the five lamps" (of the seven-
lamp Menorah). The wicks were taken out and the remainder of
the oil in the lamps was collected into a golden jug, whereupon
the lamps were cleaned dry, and then filled with new oil and wicks.

6. Next in the order of the service was the sprinkling of the
blood from the daily morning sacrifice (*Tamid*)—on the north-
eastern and south-western corners of the Altar.

7. Then the other two lamps of the Menorah in the Sanctuary
were dressed in the same manner as the five lamps.

8. Then the Ketoreth was offered on the Golden Altar.

9. Following this came the offering of the parts of the *Tamid*
which had been prepared for this purpose. They were offered on
the Outer Altar mentioned earlier (item 1).

10. Next came the meal-offering, which accompanied the
Tamid sacrifice.

11. This was followed by the baked meal-offering ("Cha-vittin")—the first part of the Kohen Gadol's offering; the second part was offered with the second *Tamid* in the afternoon.

12. It was followed by the wine-offering.

During the wine-offering the second-ranking Kohen ("Segan") raised a flag as a signal for two Kohanim to sound the trumpets, and for the Levites to begin the chanting of the "Psalm of the Day" to the accompaniment of musical instruments.

13. On Shabbos, Rosh-Chodesh and Festivals, the additional (*Musaf*) sacrifices were offered at this point.

14. On Shabbos, two spoonfuls of frankincense ("Chavittin"), which had lain all week by the "Shew-Bread" (*Lechem haPanim*) on the Golden Table in the Sanctuary, were now offered.

From then on, and until about 4:30 p.m., private sacrifices were offered.

15. The last part of the daily service was the offering of the evening-Tamid. It was followed by the offering of the second part of the Ketoreth, the meal-offering, the second half of the Bazichin, and the wine-offering—all in the same order and manner as in the case of the Morning-Tamid—and the lighting of the Menorah.

After the Evening-Tamid no sacrifices were offered until the following morning, when the daily Avodah was repeated. The parts of the Evening-Tamid were left to burn on the Altar through the night.

We have already mentioned previously that the Korbanoth and Ketoreth contained deep mysteries of communication and attachment between the Jewish people and G-d. It was therefore most imperative that the sacred Avodah in the Beth Hamikdash be carried out exactly as Divinely ordained in the Torah and transmitted through the Oral Law. Thus, even after the Beth Hamikdash was destroyed, the order of the Service in the Sanctuary was taught and preserved, in anticipation of the time when the Beth

Hamikdash will be rebuilt again (when Mashiach will appear) and the Avodah will be restored. In the meantime, our daily prayers, and our reading of the appropriate passages in the Torah and Talmud, substitute for the Avodah, and have the same effect of bringing us closer to G-d.

Furthermore, whenever we read or recite such passages relating to the Avodah in the Beth Hamikdash of old, we are reminded of the Glory of the Shechinah (Divine Presence) as it manifested itself in the Beth Hamikdash in those days. With the destruction of the Beth Hamikdash the Shechinah, too, went into "exile," as it were, together with us. It is this great "eclipse" of the Shechinah, referred to in the Torah as the "concealment (hiding) of the Divine Countenance," that has been our undoing during the present long "night" of our Galuth (exile). If the Geulah (Redemption) has not yet come, it is because we have not yet corrected all the mistakes of the past which brought about the destruction of the Beth Hamikdash. This is what our Sages meant when they said, "Each generation which does not witness the restoration of the Beth Hamikdash should regard itself as if witnessing the destruction of the Beth Hamikdash."[55] For this reason we say in our (Festival) prayers, "Because of *our* sins (not our Fathers') we have been exiled from our land." These contemplations should lead us to the obvious conclusion—a greater determination to live a better, purer and holier daily life, in accordance with the Will of G-d, as revealed to us in the Torah and Mitzvoth. This, in fact, is an essential purpose of our daily prayers.

---

55 Talm. Yerush. Yoma 1:1.

אנא בכח

PRAYER OF RABBI NECHUNIA

*We beseech, You (O, G-d), free the captive (Israel)
by Your right hand's mighty power;*

*Accept the prayer of Your people; uplift us, purify us,
O Revered One;*

*We beseech You, O Mighty One, guard as the apple
of the eye those who seek Your Unity;*

*Bless them, purify them, have mercy upon them;
Your righteousness always bestow upon them;*

*Almighty, Holy One, lead Your flock in Your boun-
tiful goodness;*

*Only-One Supreme, turn to Your people who re-
member Your holiness;*

*Accept our supplication and hearken to our cry, You
Who know all hidden things.*

This prayer is called the "Prayer of Rabbi Nechunia ben
HaKaneh," a *Tanna* (Sage) who lived at the time of the destruction of the Second Beth Hamikdash. His teachings and sayings
are to be found in various sections of the Talmud. The Talmud
relates wonderful things about the power of his prayers. However,
there is some question as to whether he was indeed the author of
this prayer. At any rate, according to the Kabbalah, and particularly the saintly Ari, this is a very holy prayer, with deep mystical
implications.

The prayer consists of *seven lines,* each containing *six* words.
The total number of words (42) signifies one of the mystical
Divine Names which, spelled out in the Holy Tongue, has the
numerical value of 42. The seven lines symbolize the Seven

Divine Middoth (Attributes) by means of which G-d rules the
world. The seven branches of the Menorah have a similar meaning. Hence the frequent recurrence of the number "seven" in the
Torah and in Jewish life. The number six, likewise, has a deep
mystical meaning. It is related to the six wings of the Seraphim
(angels) which Isaiah saw in his prophetic vision, pronouncing
the Kedushah ("Holy, holy, holy . . .") and proclaiming G-d's
Unity in all the worlds.[56] This is also why the verse "Shema," by
which we pronounce G-d's Unity, contains six words.

While the average worshipper is not expected to delve into all
the mysteries of the Kabbalah, everyone is expected to know, at
least, the meaning of the words.

This prayer is concluded with the familiar verse, "Blessed be
the name of His glorious Kingdom forever and ever."

איזהו מקומן
MISHNAH: ZEVACHIM

After the reading of sections of the Torah, on the subjects of
Korbanoth and *Ketoreth,* followed by Talmudic studies and the
Prayer of Rabbi Nechunia ben HaKaneh, all of which was discussed earlier, there follow in the Siddur readings from Mishnayoth,[57] beginning with the Mishnah *Eizehu mekoman* ("Which
were the places of sacrifices?").

Various laws regulated the place and manner of offering of the
various sacrifices. These and other basic regulations are detailed
in the said chapter of Mishnayoth, *Eizehu mekoman.*

It will be well to review here, however briefly, the subject of
Korbanoth, so that we will have a better understanding of the
Torah and Talmudic passages relating to the sacrifices which form
part of our Siddur.

---

56 Isaiah 6:3.
57 Zevachim, ch. 5.

There were two broad categories of *Korbanoth* (1) Communal Sacrifices and (2) Private, or individual, Sacrifices.

The Communal Sacrifices (*Korbanoth Tzibur*) were offered in behalf of the whole community of Israel, the Jewish people. They included the *daily* sacrifice, called *tamid,* a lamb in the morning and a lamb in the evening; and the *additional* sacrifices (*musaf*), offered on Shabbos, Rosh Chodesh, the Three Festivals, Shemini Atzereth, Rosh Hashanah and Yom Kippur, consisting of various sacrifices in each case.

In the case of *individual* sacrifices, that is, sacrifices offered by individuals, there were the following kinds: (1) Burnt Offering (*Olah*), (2) Sin Offering (*Chattath*), (3) Guilt Offering (*Asham*), (4) Peace Offering (*Shelamim*). In addition there were three more: (1) Paschal Sacrifice (*Pesach*), (2) First Born (*Bechor*), and (3) Tithe (*Maaser*).

There were certain other individual sacrifices, connected with special situations.

Communal Sacrifices could be either *Burnt Offering,* or *Sin Offering,* (except the two lambs that were brought as *Peace Offerings* in conjunction with *Two Loaves* on Shavuoth).

The *Burnt Offering* brought by an individual was *voluntary,* when a person pledged such a sacrifice.[58]

The *Sin Offering* had to be brought in certain instances by an individual when he committed a sin unknowingly, and later discovered his mistake. These were mainly in the area of offenses against G-d.

The *Guilt Offering* had to be brought by an individual in certain cases of transgression, mainly in the area of offenses against fellow-man.

The *Peace Offering,* like the Burnt Offering, could be offered by an individual at his own will, or in conjunction with a Thanksgiving Offering (*Todah*).

---

[58] There were also certain Burnt Offerings which were *mandatory* on certain occasions.

In addition there were two sacrifices which an individual had to bring when he made a pilgrimage to the Beth Hamikdash; one was *Korban Re'iyah*, which was a *Burnt Offering*, and the other was *Korban Chagigah*, which was a *Peace Offering*.

All sacrifices fell into one or other of two main categories: (1) *Kodshei kodashim*—sacrifices of a higher degree of holiness, and (2) *Kodashim kalim*—sacrifices of a lesser degree of holiness. The first included the *olah, chattath, asham* and the *public shelamim* of Shavuoth (mentioned above). In the second category belong the various kinds of individual *shelamim*, also the *bechor*, *maaser* and *pesach*.

Except in the case of the *olah* and a certain type of *chattath*, which were burnt completely unto G-d, the *kohanim* received, as their due, certain parts of all other animal sacrifices that were brought to the Beth Hamikdash.

The parts of sacrifices belonging in the category of *kodshei kodashim* could be eaten only by *male* kohanim; those belonging in the category of *kodashim kalim* could be eaten by the *whole* household of the kohen, including servants.

In the case of individual *shelamim*, the major portion of the animal (except the parts offered on the *mizbe'ach* [altar] and those due to the kohanim) belonged to the person bringing the sacrifice. This is one of the reasons why this kind of sacrifice was called *shelamim* ("peace offering") for it created peace and unity for all concerned: the offerer, the kohanim, and G-d.

Finally, the *bechor* had to be given to the kohen to be used for food; the *maaser* belonging to the owner, to be eaten by any person; and the *pesach*—could be eaten only by members of the group who joined in it. All three, of course, had first to be brought to the Beth Hamikdash, with certain portions of the fat and blood offered to G-d; only then could the kohanim and the owners have their share, which had to be eaten in purity and holiness, in a specified time.

רבי ישמעאל אומר בשלש עשרה מדות

BERAITHA OF RABBI YISHMAEL

The Beraitha of Rabbi Yishmael (taken from the Introduction to the *Sifra,* the Halachic Midrash on the Book of *Vayyikra*) appears in the Siddur as the last of the selections from the Torah, Mishnah and Talmud which have been included in the Siddur for reasons explained previously.

In this Beraitha, Rabbi Yishmael formulates the thirteen principles (*Middoth*) by which the Torah is interpreted. Its place at the beginning of the *Sifra* is explained by the fact that most of the Halachoth in this Halachic Midrash are derived from the application of these principles. However, these principles are frequently applied throughout the Talmud when it traces the sources of the various laws in the text of the Torah, both the laws which are explicitly mentioned in the Torah, as well as those laws which are implied in the text, and are inferred by means of any of the said thirteen principles.

It should be remembered that the Torah (the Five Books of the Pentateuch) which was given to the Jewish people through Mosheh Rabbenu, and written down by him (hence, *Torah shebiKthav,* "Written Torah") was given to, and transmitted by, Mosheh together with its interpretation. In other words, the Written Torah was given together with the Oral Torah (*Torah shebe'al Peh*), or *Masorah* (Tradition). The latter was not written down by Mosheh, but transmitted orally by him to Joshua, who in turn transmitted it to the Elders, and they to the Prophets, and the latter to the Men of the Great Assembly, who handed it down to the *Tannaim,* the Sages of the Mishnah. In the last generation of the Tannaim, the whole body of the Oral Law was arranged and recorded by Rabbi Yehudah haNassi, in the form of the Six Orders of the Mishnah. Subsequently, the Mishnah itself was explained and expounded by the disciples of the Tannaim, called

the *Amoraim,* and their disciples, as well as by subsequent generations of Torah scholars, called *Rabbanan Seburai.* When this vast
accumulation of knowledge, called *Gemara,* was also recorded
alongside with the Mishnah, the *Talmud* was completed. But
although the Oral Law (the *Talmud Bavli* and *Talmud Yerushalmi, Midrashim,* etc.) was now also written down, it still re-
tained its original title *Torah shebe'al-Peh* ("Oral Law") to distinguish it from the *Torah shebiKthav* ("Written Law").

Thus, the thirteen principles of interpretation were themselves
part of the Oral Law, transmitted from generation to generation,
since the time of Mosheh Rabbenu. Rabbi Yishmael merely formulated and defined them, and listed them. They follow below,
together with a brief explanation:

1

קל וחומר

Deduction *from minor to major,* and *vice versa.*

An example of a simple *Kal vaChomer* is found in the passage
where Mosheh says to G-d, "If the children of Israel did not listen
to me, why should Pharaoh listen to me?".[59] Rashi comments on
this verse that it is one of ten instances of *Kal vaChomer* mentioned in the Torah.[60]

The actual application of this principle is based on the passage
in the Torah,[61] speaking of Miriam's punishment for slandering
her brother Mosheh. That passage, in effect, declares that "had
Miriam angered her father to the extent of her father spitting in
front of her, she would have been held in contempt and isolation
outside the camp for seven days; how much more so when she
angered G-d." By inference, she would be deserving of at least
double the punishment, that is, expulsion from the camp for

---

[59] Exod. 6:12.
[60] See Ber. Rabba ch. 32.
[61] Num. 12:14.

fourteen days. Yet G-d ordered her expelled for seven days only. Here the Torah teaches that in applying the *Kal vaChomer*, the *inference must be limited to the original premise;* no more and no less. In other words, if the law is such-and-such in a lighter case, it certainly could be no more lenient, but also *no more severe,* in a graver case.

The same principle applies in the reverse. If in a graver situation the Torah shows a certain leniency, we can infer that the leniency should certainly apply in a lighter case; again, no more and no less.[62]

2

גזרה שוה

Inference from a *similarity of words or phrases* in two different texts in the Torah. This means that when an identical, or similar, word, or expression, is found in the Torah in two separate cases, it is an indication that there is an analogy between the two, and that one case complements the other. An example of the application of this principle is found in the law of prohibiting the tearing out of one's hair as a sign of mourning, in the manner of the heathen.[63] Elsewhere[64] a similar prohibition is stated in reference to *Kohanim.* In both cases the word קרחה ("making baldness") is used. *According to Tradition,* this is a case where the principle of *Gezerah Shavah* is to be applied, to infer that just as in the case of Kohanim the prohibition refers to *any part* of the head, so in the case of ordinary Jews; and just as in the case of the latter, the prohibition refers to mourning after the dead, so it is also in the case of the Kohanim. We underscored "according to Tradition," because this principle (as also the others) cannot be used freely, but only where it has been transmitted by Tradition.

---

[62] E.g. Mishnah, Zevachim 49b.
[63] Deut. 14:1.
[64] Lev. 21:5.

3

בנין אב

The *establishment of a precedent,* or general rule, to be extended to similar cases. For example, the Torah permits the preparation of food on the Festival of Pesach.[65] Since Pesach is the first of all the festivals, it serves as a precedent for all other festivals in regard to the permissibility of preparing food on any Yom Tov.

The said principle may be based on one text, as in the instance just mentioned, or on two texts. As an example of the latter may be cited the law regarding defects or deformities. The definition of physical defects is derived from two texts in the Torah, one dealing with defects in *humans,* which disqualify a Kohen from serving in the Beth Hamikdash,[66] the other specifying defects in *animals,* which disqualify them from being offered as sacrifices.[67] The texts are taken together to determine what constitutes a defect, whenever the word "defect" is mentioned in the Torah, be it in regard to animal or man.

4

כלל ופרט

A *general rule followed by a particular* (or particulars). In this case, the general rule is qualified by, and limited to, the particulars, and no more. For example, it is written, "When any man of you bring a sacrifice unto G-d, of a beast, of cattle, or of sheep."[68] "Beast" is a general term which might include also kosher wild animals. But the general term "beast" is followed by specific particulars, namely, "cattle" and "sheep," and therefore limited to

---

65 Exod. 12:16.
66 Lev. 21:20.
67 Lev. 22:22.
68 Lev. 1:2.

these only. Hence wild animals are excluded, and not permitted to be offered as sacrifices.

5
פרט וכלל

A *particular term followed by a general term*. In this case, the general term determines what is to be included. An example of this principle may be found in the law of returning lost property. It is written, "And so you shall do to his ass and to his garment."[69] These are specified categories which would rule out any other. However, the text continues, "and so you shall do to *any lost thing* of your brother," which is a general statement, making it a commandment to return any lost articles that could be identified by the owner.

6
כלל ופרט וכלל

A *general term, followed by particulars, followed again by a general term*. Here the particulars specified in the text are not exclusive (as in No. 4), but they are considered as *collective* terms, to include anything which has similar characteristics, excluding things which lack these characteristics. A case in point is the law of safe-keeping, or trusteeship. It is written in the Torah, "If a man deliver unto his friend money or utensils to keep . . .".[70] The statement opens with a general proposition ("if a man deliver to his friend"), then continues with particulars ("money or utensils"), and again with a general term ("to keep"). Applying the above principle, the inference is that not only money or utensils

[69] Deut. 22:23.
[70] Exod. 22:6.

are covered by this law, but also all such articles that have the characteristics of *money* and *utensils,* namely, (1) have intrinsic value, and (2) are movable. Accordingly, the law does *not* cover such things as a field, because it is immovable, nor a credit note, because it has no value *of its own* (except the "paper" on which it is written).

7

מכלל שהוא צריך לפרט, ומפרט שהוא צריך לכלל

A general proposition requiring a particular term to explain it, and, conversely, a *particular term requiring a general rule to complete it.*

An example of the application of this principle can be found in the law about the consecration of the First-born. It is written in the Torah, "Sanctify unto Me all the first-born."[71] This is a general proposition which, by itself, would include also a female firstling. But elsewhere[72] the Torah specifies "male only." The question would still remain. Perhaps what is meant is the first of all the male babies, even though it was preceded by a female baby? So the text specifies further—"that openeth the womb"[73]; it must actually be the *first-born* baby, second to none. It might still be asked, The text implies the first baby born *naturally*; what if there was first a baby that was delivered by means of a caesarian operation? So the text makes it clear by insisting on it being a *firstling* (*Bechor*). Thus, the general term "first-born" is explained by the specific terms, to indicate that only such a first-born is consecrated which has all three conditions: (1) male, (2) delivered *naturally* and (3) an actual firstling.[74]

---

71 Exod. 13:2.
72 Deut. 15:19.
73 Exod. 13:2.
74 Berachoth 19a.

8

כל דבר שהי' בכלל ויצא מן הכלל ללמד, לא ללמד על
עצמו יצא, אלא ללמד על הכלל כלו יצא

When a subject which is already included in a general proposition is afterward mentioned separately in order to give some new information, it is not meant to be an isolated instance, but to clarify the general proposition as well.

An example of the application of this principle is found in the law concerning the prohibition of work on Shabbos. It is written in the Torah, "You shall do no work (on Shabbos)."[75] Later, it is written, "You shall kindle no fire on the Shabbos day."[76] The kindling of fire is already included in the general prohibition of work (which covers 39 categories of work used in the building of the Sanctuary, as transmitted by Tradition); why, then, was the kindling of fire mentioned separately? The answer is: In order to establish a rule applying both to itself as well as to all other categories of work included in the general prohibition. This is to say: Just as the kindling of fire is one of the principal categories of work prohibited on Shabbos, which makes the absent-minded transgressor (who forgot that it was prohibited work) liable to bring a sin-offering *separately* (even when committed together with any other of the 39 types of work), so is any other of the 39 principal categories of work liable separately. In other words, on the basis of this principle, the law is that where a person performs two or more of the said 39 categories of work on Shabbos, forgetting that they were prohibited, he must bring a sin offering for each, and for as many, of the works which he so performed.

---

[75] Exod. 20:10.
[76] Exod. 35:3.

9

כל דבר שהי' בכלל ויצא לטעון טען אחד שהוא כענינו,
יצא להקל ולא להחמיר

*When a subject already included in a general rule is excepted
(mentioned separately) in order to specify a certain point which
is also included in the rule, this exception is intended to alleviate
and not to aggravate this particular case.*

An example of the application of this principle may be found
in the law concerning *nega'im* (blemishes, or symptoms of *tzara'at*,
"leprosy").[77] The Torah begins with a general rule about skin
blemishes,[78] specifying three *severe* symptoms, the first two of
which being signs of *tumah* (defilement, i.e., that the person is
definitely afflicted with the plague): (1) hair turned white in the
blemish,[79] (2) quick raw flesh (open sore) in the swelling of the
skin[80] and (3) if there has been no change in the skin blemish
during the first week of isolation, a second week of isolation is
required, at the end of which, if no change is noticeable, the person
is declared *tahor* (ritually clean).[81] At the same time, the Torah
specifies a "favorable" symptom, namely, a white discoloration of
the entire skin.[82]

This general rule is followed in the Torah by two particular
skin blemishes: (a) one that has developed in a "boil" which had
healed,[83] and (b) one that has developed in a spot of the skin
which had a burning by fire.[84] In each of the two cases, only one
severe symptom is mentioned, namely, hair turning white.[85]

---

[77] Sifra, on Lev. ch. 13.
[78] Lev. 13:2.
[79] Lev. 13:3.
[80] Lev. 13:10-11.
[81] Lev. 13:5-6.
[82] Lev. 13:12-13.
[83] Lev. 13:8.
[84] Lev. 13:24.
[85] Lev. 13:20, 25.

According to the said principle, therefore, we say that the intent of each of these two exceptions is to alleviate the case, and not to aggravate it. This is to say, we apply to these cases the rule of the *favorable* symptom (whiteness of the whole skin), but not the rule of the *severe* symptoms (Nos. 2 and 3, mentioned above), except the one mentioned specifically (hair turning white).

10

כל דבר שהי' בכלל ויצא למעון מען אחר שלא כעניגו,
יצא להקל ולהחמיר

When a subject already included in a general rule is excepted, in order to specify a certain point not covered by the general rule, the exception is intended to alleviate in some respects and to aggravate in other respects.

An example of the application of this principle is found in connection with the law of *nega'im* (blemishes), when affecting the *head* or *beard*.[86] However, here the Torah introduces a *new* symptom, not previously included in the general rule, namely, *yellow* hair as a sign of *tumah*.[87] Hence, according to the present principle, the Torah indicates that the purpose of the exception is to apply to it the severity of yellow hair, as a sign of *tumah,* while giving it the leniency of white hair *not* being a sign of *tumah* in this case (though white hair is a symptom of *tumah* in other skin blemishes).

11

כל דבר שהי' בכלל ויצא לדון בדבר חדש, אי אתה יכול
להחזירנו לכללו, עד שיחזירנו הכתוב לכללו בפרוש

A subject already included in a general rule and afterwards excepted in order to deal with a new matter, cannot be reincluded in the general rule unless the text expressly does this.

---

[86] Lev. 13:29.
[87] Lev. 13:30.

By way of an example: A *metzora* ("leper"), having been
cleared of his leprosy, had to bring certain sacrifices for atonement,
among them a he-lamb as a guilt offering (*asham*). (One of the
reasons for his requiring atonement was the fact that his being
afflicted with the plague was a punishment for *lashon-hara,* evil
tongue and defamation, whereby he isolated people from one another. He was, therefore, smitten with the plague and isolated from
the community, so that during his isolation and affliction he could
think and repent.) The Torah states that this he-lamb was to be
sacrificed in the same place where any sin-offering and burnt-
offering was sacrificed, that is, in the northerly corner of the altar.
The text then goes on to say, "for as the sin-offering so is the
guilt-offering."[88] Now, this general rule is already mentioned
once.[89] It was, however, necessary to restate it because the case of
the leper's guilt-offering was excepted from the general rule by
the introduction of a new law attending it, namely, smearing some
blood of the sacrifice on the right ear, thumb, and large toe of the
cured leper[89a] (a ceremony not required in the usual case of any
other guilt-offering). Consequently, one might have thought that
the exception applied also in other respects (e.g., burning of the
fat on the altar, etc.). Hence the re-inclusion of this particular
case into its original category, or general rule.

12

דבר הלמד מעניינו ודבר הלמד מסופו

A subject inferred from its context, or from the subsequent text.
For example, one of the Ten Commandments is "You shall not
steal."[90] Our Rabbis declare that this refers to stealing (kidnap-

---

88 Lev. 14:13.
89 Lev. 7:1.
89a Lev. 14:14.
90 Exod. 20:13.

ping) a human being, which is punishable by death. They infer this from the fact that this "stealing" appears in the same context with "You shall not murder," etc., which the Torah (elsewhere) clearly makes a crime punishable by death. On the other hand, the text "You shall not steal, neither shall you deal falsely," etc.[91] refers to stealing money, or valuables, which is not subject to a death penalty.

An example of the application of the second part of this principle is found in the law concerning a plague on a house. It is written, "When you come in the land of Canaan . . . and I put a plague of leprosy in a house, in the land of your possession."[92] The Torah does not specify here as to what kind of a house, a wooden one, or a brick one. Later on, however, referring to the afflicted house, the text mentions specifically, "its stones, timber and mortar."[93] Thus the text later clarifies what type of a house is subject to this law.

13

וכן שני כתובים המכחישים זה את זה, עד שיבוא הכתוב
השלישי ויכריע ביניהם

When two texts contradict each other, they can only be understood by a third text which reconciles them.

For example, it is written, "And I will speak unto You (Mosheh) from above the *kapporeth*."[94] The *kapporeth* was the golden cover of the Ark in the *Holy of Holies*. Another text says, "And G-d spoke unto him from the tent of meeting."[95] The "tent of the meeting" (*ohel-moed*) was the *Sanctuary at large*. Thus,

---

91 Lev. 19:11.
92 Lev. 14:34.
93 Lev. 14:45.
94 Exod. 25:22.
95 Lev. 1:1.

the two verses seem to contradict each other. However, the two texts are reconciled by a third, "And when Mosheh *came into the tent of the meeting . . .* he heard the *Voice speaking unto him from above the ark-cover* (*kapporeth*) that was upon the ark of testimony, from between the two cherubim; and He spoke unto him."[96] In other words, Mosheh was spoken to *in the Ohel-moed,* but the *Voice came* unto him from above the ark-cover in the Holy of Holies.

The Thirteen Principles of Torah interpretation, as already mentioned, are part of the Oral Law, or Tradition, (*Torah she-be'Al-peh*), which came down to us together with the Torah at Mount Sinai. Without this Oral Law, the Torah would be a closed book to us. We would not know what the Torah meant. This is true of *all* parts of the Torah, the narratives (the events related in the Torah) as well as its legal sections (laws and regulations governing our daily conduct); but it is particularly true in regard to the latter. Just how wrong can be those who attempt to inter-pret the Torah without the Tradition handed down to us from generation to generation, from Mosheh Rabbenu to this day— can be seen from the *Karaite* sect. This was a Jewish sect which came into being in the second half of the 8th century. It rejected the Tradition (Mishnah, Gemara, and later Rabbinic sources) and claimed to rely only on the Written Law (*Mikra*) itself. Thus, for example, they interpreted the words of the Torah, "You shall not kindle a light on the Shabbos day," literally, and sat in com-plete darkness the whole day of Shabbos, from Friday evening to dusk on the following day. Similarly, the Biblical prohibition of boiling a kid's flesh in its mother's milk was interpreted literally, so that they did not consider themselves obliged to observe the Jewish dietary laws as we know them; and so forth. This sect, as other sects which broke with Jewish Tradition, eventually dis-appeared, since they excluded themselves from the Jewish people,

---

[96] Num. 7:89.

which is "a people only by virtue of the Torah and Tradition from Sinai."[97] A similar fate awaits other Jewish sects and movements which preach their own form of "Judaism" which is not the true traditional faith and practice. Their misguided followers will either return to the true Jewish fold, or they will in due course, unfortunately, assimilate with the non-Jewish environment.

The Beraitha of Rabbi Yishmael concludes the section of *Korbanoth* ("Sacrifices") in the Siddur. It is therefore appropriately followed by a short prayer, taken from *Pirkei Avoth*.[98]

> *May it be Your will, O G-d, and the G-d of our Fathers, that the Beth Hamikdash be rebuilt speedily, in our time, and grant our portion in Your Torah.*

For, while prayer now takes the place also of the sacrifices in the Beth Hamikdash of old, we pray for the rebuilding of the Beth Hamikdash and the restoration of the holy service in it, in our holy city of Jerusalem, which will come to pass when Mashiach will come.

"Grant us our portion in *Your Torah*" emphasizes that every Jew has a portion in *G-d's* Torah (not the "Torah" invented by any man), and it is in this Torah from Sinai that we desire to have a share.

This prayer is followed by *Kaddish* (*d'Rabbanan*).

---

[97] Saadia, Emunoth v'Deoth 3:7.
[98] Avoth 5:20.

הודו

HODU
(GIVE THANKS)

*O give thanks unto the L-rd, call upon His Name;
make known His doings among the peoples. . . . O
you seed of Israel His servant, you children of Jacob,
His chosen ones. He is the L-rd our G-d; His judgments are in all the earth. Remember His covenant
forever, the word which He commanded to a thousand
generations; (the covenant) which He made with
Abraham, and His oath unto Isaac; and confirmed the
same unto Jacob for a statute, to Israel for an everlasting covenant. . . .*

*Sing unto the L-rd, all the earth; proclaim His
salvation from day to day. . . . And say you, Save us,
O G-d of our salvation, and gather us and deliver us
from the nations, to give thanks unto Your holy
Name, and to triumph in Your praise. Blessed be the
L-rd, the G-d of Israel, from everlasting even to ever-
lasting. All the people said, Amen, and praised the
L-rd. . . .*

*And He is merciful, forgives iniquity, and destroys
not: yes, many a time He turns His anger away, and
does not stir up all His wrath. . . . Rise up (O G-d)
for our help and set us free for your loving-kindness'
sake. . . .*

110

This prayer, of which we cited only a few sentences above, introduces the second part of our morning service. It consists of two major sections from the Book of Chronicles,[1] the Book of Psalms,[2] and other selections.

The first part of *Hodu* comes from the first book of Chronicles. King David composed this prayer, and the famous singer Asaph and his choir sang it in the Sanctuary on the day when the Holy Ark was returned to Jerusalem. The first section which ends with the words, *Al tig'u bimshichai* ("touch not my anointed ones"), was said daily in the Beth Hamikdash right after the offerings, and refers to the miraculous restoration of the Holy Ark from the hands of the Philistines. The Psalmist takes the occasion of the transport of the Ark into the Sanctuary to thank G-d for this miracle and for the many other miracles He wrought on behalf of the Jewish people.

The second section, which begins with *Shiru Lashem* ("Sing unto G-d") and ends with *Vehallel Lashem* ("and praise G-d"), was said in the Temple every evening, right after the completion of the offerings. It pictures the future as promised to us in the holy Scriptures, when G-d will be recognized by all men, and Israel will be respected as the true servants of G-d. Even Nature will then join in the jubilation and thanksgiving to the Creator. The various nations will bring their offerings and will emulate Israel in the service of G-d. The last two sentences of this second section are summations of the two thoughts contained in the first and in the second part of *Hodu,* namely the expression of gratitude for His grace and mercy, and prayer for the happier and better future, as signified by the three expressions: *Hoshienu* ("save us"), *vekabtzenu* ("and gather us"), *lehodoth* ("to thank"). But at all times, we say: *Baruch Hashem Elokei Yisrael min ha'olam ve'ad*

---

[1] Chron. I, 16:8-36.
[2] Ps. 103:10-15; 96:23; 106:47-48.

ha'olam ("Blessed is the L-rd G-d of Israel in this world and in the world to come").

Thus we can see that the prayer *Hodu* fits very well into the place given to it by our Sages, right after the daily offerings, as it was said in the holy Temple. We can also understand from its contents why the first part was said in the morning and the second part in the evening. For, according to the Psalmist, the morning prayer is mostly devoted to the expression of thanks for G-d's help and grace, while the evening prayers are requests for future help: *Lehagid baboker chasdecha ve'emunathcha baleiloth,* "to tell in the morning of Your kindness and of Your faithfulness in the nights."[3]

The concluding part of *Hodu,* which is composed of passages from different psalms, follows in logical sequence. It speaks of G-d's hearing our prayers, even though the Beth Hamikdash does not exist any longer and we cannot offer our sacrifices, and even though the holy Ark, of whose miraculous salvation the first part has spoken, has disappeared. Prayer is not bound to the Temple, or the Ark. G-d hears the requests of the praying community even though the individuals, taken by themselves, may not be worthy of help, for He is merciful: *Vehu rachum yechaper avon.*[4] This thought is carried further in the next few passages from Psalms, which tell us that G-d's faith and love are eternal and therefore not dependent upon the existence of the Temple and the presence of the holy Ark and of offerings.[5] Yet, in order to make sure that these vital necessities of the perfect life of the Jews are not underestimated, the prayer stresses again the importance of the holy Temple as the seat of Divine grace and mercy in the future, with Israel foremost among all nations in the service of G-d. In this future we believe, not because of confidence

---

3 Ps. 92:3.
4 Ps. 78:38.
5 Ps. 40:12; 25:6.

in ourselves, but because we have faith in, and hope for, the help of the L-rd: *Lashem hayeshuah* . . . ("Salvation belongs to G-d").[6] Even though the present does not seem to justify such confidence, we see the dawn behind the night, and we end this chapter of confidence with the jubilant exclamation: "And as for me, I have trusted in Your loving kindness; my heart shall be glad in Your salvation; I will sing unto the L-rd, because He has dealt bountifully with me."[7]

מזמור שיר חנוכת הבית
(PSALM 30)

In *Nusach Ari,* Psalm 30 of the Book of Tehillim follows the prayer of *Hodu,* while in *Nusach Ashkenaz* this Psalm is at the beginning of the Morning Prayer proper. In either case it is recited before *Baruch She'amar,* as a fitting introduction to *Pesukei d'Zimra.*

It is not known when, precisely, this Psalm found its way into the Siddur. In the earliest printed Siddurim this Psalm was not included in the Morning Service, except in Sfardic and Yemenite Siddurim where it was included in the Sabbath prayer only. Nor do such great authorities as Abudraham, Tur, and others, mention it.

It is known, however, that the saintly Ari definitely incorporated this Psalm into the *Nusach Ari,* and eventually it found its way also into *Nusach Ashkenaz* and all other Siddurim. The saintly Ari also revealed some of the hidden aspects and meanings of this Psalm, such as pointing to the fact that the Name of G-d is mentioned ten times in this Psalm, corresponding to the Ten Commandments; that from the first mention of G-d's Name to the end of the Psalm there are 91 words, corresponding to the

---

6 Ps. 3:9.
7 Ps. 13:6.

numerical equivalent (26 plus 65) of the combination of G-d's
Name as it is written (*yud-kei,* * etc.) and pronounced (*aleph-
daleth,* etc.), the meaning of which is explained in the Kabbalah,
and so forth.

As an introduction to *Pesukei d'Zimra,* Psalm 30 is particularly
fitting for several reasons:

(1) King David composed this sacred Psalm for the Dedication
of the House (the Beth Hamikdash) which was to be built by his
son, King Solomon. It is also a prophecy for the future Beth
Hamikdash which will be built by Mashiach. Now, in the absence
of the Beth Hamikdash, the house of prayer is called *Mikdash
Me'at*—a "Sanctuary in Miniature."[8] Our prayer in the synagogue
has, for the time being, replaced the Divine Service in the Beth
Hamikdash, but we constantly reaffirm our fervent hope that the
Beth Hamikdash will soon be rebuilt by Mashiach and the Service
restored as in days of old. Then we will indeed sing a Song of
Dedication of the House.

(2) As we are about to begin our prayers, we must have full
confidence that our prayer will be heard; that G-d will accept
our prayer. This is what King David assures us in this Psalm,
when he declared,

> *O, G-d, my G-d, I cried unto You, and You healed me.*

Moreover, even when things seem so desperate that a person
feels he is on the brink of doom, there is hope in G-d, as the next
verse declares,

> *O G-d, You have brought up my soul from She'ol
> (grave),*
>
> *You have kept me alive from descending to the pit. . . .*

---

*Because it is forbidden to spell out G-d's Name, the letter *Hei* is referred to here
and elsewhere as *"Kei."*

8 Ezekiel 11:16.

If G-d helps one out of a desperate situation, why did He place one there at all? The answer is found in the following verse:

> *For His anger is but for a moment; life is in His desire.*
>
> *In the evening, weeping may tarry, but in the morning—joy.*

This means, first of all, that when a person has incurred G-d's displeasure and brought suffering upon himself, it is only temporary; relief is sure to come as morning follows night. More importantly, in the very suffering there is a hidden good, for G-d desires life; and from the grief itself comes joy.

The ups and downs in life are part of G-d's merciful Providence; they are for our own good—to remind us that we constantly depend on G-d. If a person were always prosperous, he would become arrogant, as King David said,

> *Yet I thought in my prosperity that I shall never fall!*

And King David continues, ["Now I know that"]—

> *O G-d, in Your favor You stood me up like a mighty mountain; but when You hid Your Face, I was confused.*

[Therefore]

> *Unto, You O G-d, I will call; unto G-d I will make supplication.*

To know that G-d hears our prayers; to realize our dependence on G-d; to understand that even in "anger" G-d is merciful; to feel certain that we are never rejected by G-d; nor must we ever reject G-d, or give up hope—these are very foundations of our daily prayer.

(3) Having understood all the above, we can dismiss all sad thoughts from our mind, and sing G-d's praise *with joy.* Indeed,

we are commanded to "serve G-d with joy" at all times, and it is necessary to attune our thoughts to a happy frame of mind. This Psalm helps us to attain this, for even if things are not as we would like them to be, we can say with King David in absolute confidence:

> *You have turned for me my mourning into dancing;*
> *You have removed my sackcloth and girded me with*
> *gladness. In order that glory sing praise unto You, and*
> *not be silent; O G-d my G-d, I will for ever thank*
> *You.*

In addition to the profound contents of this sacred Psalm which make it so fitting a "foreword" to the *Pesukei d'Zimra*, the very words at the beginning and end of the Psalm (*Mizmor . . .* and *lema'an yezamercha*) share the same root as *Pesukei d'Zimra*.

In *Nusach Ari*, Psalm 30 is followed by several familiar Biblical verses (mostly from Tehillim), and the short Psalm 67. The central theme of these additional passages is G-d's reign upon all the earth. Thus, while we recognize our good fortune in that G-d has been especially gracious to us in bringing us close to Him, we hope and pray for the day when all the nations of the world will also acknowledge G-d and fear Him. This will come to pass with the fulfillment of the prophecy,[9] when "on That Day" (at the coming of Mashiach) G-d's Unity will be recognized throughout the world.

---

[9] Zechariah 14:9.

פסוקי דומרה
PESUKEI D'ZIMRA

ברוך שאמר
BARUCH SHE'AMAR

"Baruch She'amar" continues the prayer of gratitude that was started in *Hodu,* and in which G-d is praised as the creator and originator of all phenomena of nature and history. This section, called *Pesukei d'Zimra,* begins with the blessing of Baruch She'amar and ends with Yishtabach.

The real blessing of Baruch She'amar begins with: "Baruch . . . hakeil ha'av . . .". The preceding introductory sentences contain the various interpretations of G-d's holy Name. Therefore Baruch She'amar is to be considered one of the outstanding pieces of our regular prayers. According to Tradition it was revealed to its authors, the men of the Great Sanhedrin, the "Anshe Knesseth Hagedolah," from heaven. Therefore it has to be said standing, Tzitzith in hand, so that we may remember of Whom we speak. The reason why these sentences explaining the various versions of G-d's Name are put ahead of our prayers, can be seen from the comment of the Midrash to the passage of Psalm 91: "Why does Israel pray in this world without being heard? Because it does

117

not know the Holy Name of G-d."[9a] By knowledge of His Name is meant knowledge of His attributes, namely, knowledge of His might and all-embracing love. Therefore, instead of mentioning the "Shem Hameyuchad" after the word "Baruch," as in other blessings, G-d's Name is here circumscribed by its various forms, describing His actions.

The first sentence of Baruch She'amar is: "Blessed is He, Who has created the world by His word." In order to complete this idea of G-d as the Creator by the mere Word, the passage *Baruch oseh bereishith* has been added to stress that the creation was *Yesh me'ayin*. This has always been interpreted by our great Sages as the Divine creation of the world *out of nothing,* in contrast to the belief of other people who claimed that G-d may have been the Creator, but He used an eternal matter, a stuff of which He formed the world. This agrees with the general use of the word "reishith" which means always an absolute beginning.

G-d makes His promises come true. Both good and bad are to come true, once G-d has decided so, irrespective of circumstances. However, the good will be given even though man may not deserve it. The bad is meted out when G-d sees that the evildoer will not change his ways. Therefore we say in Baruch She'amar: *Baruch gozer umekayem,* wherein *gozer* means the final decision of G-d to do as He planned, or decided.

Baruch merachem al ha'aretz, the Divine attribute of mercy. That this Divine mercy is perhaps the most essential, can readily be seen from Rashi's explanation of the first sentence of the Chumash. G-d gave loving mercy preference to the justice, for our world could not exist on justice alone because of our shortcomings.

Baruch meshalem sachar tov liyereiav, is a continuation of the second and the third, for the attribute of merciful love leads

---

9a Yalkut 843.

to the characterization of G-d as the One Who rewards those that fear Him and observe His commands.

Baruch chay la'ad vekayam lanetzach, G-d is eternal, as we say in "Adon Olam": *He was, is, and will be,* in the past, present and future alike. It is with a definite purpose in mind that we express that He is always the same, alive and active, not only the Creator of the universe in the beginning, but the *chay la'ad vekayam lanetzach,* the One Who is always present. For many other religions have recognized and conceded the existence of G-d and His creation of the world. But to them He was only in the past; He left the world to its own fate after He had wrought it. Since then, they claim, He had no relation to the world at all. They don't believe in His providence in the present and the future. To them everything that happens, happens by necessity according to the unchanging laws of Nature. In contrast to that conception we believe and say so in our prayer that G-d is eternal, yet not separated from the world. Everything and anything that happens anywhere, from the growth of the grass to the greatest revolution in history, is due to His everlasting and everactive providence.

Baruch podeh umatzil, according to the meaning given by our Sages, pictures G-d as the One Who gives life back to those who have lost their right to existence. When G-d accepts penitence of a former sinner, He returns the right of life to a man who had been lost morally. The word *podeh* is usually interpreted to mean salvation from physical distress. The classical example for this double salvation is the redemption of the Jewish people from the slavery of Egypt where it was saved at the moment when it had reached the low of physical and moral decline. It is in this attribute of the Redeemer that G-d's Name is here expressed.

Baruch Shemo—it seems impossible for us to call something by a name that is outside of our experience and knowledge. How then do we know the "Shem" of G-d, when He certainly is the

One being that is beyond our capacity to grasp and to know? But G-d revealed Himself to Israel, and only our forefathers proved themselves worthy of such knowledge. Later on, when Israel left Him, He revealed Himself to the prophets to bring the knowledge back to the Jewish people and make them change their ways. Therefore we are called the "Am Hashem," the people to whom G-d has revealed His Being, and we thank G-d for this revelation in our prayer, for otherwise we would never have been able to find Him.

Referring to these enumerations of the Holy Name of G-d, the following blessing of *Baruch She'amar* states that He is praised by His people as the merciful and loving Father. But since G-d is also the King of the entire universe, His great Name will always be glorified and blessed, irrespective of our praise: "Melech meshubach umepho'ar adei ad." With this precaution against any misunderstanding of the role of human praise of G-d, we start our "Pesukei d'Zimra."

The two main expressions of praise in Baruch She'amar are (a) *Hillul* and (b) *Shevach*. The first means general praise and all-out surrender to the G-d of the Creation. The second, *shevach*, refers to special praise as consequence of our being able to recognize and understand specific manifestations of G-d by hard thinking, and learning the ways of G-d in nature and history. It always refers to the praise given by the small circle of the true servants of G-d who devote their entire lives to the study of Torah and His work in the world: *Meshubach umepho'ar bilshon chasidav veavadav. Hillul,* however, is the praise given by the entire community: *Mehullal bephi amo,* that grows out of the study and recognition of His Being as the only G-d of all life: *Yachid chay ha'olamim.* And we end up with the blessing of both *Shevach* and the *hillul* that grows out of *shevach: Melech mehullal batishbachoth.*

מזמור לתודה
(PSALM 100)

Psalm 100—a "Hymn of Thanksgiving"—used to be recited when a Thanksgiving offering was brought in the Beth Hamikdash of old.

The Thanksgiving offering included ten loaves of *leavened* bread. This offering, as well as that of the Two Loaves which were offered on Shavuoth, were the only exceptions where leavened bread was offered in the Beth Hamikdash; all other meal-offerings were of *unleavened* bread, i.e., Matzoth. For this reason Psalm 100 is omitted from our prayer on Erev Pesach and Chol-Hamoed Pesach, because leaven is then forbidden. Nor do we say this Psalm on Shabbos and Yom Tov, because no Thanksgiving offerings were accepted from individuals during these days, which were reserved for the *public* sacrifices (that is, those brought in behalf of *all* the people), and special festival sacrifices.

According to Jewish Law, a Thanksgiving offering is due on four occasions of miraculous escape from danger: (1) Crossing the sea, (2) Crossing a desert, (3) Release from captivity, and (4) Recovery from a serious illness.

It is customary, nowadays, in all cases of a narrow escape from serious danger or injury, to recite a special blessing—*Hagomel* (". . . Who recompenses the undeserving with good, for having recompensed me with good"). The blessing is recited in the synagogue, when called up to the reading of the Torah, and the congregation responds: "He Who recompensed you with good should recompense you with all good always."

However, the Hymn of Thanksgiving (Psalm 100) is recited daily (with the exceptions mentioned above), because actually we enjoy G-d's miracles every day, without being aware of them. Indeed, our Sages declared, "A person does not recognize the

miracle that happens to him."[10] The familiar prayer of *Modim,*
in the Shemone Esrei, contains the words: "We thank You . . .
for Your miracles which are with us every day, and for Your
wonders and benevolent acts at all times, evening, morning and
noon."

What is a "miracle"? We usually think of a "miracle" as
something "supernatural," like the miracles and wonders which
G-d performed for our people in ancient Egypt through Mosheh
Rabbenu and Aharon. These and similar miracles of which the
Torah tells us were certainly "supernatural," because G-d clearly
changed the laws of Nature for our sake. But miracles do not
necessarily have to be so extraordinary as to break the laws of
Nature. Miracles occur every day in the "normal" course of the
every-day life without our being aware of them.

Thus, there are two ways in which G-d's benevolent Providence
manifests itself: an "extraordinary" or "supernatural" way, and
an "ordinary" or "natural" way. In the first instance G-d's Providence is "revealed" and makes us take notice of it; in the latter
instance G-d's Providence is "hidden"; things appear to run so
"normally" that we take them for granted. In our sacred literature
the two ways of G-d's Providence are symbolized by the two
Divine Names, the four-lettered Name (*Yud-kei,* etc.) and the
five-lettered Name (*Elokim*). The first symbolizes G-d's Providence as it appears to us in "supernatural" powers "over and
above" Nature; the second symbolizes G-d's Providence as it acts
through and within Nature (*Elokim* is the numerical equivalent
of *ha-teva,* Nature). A simple illustration, in terms of human
experience, is this: When a person is well, that is, in "normal"
health, he does not pay much attention to the wonders and
miracles of the human body and mind; nor does he give much
thought to the fact that good health is a gift from G-d. It is only

---

[10] Niddah 31a.

when a person becomes seriously ill that he realizes how much he truly depends upon G-d's mercy.

Obviously, true Divine service is not service inspired in times of distress, or danger, or any other special occasion. We must *always* be aware of G-d's benevolent Providence, and this is expressed in the declaration that G-d (*Yud-kei,* etc.) is *Elokim.* The same Supernatural Power that created the world also directs all its affairs, however "natural" they appear.

Now, taking a closer look at Psalm 100, we can see that it has a three-fold theme:

(1) *Serve G-d with joy* (v. 2).

(2) *G-d* (*Yud-kei,* etc.) is *Elokim* (v. 3).

(3) *G-d is good; His loving kindness is everlasting* (v. 5).

These are very basic principles of our faith, and they follow here in logical order: Having experienced G-d's special favor and direct Providence, we are moved to "shout for joy" (v. 1) and to serve G-d with joy and heartfelt gratitude. On further reflection, we realize that G-d's Providence, in whatever way it manifests itself, comes from the same benevolent G-d. Therefore we declare: G-d is always good and faithful.

If to "serve G-d with joy" is a spontaneous feeling, the natural response to a miraculous salvation, it could quickly evaporate, unless it was followed by deep reflection on G-d's Providence. That is why the next verse begins with *Know*—*Know that G-d* (*Yud-kei,* etc.) *is Elokim; He has made us, and we are His, His people and the sheep of His pasture.*

The Unity of G-d, which is emphasized in this verse, is closely linked with the Jewish people. It is the Jewish people that recognize the true Unity of G-d (Monotheism) and express it in every aspect of the daily life. We are constantly aware that He is our Maker, and that we belong to Him, which means that we have to serve G-d with all our life and all our possessions; we are His people and sheep, which means that He is our King and Shepherd, always taking care of us. Therefore we invite everybody to join us in giving thanks and praise to G-d:

Enter His gates with thanks, His courts with praise;
Give thanks unto Him, bless His Name.
For G-d is good; His loving kindness is everlasting;
And His faithfulness from generation to generation.

יהי כבוד

YEHI CHEVOD

Yehi Chevod is composed of different passages from various psalms. It is a prelude to the actual *Pesukei d'Zimra* which consist of the six last psalms of Tehillim.

Our Sages gave the following explanation for its addition into the service at this place. It contains twenty one names of G-d, just as many as there are sentences in the immediately following "Ashrei." This figure twenty one has a special meaning, for it represents the numerical value of the letters in the name "Aleph-Kei-yud-Kei," in which G-d revealed Himself to Mosheh in the desert.[10a] Rashi explains that this name of G-d characterizes His might and yet at the same time His readiness to help and console. The first of these two attributes of G-d is expressed in *Yehi Chevod,* and the second in Ashrei. Thus, these two prayers are the illustration of "Eheyeh asher eheyeh," and are arranged around the numerical value of Eheyeh, twenty one.

The first sentence of *Yehi Chevod* is taken from Psalm 104, which has been called the greatest hymn to the Creator and His creation. The creation of the world is the form in which G-d's greatness and unlimited power are visible to man. This recognition

10a Exod. 3:14.

of G-d, which began with the creation of the first man at the dawn of Creation, will spread further and further, until all parts of the Creation will fully share it. Heaven and earth will join in the jubilation and joy over the true kingdom of G-d, for then all nations will bow to His rule.

The second half of *Yehi Chevod* describes G-d as the absolute ruler over all history. It tells of His omniscience and omnipotence, that is, His unlimited knowledge of, and power over, everything that happens. All evil planning and intrigues of nations come to naught before Him. Whatever they may desire and try, they cannot avoid the fate that is theirs by Divine ruling. Willy-nilly, the world has to develop towards the goal that G-d has set for it, namely the change of their evil ways and the recognition of G-d, of which the first part of the prayer has spoken. Even if Israel may at times not live up to His expectations and commands, He will not turn away from them completely, for He is a G-d of mercy. He fulfills what He has promised, even though we may not deserve it. *Yehi Chevod* ends with this beautiful promise for the future that G-d will forgive our iniquity when we call to Him and that He will restore us to our glory, when He will return to Zion.

This idea of G-d's mercy and loving care, serves as an introduction to the next prayer, Ashrei.

אשרי

ASHREI

Ashrei (Psalm 145) introduces a series of Psalms which have been inserted into the daily morning service at the suggestion of Rabbi Jose, who said: "May my share be with those who complete *Hallel* every day."[10b]

10b Sabbath 118b.

Our Sages tell us: "Whoever says this Psalm (145) three times daily, will have a share in the future world."[11]

This Psalm contains letters of the entire *Aleph-Beth* (except the letter *nun*) in correct order at the beginning of each sentence. It also includes the passage: "You open Your hand and feed each creature willingly,"[11a] which is a statement of the Divine Providence caring for every form of life. The specific importance of *Ashrei* is therefore expressed in the two thoughts that G-d's praise is sung in all letters, which means in all possible forms of human expression, and that He takes care of all creatures.

Psalm 145 proper really begins with *"Tehilah l'David."* Our Sages supply the reason why the Psalm is introduced with the verse *Ashrei* (*"Happy are they that dwell in Your house; they will be ever praising You."*)[11b] For the Minchah service begins with Psalm 145, and the verse of *Ashrei* was put before it, as an introduction and fitting beginning. This introductory verse stuck to Psalm 145 even though, in the morning, this Psalm figures in the middle of the service.

There is also a very good reason why this Psalm was framed by two other passages, namely, in the beginning, *"Happy is the people whose fate is such, happy is the people whose G-d is the L-rd,"* which is the last verse of the immediately preceding Psalm 144, and *"But we will bless G-d from this time forth and for evermore; praise You G-d,"*[11c] at the end. For these two sentences throw the proper light upon the contents of Psalm 145.

The Jewish view of G-d differs essentially from that of other peoples in the conception of His Providence and mercy. "Don't be like others," calls Rabbi Akiba to the Jewish people, "who honor their gods when they fare well and curse them when they suffer

---

11 Berachoth 4b.
11a Ps. 145:16.
11b Ps. 84:5.
11c Ps. 115:18.

bad luck. . . . You are Jews; when G-d brings you happiness praise Him, and when He causes you suffering, praise Him too."[11d] This recognition of the all-merciful love of G-d, which is always good to us, regardless whether it appears to us to be good or bad, is expressed in the various sentences of Psalm 145, which praise alternately His greatness, mercy, justice, providence, and omnipotence, to show that everything that happens does so because it fits into the Divine scheme of the universe, and therefore, is bound to be good.

The letter *"Nun"* is missing in the Aleph-Beth of *Ashrei* because, as our Sages explain, it is the initial letter of the word *nefilah,* meaning downfall. However, King David did not leave it out completely. The next sentence that begins with *"Samech,"* expresses the thought that G-d supports and raises the falling.

Psalm 145 is brought to a conclusion in the last sentences which praise G-d as the One to Whom all the living have to look for their support; as the One Who is *"Chasid,"* merciful beyond the strict demands of justice, to those who call upon Him in true devotion. The very final passage of Psalm 145, sums up with the statement that Israel will never stop praising G-d's glory, until "all flesh bless His holy Name for ever and ever."

מזמורים קמ"ו – ק"נ
PSALMS 146 - 150

The five psalms that follow *Ashrei* are songs of praise—*Pesukei d'Zimra.* They were written by King David, Divinely inspired, who sang G-d's praises and expressed his burning love for G-d in his Book of Psalms. Psalms 145-150, which are included in our morning prayers, are the concluding chapters of this holy book of the Bible.

11d Comp. Yalkut on Ps. 101:1.

Like a masterpiece of music these psalms start out quietly with
a single voice—the praise of the individual as he faces G-d by
himself. The volume and sound increase as more and more voices
join in the chorus of praise to G-d's glory. The finale of the
symphony is reached when the entire universe shouts out the
triumphant call of "all that breathes praises G-d."

The contents of these Psalms bring to a conclusion the thought
that was started with *Yehi Chevod,* in which G-d is acclaimed as
the Creator, and that was continued in *Ashrei,* with the detailed
description of His loving Providence and omnipotence. In the
five stirring chapters following, the individual Jew, then Nature,
and finally the entire world pay homage to Him for their existence.

In the first of these Psalms, *Haleli nafshi et Hashem,* ("Praise
the L-rd, my soul), King David speaks for the Jews as he praises
G-d for His help, disavowing all trust in human strength and
power. Human help is but temporary, and rarely unselfish. G-d's
help, however, is eternal and dependable. It comes to the poor
and rich alike. It supports the orphaned and the widowed and
protects the just from the unjust.

The second of the five psalms passes from the glorification of
the *Hashgachah Peratith,* the *individual* Providence, to the *Hash-
gaschah Kelalith,* Providence to the *community.* G-d's special care
for the Jewish people is expressed in relation to His order and
rule of Nature. Nature is maintained by Him, depending on His
mercy for its existence; it is governed by unchanging laws, the
laws of Nature, which He alone had created and embodied in
Nature. Israel, too, had been presented with unchanging *Chukim
and Mishpatim* (statutes and laws)—Divine laws, the acceptance
of which put the Jewish people in a unique place in G-d's direct
and personal guidance of the universe. For this distinction of
having been given special privileges and duties we sing His glory:
Praise you the L-rd, for it is good to sing praises unto our G-d.

The expression of heartfelt praise of Psalm 147, is continued into Psalm 148 where the entire universe is put aflame with the glory of the Creator. Heaven and earth and all their hosts: the angels, the planets and all the heavens above; the sea monsters, fire, hail, snow, stormy wind, mountains and hills, fruit trees and cedars, wild beasts and all cattle, creeping things and winged birds, kings, princes, judges, old men and children, everything that lives on the earth below—in short, the whole vast universe joins in one mighty chorus of the L-rd's glory. For everything exists only by His word.

The psalm concludes with a vision of the future. For, while Israel and the whole of Nature are even now all out in their daily praise of the L-rd, the kings, princes and judges on earth will eventually follow the example of Israel to recognize G-d's absolute authority. Then this now persecuted nation will rise and surpass its old glory, as the true servants of the true L-rd.

This vision of the future is continued by King David in the next psalm, where he sees the time when the entire mankind will unite and the whole world will resemble one big Temple that resounds with the great new song of praise to the L-rd: *Shiru lashem shir chadash* ("Sing you unto the L-rd a new song"). Led by Israel the then new mankind will recognize the Creator. By then the enemies of the L-rd will have suffered His judgment, civilization will be purified and atoned, and there will be nothing to disturb the all-pervading holiness: *Halelu kel bekodsho* ("Praise you the L-rd in His sanctuary"), of which the last psalm speaks.

In the last psalm all voices have now united in the hymn to the L-rd. They jubilate and glorify Him with thirteen expressions of glory (the Hebrew text contains thirteen expressions of "praise"). All instruments and voices of the living pour out their souls to express their longing, hopes and wishes. The universe will be like one whole: one spirit, one soul, united in acclaim of the Divine reign: *Kol haneshamah tehallel kah* ("All souls will praise the L-rd").

This is also the great and proper finale of the Book of Psalms which throughout the centuries has been the source of solace in all human sorrow, the expression of the soul in prayer and faith. It certainly is most suitable to take such an important place in our daily service, to serve as an introduction to the culmination of our morning prayer in the *Shema* and the *Shemone Esrei*.

ויברך דוד

THE BLESSING OF DAVID

The prayer we are going to discuss now consists of two parts. The first part, from the beginning of the prayer *Vayevarech David* (David blessed) to *Tifartecha* (Your glory), consists of four verses from Chron. I (Chap. 29); the second part is taken from Nehemiah (Chap. 9).

The connection between these two will become more apparent if we consider the impressive declarations by King David and Nehemiah, respectively.

When King David felt that his last days had come, he gathered all the princes of Israel and the captains of his host. Then King David stood up upon his feet and made a moving declaration in which he informed them that his greatest hope in life was to erect the Beth Hamikdash, where the people of Israel could serve G-d with all their heart. But G-d told him that he, a man of war, could not build the Beth Hamikdash, but that his son Solomon, who would succeed him, would build the Holy Temple. And, in a final farewell, David blessed the L-rd before all the congregation. These moving words now form part of our daily prayer.

Many years later, after the exile in Babylon, when the children of Israel began to return to their own land and rebuild it, their leader Nehemiah also summoned the children of Israel. After calling upon them to return to G-d with all their heart, he commanded them to stand up and bless G-d, the Creator of heaven and earth, Who sustains all life and Who had chosen Abraham and made a covenant with him, and then chose his children and freed them from the Egyptian exile with great miracles and wonders.

It will be seen that the previous chapters of *Pesukei d'Zimra* which we have already discussed, all of which are intended to make us understand the glory and power of G-d, have been leading up to this prayer where the meaning and purpose of all blessings is so clearly stated—the realization that we owe everything to our dear G-d.

This prayer in turn leads to the *Shirah,* the Song at the Sea, which is the climax of all the *Pesukei d'Zimra.*

Because of the importance of this prayer, and because of the fact that these words were pronounced standing, both by King David and Nehemiah and their audiences, we say this prayer also standing.

It is customary also, in many congregations, to take the charity box around when this prayer is recited in the synagogue, to give the worshippers an opportunity to give charity. This lends further weight to the prayer in which we proclaim that everything belongs to G-d, including our possessions, and therefore, it is only fitting that we give part of our possessions to charity.

ויושע – אז ישיר

THE SONG AT THE SEA

The great event of the Exodus from Egypt was attended by extraordinary miracles and wonders, especially in its final phase— the miraculous crossing of Yam Suf (Reed Sea, generally called Red Sea). It was after witnessing the Divine revelations at Yam Suf that the children of Israel attained the highest degree of awe and fear of G-d and, at the same time, a profound trust in G-d and in Mosheh, His servant. Thereupon, Mosheh and the children of Israel were inspired to sing the *Shirah* (Song), known as *Shirath HaYam* (Song at the Sea).[12]

The phrase *vaya'aminu baShem ubMosheh avdo*[13] (and they believed in G-d and in His servant Mosheh) calls for comment.

The Hebrew word *vaya'aminu,* as in the word *emunah* which is generally translated by "belief" or "faith," means a great deal more than "faith" in its ordinary meaning. Faith implies complete, blind acceptance of something not supported by reason. Where people see and hear something with their own eyes and ears, they do not need to have "faith" in the existence of that thing. Similarly, the Jewish people, having seen with their own eyes the Divine revelations at the Crossing of the Red Sea, did not have to rely on "faith" to believe in G-d; they *knew* and *experienced* G-d's Presence, for they *saw* G-d's "Mighty Hand" as it triumphed over Pharaoh and the Egyptians. Indeed, our Sages say that "(even) a maidservant saw at the Sea what Ezekiel and all other prophets did not see."[14] For, all the prophets (except Mosheh Rabbenu) saw prophetic *visions* and *images* while mostly in a trance, whereas the Divine revelations at the Sea, (and the subsequent greatest revelation of all at Mount Sinai), was something which the entire Jewish people experienced with all their senses and faculties. This is why each and every one of them could sing: "*This* is my G-d, and I will glorify Him,"[15]—as one points to something before his very eyes.

It is this personal experience which the children of Israel of that generation conveyed to the next generation, and that one to the next, that was transmitted from father to son to the present day; transmitted *uninterruptedly,* and by thousands upon

---

12 Exod. 14:30—15:19.
13 Exod. 14:31.
14 Mechilta on Exod. 15:2.
15 Exod. 15:2.

thousands of men and women, since there has never been a break in Jewish history from the time of Abraham to this day.

Thus, we cannot speak of the Jewish "faith" in the same sense as the other major "faiths" of the world. All other faiths are based on acceptance of certain dogmas and beliefs. In *Emunath Yisrael* the word *Emunah* denotes our steadfast, constant, complete trust in G-d and dependence upon Him. Our trust in G-d is not based on "hearsay," nor on philosophical or logical proofs, but on the personal eye-witness experience of a whole nation, transmitted from father to son in every exact detail, which is as though we ourselves had witnessed and experienced it at the Crossing of the Red Sea and, six weeks later, at Mount Sinai.

It follows, that in reciting the passages from the Torah about *Keri'ath Yam Suf* in our daily Morning Prayer, we do not merely recount that important historical event, but also reaffirm our trust in G-d.

The verse "G-d will reign for ever and ever"[16]—the last verse of the Shirah—is repeated twice, indicating that the Shirah ends here. (Similarly, the last verse of the Psalms recited in *Pesukei d'Zimra,* is repeated, to indicate the conclusion of the Book of Psalms.) Then follows the Aramaic version of this verse, and several other verses. The theme of these verses is the future and final redemption of our people, and the great Divine revelation which will usher in the Messianic era, when "On that day G-d will be One, and His Name One," that is to say, when G-d's *unity* will be recognized by all.

The saintly Shaloh and other authorities pointed out that the Shirah should be said standing, and with joy, as if we ourselves were actually standing at the shore of Yam Suf and singing it with Mosheh Rabbenu. In the holy Zohar, the importance of saying the Shirah with *kavanah* (concentration) is especially emphasized.

---

[16] Exod. 15:18.

יִשְׁתַּבַּח

YISHTABACH

With the prayer of *Yishtabach* the *Pesukei d'Zimra* come to an end. This prayer is really a blessing, but it does not begin with the customary *Baruch* because it is regarded as the conclusion of *Baruch She'amar*. But *Yishtabach* concludes with a blessing, and thus the *Pesukei d'Zimra* begin with a blessing and end with a blessing.

The prayer of *Yishtabach* begins with the words "Praised be Your Name," and contains fifteen expressions of praise (song, praise, hymn, psalm, strength, dominion, victory, greatness, might, renown, glory, holiness, sovereignty, blessings and thanksgivings).

The number fifteen is not an accident but has a deep significance. We find this number again in the psalms, in the fifteen consecutive psalms beginning with *Shir Hamaaloth* (A Song of Degrees)[17] which were recited by the Levites in the Holy Temple as they ascended the fifteen steps leading to the Sanctuary.

The figure fifteen represented in the Hebrew alphabet by the *Yud* and *Hei,* form the Divine Name. We find these two symbolic letters also as the first of the four letters *Yud-Kei-Vav-Kei* of G-d's Name. The prophet Isaiah said, "Trust you in the L-rd forever, for in G-d (*Yud-Kei*) the L-rd, is the rock of the worlds."[18] We find these two letters again in the psalms which

---

[17] Ps. 120-134.
[18] Isaiah 26:4.

we recite in the *Pesukei d'Zimra,* each beginning and ending with the Haleluyah (*Yud-Kei*), "Praise you the L-rd."

The prayer concludes with the words *Chay Haolamim*—"the Life of the worlds." This conclusion of the *Pesukei d'Zimra* is a very fitting one. We have been praising G-d, His might, wisdom and kindness; we have extolled Him as the *Creator* of everything that exists and breathes. But He is not merely the *Creator* of these things; He is the very Life of all these things. He is the origin of life and He is Life, the never-ending and never-resting energy and driving force of the whole universe. We begin the *Pesukei d'Zimra* with "Blessed be He Who spoke and the world came into existence." We conclude with "He is the only King, the Life of the worlds."

קדיש – ברכו

KADDISH — BARECHU

The prayer *Yishtabach* is followed by *Barechu*, which is recited by the reader and is responded to by the congregation. *Barechu* is not said when one prays at home, where there is no *Minyan* (a congregation of ten). However, in the synagogue the reader recites *Kaddish* before *Barechu*. Let us then try to learn something about this sacred prayer of *Kaddish*.

Kaddish is recited several times in the course of the synagogue service. But it is not always recited by the reader alone. Often several worshippers recite this prayer together. They are mourners who recite the *Kaddish* for the soul of a close relative. But there are other kinds of *Kaddish*. There is the *Kaddish d'Rabbanan*, which includes a prayer for the Rabbis, scholars and students of the Torah. This *Kaddish* is recited at the conclusion of a period of study of the Talmud, or Mishnah. There is one such *Kaddish* in the early stage of the daily morning prayer, and in some congregations where "Ein-kelokeinu" is said daily (and not merely on Shabbos and festivals) it is said again after this prayer.

The *Kaddish* with which we are concerned here (that is, the *Kaddish* before *Barechu*) is called "Chatzi-Kaddish," meaning "Half-Kaddish," for it is not concluded. There is the *Kaddish-Shalem* ("full") and *Kaddish-Tithkabel*. The former is the Mourners' Kaddish; the latter is recited only by the Reader.

136

Before we turn our attention to the *Half-Kaddish,* let us learn something about the origin of this sacred prayer.

If you are familiar with the Hebrew langauge, you will see at once that this prayer is not in Hebrew, but in Aramaic, which is also the language of the Talmud Bavli. The reason is that this prayer was composed during the Babylonian exile, when the Jews had acquired the Babylonian dialect, Aramaic. It was composed, like most of our prayers, by the *Anshe Knesset Hagedolah*—the Men of the Great Assembly. It is based on the wording of Ezekiel's prophecy[19] in which *Kiddush HaShem,* the sanctification of G-d's Name, is placed in the center of the national duty of Israel, upon which the deliverance of the Jewish nation was dependent. *Kaddish,* of course means "holy," and begins with the words *Yithgadal veyithkadash,* etc. (Magnified and sanctified be His great Name).

Here is the translation of the *Half-Kaddish:*

Reader: Magnified and sanctified be His great Name (Cong.— *Amen*); in the world which He has created according to His will and will establish His kingdom, and bring forth the Redemption and hasten the Messiah (Cong.—*Amen*); during your life and during your days, and during the life of all the house of Israel, even speedily and at a near time, and say you, Amen.

Cong. and Reader: Let His great Name be blessed for ever and to all eternity blessed.

Reader: Blessed and glorified, exalted, extolled and honored, magnified and lauded be the Name of the Holy One, blessed be He (Cong.—*Amen*); though He is above all blessings and hymns, praises and consolations, which are uttered in the world; and say you, Amen (Cong.—*Amen*).

Now, read the above carefully again and again, and try to get the full significance of this sacred prayer.

---

[19] Ezekiel 26:4.

It is the duty of our people Israel to make G-d's Name great and holy in the world. How do we accomplish this? Our Torah which is our way of life, teaches us. Everything about our daily life, *if* it is conducted according to the precepts of the Torah, is attuned towards this end. By fulfilling the daily precepts, by leading a clean, honest and moral life, by observing the Sabbath and festivals, we give living evidence of G-d's sovereignty. "There lives a G-dly people," the nations of the world will say, "truly a 'kingdom of priests and a holy nation.'"

Of course, we live in exile; in some countries Jews are persecuted and downtrodden, because the world about us has not yet accepted the true sovereignty of G-d. But G-d will surely establish His kingdom and hasten the Redeemer. However, the coming of the Redeemer is closely linked with *your* life, *your* days and the life of all the house of Israel. Every one of us has to do his share in order that we hasten the coming of Messiah in our own days.

And here comes the principal response of the *Kaddish*, in which the entire congregation joins fervently: *Let His great Name be blessed forever and to all eternity blessed.* Our Sages tell us[20] that he who responds most fervently and with all his heart with these words of the *Kaddish*, is forgiven his most serious sins, for surely this declaration, if it is sincere, amounts to the highest form of cleavage to G-d. Small wonder *Kaddish* came to be regarded as one of the most solemn hymns of our prayers.

Then follow various expressions of praise, and realizing that we cannot possibly express G-d's holiness in words, we conclude with the words that He is above all blessings and hymns, etc. which are uttered in the world.

Kaddish, as already mentioned, may be recited only in the midst of a congregation of at least ten adult Jews (from Bar-Mitzvah and older), and standing. It should be carefully listened to, and

---

[20] Sab. 119b.

Amen and *Yehey shemey rabba* should be answered sincerely and fervently.

The "Half Kaddish" which follows *Yishtabach* (when the Morning Prayer is recited in the Synagogue) introduces a short benediction which is opened by the Reader and responded to by the Congregation.

Reader: Bless you G-d Who is blessed.

Cong. and Reader: Blessed is G-d Who is blessed for ever and ever.

This is a summons, or call, by the Reader to join him in praising G-d. We find a similar "invocation" which is called "Zimun," in the case of Grace After Meals, when three or more persons have eaten together. There the words are somewhat different, but the idea is the same. It is explained in the *Zohar* that all Mitzvoth must have preparation; we do not want to perform the sacred Mitzvoth like automatons, without proper mental preparation. We want to pause to think of the great significance of the Mitzvah we are about to perform. In prayer, we want to stop to consider before Whom we are standing, to Whom we are praying, Whom we are praising. That is why when we begin the second part of our Morning Prayer, the part which leads to the *Shema* and *Shemone Esrei,* we begin it with this "invocation" or summons.

This same benediction is said at the beginning of the Evening Prayer, for the same reason. It is also said every time the Torah is read in the synagogue, when it is repeated by each worshipper who is "called up" to the Torah.

This benediction is a very ancient one, and its origin was not merely a preparation to the important service that followed, but also a declaration that G-d alone is to be blessed and praised, and He alone is to be served. Thus the Jews rejected the service of the idol-worshippers who served many deities.

Barechu is recited standing, and with a special bow of the head in reverence to the One and Only G-d.

יוצר אור

YOTZER OR

INTRODUCTION TO THE SHEMA

With the blessing of *Yotzer Or* (Who forms light) the second part of the Morning Service begins, of which the *Shema* is the outstanding prayer. As we shall see later, the *Shema* is the heart of the Morning Service, for it is our Confession of Faith, our Oath of Allegiance to G-d. But before we can properly make that most important declaration: The L-rd Our G-d the L-rd is One, we must realize the greatness of G-d, His majesty and might, and above all, what the meaning of One is.

To help us to realize all this, and thus enable us to attain the proper spiritual mood and real understanding of the *Shema,* our Sages have instituted two introductory prayers. The first is *Yotzer,* which begins with the blessing *Yotzer Or* and concludes with the blessing *Yotzer Hameoroth* (Creator of the Luminaries). The second is *Ahavath Olam* (Everlasting love), or *Ahavah Rabbah* (Abounding love), as it is recited in certain congregations. The latter concludes with the blessing, "Who has chosen His people Israel in love."

We shall now consider the first of these prayers, which opens with the blessing:

> *Blessed are You . . . Who forms light and creates darkness, Who makes peace and creates all things.*

140

This blessing is not to be understood as an expression of gratitude for the new day. For this we have already thanked G-d in the beginning of our Morning Blessing. Here we are making an important declaration that G-d is the Creator of both Light and Darkness, of Good and Evil; in other words, that there is only One Creator. This is a very important declaration, and the very essence of our faith, for in ancient times some people (such as the Persians) believed that there were two gods: one a good one, who created light and all good things, and another, an evil one, who created darkness and all evil things. We Jews believe that there is only One G-d Who created both light and darkness, Who created *all things*.

This blessing is based on a verse in Isaiah which reads, "I am the L-rd, and there is none else; I form light and create darkness, I make peace and create evil."[1]

You will notice that the blessing differs a little from Isaiah. This is because we do not wish to finish a blessing with the word "evil."

The words *"Who makes peace"* are very significant. We have mentioned before how people were misled by the things they saw in daily life which were so contradictory: light and darkness, life and death, peace and war, good and evil. This made them think there were two gods who were continually fighting each other for supremacy. But we Jews, from the days of Abraham our father, have been proclaiming daily that the L-rd is One, that He created all things, and that it is one of His Divine powers to "make peace" among things so contradictory. Nothing is more contradictory than our body and our soul, but it is the Maker of Peace that keeps our body and soul together. Thus the meaning of the blessing of *Yotzer Or* is clear: G-d is the creator of both light and darkness, because He is the Divine Peace Maker and the Creator of *all things*.

[1] Isaiah 45:7.

המאיר

HAMEIR

We begin this prayer by praising G-d "Who gives light (*Hameir*) to the earth and them that dwell thereon." This, G-d does *in mercy.* "Light" is good, as we learned in the first few verses of Genesis—"And G-d saw the light that it was good, and He divided between the light and between the darkness." We Jews are grateful to G-d for giving light to the inhabitants of the earth. Though other people may take it for granted and do not give it a thought, we Jews praise G-d in our daily prayers for this. Moreover, we realize that there is Divine mercy in the *way* He bestows His gifts upon us. There is a slow and gradual transition from night to day and from day to night. The sun does not rise overhead instantaneously, but slowly and gradually. This gives us a chance to get used to the light and heat of the sun, and we are not blinded by its dazzling brightness without warning. Similarly, the sun does not disappear without warning, and we can adjust ourselves to the night.

We continue the prayer with the words, "and in His goodness renews the Creation every day continually." These are very important words, full of great significance. We well realize that there is a Creator Who created this great universe. Similarly, one realizes that G-d created this universe with infinite wisdom. What people often forget is that this creation was not a single act, like someone making a piece of furniture and there it stands on its feet; but the miracle of the Creation is a daily occurrence. *Every day continually* G-d renews the work of the Creation. Why is it that when someone makes a piece of furniture he can go away and the thing will not fall to pieces? It is because the man did not create anything new, but merely changed the form of the material he was working with. But G-d created the world out of *nothing,* and every day continually, every instant, He repeats this miracle of creation so that it should not turn to nothingness.

The concept of *continuous creation,* namely, that G-d creates the world anew continuously, giving it life and existence without interruption, will be better understood by the example of an electric clock, which must have electric current all the time in order to function. The moment the flow of electricity is cut off, the clock stops. There is this difference, however: In the case of the clock, it will merely cease to function when its power is cut off; the clock itself will remain intact. In the case of the world, the world would *cease to exist* the moment G-d turned His attention away from it.

Here is another example: I take a stone and throw it upwards into the air. The stone will fly up and continue to rise as long as the force of my hand which threw it up is behind it; the moment that force is spent, the stone will fall back. So it is with the world. The world has no existence of its own, except the will of G-d that brought it into existence. If G-d should for a moment take away His will, the world will return to "its former state"—to *nothing.*

What does this mean further?

It means that everything exists by G-d's mercy, and that we owe every moment of our life to G-d.

It means also that G-d *knows* everything that there is in the world, for, as we pointed out before,[1a] it is this knowledge and constant attention of the Creator that makes it possible for everything to exist. Every man, every animal, every blade of grass and grain of sand are known to the Creator. By the same token, not only our deeds, but our thoughts, too, are known to G-d.

It means, further, that G-d guides the world and determines the fate of everything, big or small.

1a See p. 78 f.

Thus we Jews always see the power of the Creator in the things surrounding us, which could not exist were it not for the fact that the Creator continually *renews* the miracle of the Creation.

The next verse of this prayer is borrowed from the Psalms, "How manifold are Your works, O L-rd! In wisdom did You make them all; the earth is full of Your possessions."[2] We look upon the sun, the moon, the stars, the sea, mountains and all the big and small things which fill our universe, and we realize that G-d created them all, and that all are His possessions; all exist by His mercy and all bow before His Divine majesty. From days immemorial, when some people worshipped the sun, others the moon, still others worshipped fire or various forces of nature, we Jews proclaimed that there was One Creator, and that all things He created have no will of their own and no power of their own, but are all G-d's creatures. Therefore to Him alone we owe allegiance, and Him alone we worship. This is the meaning of the following words of the prayer: "O King, Who alone was exalted from aforetime, praised, glorified and extolled from days of old." And realizing this, it is only natural that we should address our petition to Him alone: "O ever-lasting G-d, in Your abundant mercies, have mercy upon us, L-rd of our strength, Rock of our stronghold, Shield of our salvation, You Stronghold of ours!"

Now comes a paragraph in which G-d is praised with 22 words, or attributes, in the order of the Hebrew alphabet, developing the theme that the Heavenly bodies declare the glory and holiness of G-d. This theme finds its final expression in the words of the prophet Isaiah who described the worship rendered to G-d by the angelic hosts, "Holy, holy, holy is the L-rd of Hosts, the whole earth is full of His glory."[3] To this we will refer later. We shall

---

[2] Ps. 104:24.
[3] Isaiah 6:3.

merely add here a few words on the significance of the acrostic of the Hebrew alphabet in this prayer.

The Midrash[4] says on the verse, "Nagila venismecha bach" (we shall be glad and rejoice in You), that the word *Bach,* consisting of the two Hebrew letters "Beth" and "Chaf," has the numerical equivalent of twenty two, that is, the number of letters in the Hebrew alphabet. At the height of our Divinely inspired joy and happiness we want to use all the twenty two letters of our Alphabet to praise G-d, for in these twenty two letters our holy Torah has been written, and in these twenty two letters the world was created, and these letters in themselves, in their pristine origin, are considered "names" or attributes of G-d.

תתברך

TITHBARACH

The prayer "Hameir" by which we praise G-d, the Creator of the luminaries, using all the twenty two letters of the Hebrew alphabet in doing so, is followed by the prayer "Tithbarach lanetzach Tzurenu" (Be You blessed for ever, O our Rock).

The prayer vividly describes how the heavenly angels offer their praises to G-d, and is based on a description by the Prophet Isaiah. The angels' prayer is called "Kedushah" (Sanctification), because it begins with the words "Kadosh, kadosh, kadosh" (Holy, holy, holy is the L-rd of Hosts; the whole earth is full of His glory).[5]

It should be mentioned here that the Kedushah is said by us three times during the morning prayers: Before the *Shema* (that is, at the stage where we are now), during the repetition of the *Shemone Esrei,* and finally in the prayer of "Uva l'Zion" (And the Redeemer shall come unto Zion).

---

4 Shir Hashirim Rabba on v. 1:4.
5 Isaiah 6:3.

It is natural for us to turn from the luminaries to the angels. For as we look up to the sky and marvel at G-d Who "designed and formed the rays of the sun," we look further into heaven and "behold" the angels worshipping G-d in trembling fear and awe before the majesty of their Creator. The picture so vividly drawn before our eyes by the great prophets Isaiah and Ezekiel is indeed awe-inspiring, and goes a long way to prepare us for the great prayer of Shema.

Our Sages tell us in the Talmud that the angels in Heaven offer their praises to G-d *after* we say our prayers on earth. The Kedushah should therefore have been placed at the end of our prayers, not before the Shema. However, as already explained in connection with the prayer "Hameir," we want to proclaim that G-d is one, and that all else has been created by Him and pay homage to Him alone, contrary to the belief of worshippers of the sun, moon and other heavenly creatures.

The angels are called "messengers." The Hebrew word for angel, "mal'ach," actually means messenger. The angels are not independent, but they are created for a special purpose. Our Sages say that every day G-d creates angels from the River of Fire, and after they fulfill their purpose and chant their hymn of glory to G-d, they expire.[6] There are, of course, the Ministering Angels that have a continuous existence. They are the highest created intelligences, whose comprehension of G-d is all the greater because of their proximity to Him. But their comprehension of G-d is only matched by their humility and self-effacement in the awesome presence of their Creator, which is expressed in moving adoration. In the words of the prayer:

> *All of them are beloved, pure and mighty and all of*
> *them in dread and in awe do the will of their Master;*
> *and all of them open their mouths in holiness and*

---

6 Chagigah 14a.

purity, with song and psalm, and bless, praise, glorify,
revere, sanctify and proclaim the sovereignty of the
Name of the Divine King. . . .

The prayer goes on to describe that "they all take upon themselves the yoke of the kingdom of heaven, one from the other. . . ."
It should be remembered that a "yoke" is put on animals not for
the purpose of torturing them, but to enable them to pull together
in harmony. In the same way we speak of the "yoke of the kingdom of heaven" in relation to ourselves. It means that not only
must we accept the sovereignty of G-d, but that we should all
"pull together" to further G-d's reign upon the earth. We bear
this "yoke" willingly and joyfully, knowing that the precepts and
commandments of G-d, far from enslaving us, give us real
spiritual freedom and unlimited power and control over the
passions and weaknesses of our human nature.

There is a great deal of preparation going on among the
angelic hosts before they utter their prayers, "to sanctify their
Creator in serene, pure utterance of sacred harmony, all of them
like one declaring in trembling and proclaiming in fear: 'Holy,
holy, holy. . . .' "

"Holy," in Hebrew means "separate." To say that "G-d is holy,"
is to say that G-d is separated from, and unaffected by, the world
He created. The repetition of the word "holy" three times is
explained in the Aramaic translation of the Kedushah in the
prayer of *Uva L'Zion*: "Holy in the heavens above, the abode of
His glory; holy on earth, the work of His might; holy for ever
and ever."

Yet, though G-d is separated and aloof from all the worlds
He created, "all the earth is full of His glory." G-d is both "above"
the world and "within" the world. Through the power of His
attribute of "might" (*Gevurah*) He can limit and concentrate
some of His infinite Being into this finite world. Indeed, as we
have noted in connection with the idea of *continuous creation*,

were it not for the continuous flow of His power, the world could not exist for a moment.

There is yet another meaning in the words, "all the *earth* is full of His glory." The angels themselves recognize that the essential aspect of G-d's glory is concentrated in the lowest of all worlds, the earthly world. It is here on earth that man was bestowed with the privilege of the Torah and Mitzvoth, constituting G-d's wisdom and will. By studying the Torah and observing the Divine precepts, man can attain spiritual heights inaccessible even to angels. Angels have no choice, no freedom whatever, while man has been given a free will, and free choice of action to do good or evil. Thus, man is in a better position to appreciate the good by contrasting it with evil, and by shunning evil and doing good he can enjoy unlimited spiritual advancement, which has been denied the angels.[7]

יוצר המאורות

YOTZER HAME'OROTH

Continuing in the same vein, this last section of the first blessing before the Shema sums it up:

> To the blessed G-d they {the angels} offer melodious strains . . . for He alone works mighty deeds, makes new things . . . He is the Lord of wonders Who in His goodness renews the creation every day continually. . . . Blessed are You, O G-d, Creator of the luminaries.

As usual in the case of long blessings, which conclude on the same thought as they begin, this blessing begins and concludes

---

7 Lik. Torah Berachah 98a.

on the idea that G-d has never stopped for a moment the process
of creation, with all that it implies in terms of particular Divine
Providence (*Hashgachah Peratith*), as noted above.

We bless G-d as the Creator of the "luminaries" (lights).
Here we have in mind not only the physical lights, the light of
the sun and moon and other forms of light, but also "lights" in a
deeper sense, the light of the Torah and Mitzvoth, as it is written,
"A Mitzvah is a lamp, and the Torah is light."[7a]

אהבת עולם

AHAVATH OLAM

Ahavath Olam is the second of the two blessing-prayers that
come before the *Shema*. But unlike the first, it does not begin
with a *Berachah,* because, in a sense, it is the continuation of
the first.

At the same time it is a perfect, final introduction to the *Shema.*

The two points will become clear as we read the words of this
prayer carefully.

Ahavath Olam—*"With everlasting love have You loved us,
O G-d our G-d."*

These are the opening words of this prayer which speak of
G-d's love and kindness to us in giving us the Torah. We pray
that G-d, Who has taught our ancestors the laws of life, be
gracious also unto us and give us proper understanding of His
teachings. "Enlighten our eyes in Your Torah, and let our hearts
cleave to Your Commandments," we pray.

The sentences that follow contain the wishes and prayers that
mean most to every faithful Jew: that G-d grant us understanding
"to obey, learn, and *teach,* to keep, practice, and uphold all the

---

[7a] Prov. 6:23.

words of instruction in Your Torah." It is not only for ourselves that we pray, but also for our children, and for all our brethren.

We further pray that G-d give all of us the wisdom to be single-hearted and undivided in our loyalty to G-d and to the Torah. Here we give expression to the sincere feeling of responsibility towards one another, and we pray that G-d help us translate this feeling into proper deeds.

We do not complain about the difficulties we have experienced in the centuries of our exile, but we do pray that G-d gather our exiles from the four corners of the earth and lead us upright to our sacred land, so that we might better be able to worship Him, and serve as a model nation to the whole world.

We conclude with the words:

> O bring us in peace from the four corners of the earth, and lead us upright to our land. . . . You have chosen us from all peoples and tongues, and have brought us near, O our King, unto Your great Name with love, to give thanks unto You, proclaim Your unity, and love Your Name; Blessed . . . Who has chosen His people Israel in love.

Thus the first and the last word of this moving prayer is "love." We are moved by the unending love which G-d has shown us from the days of Abraham. Having proclaimed the wonders of the Creation in the previous blessings and prayers; how G-d created everything and how He takes care of everything and everybody, man, beast, and bird; how in His goodness and mercy He sustains the whole world; how He has chosen us from all peoples and given us His Torah,— we can readily appreciate the words in the *Shema*: "You shall love G-d your G-d. . . ."

Were it not for the prayers and blessings leading up to the *Shema,* we could not very well understand the command, "You shall love G-d." For after all, "love" is a feeling; you cannot order it. It is a feeling which has to be cultivated and developed. When you learn about the fine qualities of the other person, when you realize that he is devoted to you and loves you, then you begin to feel the same about him. It is the same thing in our relationship to G-d. It is only after we realize His greatness and goodness, and His everlasting love for us, that we are filled with deep love for our dear Father and King: only then can we sincerely exclaim: "O our Father, merciful Father!" as we do in this prayer.

"You have chosen us from all peoples and tongues . . . and brought us near to Your great Name . . . to proclaim Your unity. . . ." We have been chosen not for the purpose of leading an easy life, nor for the purpose of imposing our dominion over other peoples, but for the purpose of proclaiming that G-d is one, the Creator and Ruler of the earth. We have been chosen to spread the light of the Torah among the nations of the world and the "laws of life" which G-d has taught our ancestors.

These words lead immediately to the words of the *Shema*: "Hear, O Israel, G-d our G-d, G-d is One!" the keynote of all Judaism.

קריאת שמע

SHEMA

1.

The Shema contains the essence of our faith, so much so, that countless Jewish martyrs calmly and bravely faced death with the words of Shema on their lips. They did so because they knew what these words meant.

The Shema consists of three chapters, taken from the Bible.

The first chapter[8] begins with the proclamation: "Hear, O Israel, G-d our G-d, G-d is One." It goes on to tell us that we must love G-d and dedicate our lives to the carrying out of His will. We can keep this faith alive only if we bring up our children in this belief. This section also contains the two Mitzvoth of Tefillin and Mezuzah which remind us that we are Jews.

The second chapter[9] contains a promise that if we carry out G-d's commands we shall be a happy people in our land. If not, we will suffer exile and hardships in strange lands, so that by suffering and trouble we will learn the ways of G-d and return to Him. We are again reminded to teach our children our true faith, and the Tefillin and Mezuzah are again mentioned, being the symbols of practical observance of G-d's commands.

The third chapter[10] contains the commandment of Tzitzith, the distinctive Jewish garment which is a constant reminder of all the

---

8 Deut. 6:4-9.
9 Deut. 11:13-21.
10 Num. 15:37-41.

152

precepts of the Torah. We are reminded also that G-d brought us out of Egypt and made us His people, and that we accepted Him as our G-d.

This, in short, is the theme of the Shema. Now we have to understand what all this means.

A little reflection on the contents of the Shema will reveal that the Shema is the highlight of our prayers and that all the prayers recited before the Shema are really but an introduction to it.

When we speak of the *essence* of Judaism we mean the foundations upon which our whole Jewish faith rests. These foundations are mentioned in the first chapter of the Shema:

The Unity of G-d—that G-d is the Creator and He is One, and that there are no other gods.

Submission to the reign of G-d—that is, to accept the Divine discipline (all the laws and precepts He gave us in the Torah) in our daily behavior, both in regard to our duties towards G-d and our duties towards our fellow-man.

Love of G-d—to understand that we owe everything to our good G-d, our Heavenly Father, Whom we must love with all our heart and soul.

Self-sacrifice—to be ready to give our very life rather than be forced to give up our faith.

The Study of the Torah and its Perpetuation—contained in the words: "And you shall teach them deligently unto your children and speak of them (of these foundations of Judaism) when you sit in your house, and when you walk by the way, and when you lie down, and when you rise up."

All this is contained in the first chapter of Shema, beginning with the word *Shema* ("Hear!") and ending with the word *ubishe'arecha* ("and in your gates"). It is a *Mitzvah* (a Divine command) to read the Shema every day, twice: in the morning and in the evening.

When we speak of the Shema, nowever, we do not mean only the first portion, but also the following two portions. For they also speak of the same foundations (although in different words) and contain the additional precepts of *Tzitzith* and the reminder of the Liberation from Egypt.

Now, let us consider these basic principles of our faith:

The Unity of G-d: Many years ago people did not know that there is but One and Only G-d. They thought that there were many gods: a god of light and a god of darkness; a god of goodness, and a god of evil; a god of war, and a god of peace, and so on. They thought that the god of goodness wanted them to do good things, but the god of evil wanted them to do bad things. They did not know how to satisfy all the gods. They did terrible and cruel things thinking that by doing so they were making their gods happy.

Then came Abraham. Even when he was a little boy he knew there was but one G-d, Who created heaven and earth and everything. He knew that G-d was good and merciful and wanted the people to be good and merciful, so that they would be happy. He knew that G-d often puts people to the test to make them all the stronger, just as iron becomes strong when put through fire. He knew that everything G-d created and everything He does is good, but that people often bring trouble upon themselves by not knowing how to live. Abraham knew all this, and then G-d spoke to him and chose him to be the father of a great and holy nation, who would teach the whole world these truths.

Later, we received the Torah on Mount Sinai, in which G-d told us how we should live, and what we have to do in order to be happy. It is from this Divine Torah that the Shema is taken, and we repeat it every day of our lives, from the day when we are first able to speak.

Submission to the Reign of G-d: G-d is the Creator of the world. The whole world is His, and He is its King. A good king does everything for the benefit of his land and his people. He makes laws and gives orders so that the people could live in peace and harmony. Men who are near the king, know *why* he has made these laws; others who are far away, perhaps in the country, or on a farm, do not understand them. But everybody knows that the laws are made for their benefit. It does not really matter whether one knows the reason or not; the main thing is to observe the laws, for the benefit comes from *observing* them.

In the same way, but much more so, we have to accept the laws which G-d, Our Father and Our King, has given us. They are all for our benefit, even if we are too young or of too little knowledge to know their importance. Even the wisest of men cannot understand the thoughts of G-d.

The Hebrew words for this submission to G-d are *Kabbalath ol malchuth shamaim*—"accepting the yoke of the heavenly kingdom." A "yoke," as we had occasion to note, is a harness put on an animal, so that its owner can lead it on the right way; it is not for the purpose of breaking its back under a heavy load. It is for the purpose of making the animal serve in the best way, for that is what the animal has been created for.

G-d never gives us a greater burden than we can carry. It is not a "burden" at all, if we have sense enough to understand the great benefits we get from accepting this "yoke." The unhappiest man is he who does not know what he has to do and whither he has to go. We Jews are very fortunate. G-d has given us wonderful laws and regulations. If we observe them faithfully, we are the happiest people on earth. They teach us all the good and wise things. By practising them regularly in our daily life, they refine our character, for it becomes our habit—our very nature—to do what is good and right.

We are like soldiers in training. The soldier must not question the orders he receives. He must carry them out willingly and to the best of his ability. A good soldier is so well trained, that he does not have to think what to do in an emergency. He knows exactly what to do.

We are also like little children, whom a wise father wants to bring up well. A wise father does not spare the "rod" whenever the occasion requires it. When the child is too young to know why he has to wash his face and hands with soap and water, or clean his teeth, or behave like a little gentleman, he thinks all those things are unnecessary. When he grows up, he knows that but for the wise training of his father he would have become a hateful creature.

And so, when reading the Shema twice daily, morning and evening, we think of G-d's great Majesty. He is the Almighty Creator of the Universe, wise, kind, gracious, merciful. In His presence (and when are we not?) we must feel quite insignificant, even more insignificant than, by way of example, a worm in the presence of a great man. This gives us a feeling of humility. Knowing how good and kind G-d is to us, this leads us to the next thought of the Shema—love of G-d, contained in the words, "And you shall love G-d your G-d with all your heart, and with all your soul, and with all your might."

2.

And you shall love G-d, your G-d, with all your heart,
and with all your soul, and with all your might.

You may wonder how we may be *commanded* to love. If a stranger comes up to you and says to you, "You must love me," you may ask, "But why should I love you? I don't even know you." But suppose that the "stranger" turns out to be someone very close to you, someone who loves you, who has been watching over you, taking care of you, who has, perhaps, saved your life many times, who is kind, wise, generous, and so on. Would it be hard to love him then? For that matter, what about our own loving parents? We love them dearly, without even being *ordered* to do so.

Here, then, lies the explanation of the commandment to love

G-d. What it really means is to remember that we owe everything to G-d: our life, our health, our parents, our home, our being able to think, understand, speak, walk, study, play; the sunshine, the very air we breathe—everything is a free gift from our benevolent G-d.

If we consider that *G-d does not owe us* anything, and that He has given us everything simply because He is good and kind— surely we could not help but love Him!

And so the commandment to love G-d simply amounts to an obligation on our part to reflect upon and appreciate G-d's kindness to us. *Shema,* means not only *hear,* but *understand.* Of course, the more we think about it and the better we understand it, the greater will be our love for G-d. Our heart will be filled with love for G-d, with a great and intense love, a greater love than any other, a love that is truly "with all your heart, and with all your soul, and with all your might."

That is why our daily prayers do *not* begin immediately with the Shema. There is a great deal to say and to think before we come to Shema, so that by the time we come to the Shema G-d is no longer a "stranger" to us.

But what is meant by loving G-d?

When we love our parents truly, we will try to please them. We will be eager to obey them and do everything they want us to do. We will do our best never to make them angry or displeased with us in any way. We will never do anything that would show us to be ungrateful, or disrespectful.

It is the same in the case of our love of G-d. We must be eager to do all that G-d has commanded us to do. If we really love G-d, nothing will seem difficult. On the contrary. It will give us much pleasure to know that we are doing so many things for which G-d will love us all the more.

There is yet another meaning in the words *"And you shall love G-d your G-d."* The Hebrew word for *And you shall love (ve'ahav-ta)* may be read in such a way (*ve'ihavta*) as to mean *And you shall make* (G-d) *beloved* (by others). This is to say, that through you—through your actions and conduct—G-d would be loved by all who know you. If you love G-d very much, you will want all your friends to feel that way too. Maybe they don't know why they should; maybe they never think about it. You may have many opportunities to tell them.

Being a living example of love of G-d, translated into action in the daily life and conduct, in itself goes a long way to make G-d beloved by others.

> *With all your heart, and with all your soul, and with all your might.*

With all your heart. In our heart all our desires are born, the good ones and the not so good. We have a "little good man" inside of our heart that tells us always to do good things. There is another "inner man" in our heart that tempts us to do bad things. (In Hebrew they are called *Yetzer-Tov* and *Yetzer-Hara*). They are always fighting each other, one trying to drive the other out and be the sole master. The heart cannot have two masters. When one is master, the other must be slave. Who shall be the master? Of course, the "Good Inner Man." We must help him.

This, our Sages tell us,[11] is the meaning of the words "with *all* your heart." Our *whole* heart must be filled with love of G-d; there should be no room in it for the "Bad Man"; if it cannot be driven out completely, it should be subdued and kept in check, so as to have no power over our actions. The voice of the inner "Bad Man" must be silenced; when there is something we *have* to do, there should be no inner voice saying "It's too hard," or "It can wait."

With all your soul. The Hebrew word *nefesh* (soul) also means *life.* This means that if we have to choose between G-d and a G-dless life, we should be prepared to give up our life.[12] To

---

11 Sifre on Deut. 6:5. See also Zohar III, 268a.
12 Berachoth 61b, Rashi; Targum Jonathan on Deut. 6:5.

countless Jews throughout the ages these words were very real. During the time of Antiochus, during the reign of Hadrian, during the period of the Crusaders, the Inquisition, and, yes, down to the present time, Jews willingly chose torture and death rather than give up their love of G-d. They died *Al Kiddush Hashem*—for the sanctification of G-d's Name.

And with all your might. This, our Sages tell us,[13] refers to our possessions, our wealth. We must love G-d more than all our most precious possessions. It may seem strange that after speaking of *self-sacrifice,* that is, being prepared to give up our very life, we should still speak of worldly possessions, wealth, money. But, sad to say, there are some people to whom money is more precious than their lives. Some people work themselves to death, or risk their life in a mad rush for gold. Even if the love for gold is so great, love for G-d should be greater.

> *And these words which I command you this day shall be upon your heart.*

We must study the Torah and learn to recognize G-d. This we do with our head, but the result will be that these words will fill our hearts and there our love for G-d will be born, and we shall love G-d with all our heart.

Note the words "this day" in the sentence quoted above. Here we are told[14] to think of the Torah as though it has been given *this day* for the first time. The Torah should *not* be thought of as a gift given us a long, long time ago, but as something new and fresh. When a person gets a new gift, it attracts his attention and holds his interest. So should we regard the Torah, with the exciting interest of a novelty. These are not mere words, for those who study the Torah know that it can never become stale, that there is always something new which they can discover in it. For the Torah is G-d's wisdom which knows no bounds.

---

[13] Berachoth 61b; Sanhedrin 74a.
[14] Sifre on Deut. 6:6, quoted in Rashi.

And you shall teach them diligently unto your chil-
dren and speak of them when you sit in your house
and when you walk by the way and when you lie
down and when you rise up.

Here lies a very important commandment: the duty of Jewish
parents to give their children a good Jewish education. The time
to learn begins when Jewish boys and girls are young. The Torah
and its precepts should become part of their life, at home and
outside, in joy and in sorrow, in sickness and in good health.
At all times the Torah is the Jew's guide in life and his constant
companion.

Moreover, our Sages extended the duty of providing Jewish
education also to *all* Jewish children, not merely to our own.
Thus, they interpreted the word *l'vanecha* ("to your children") to
mean "the pupils," for "pupils are also called children."[15]

The words, "when you lie down and when you rise up," contain
the command that we should read the Shema twice daily, in the
morning and evening service (that is why we do not say the
Shema in the afternoon service). But "these words"—the words
of the Torah—should be studied always, whenever we have a
free moment, and we must live up to them in all our actions
and movements.

And you shall bind them for a sign upon your hand
and they shall be as frontlets between your eyes.

Here the commandment of *Tefillin* is given. This commandment makes it the duty of every male Jew, from the age of 13
years and on, to observe the precept of Tefillin for the rest of
his life. The details of the commandment were given to Moses
orally, and they are to be found in the Mishnah and Talmud (the
"Oral Law"). The details include instructions on how the Tefillin
are to be made, how they should be taken care of, and so on.

---

15 Sifre on Deut. 6:7, quoted in Rashi.

The Tefillin consist of two parts: the Hand-Tefillin and the Head-Tefillin. The former is placed on the left hand, facing the heart. The latter is placed on the head (*not forehead*) in the center (this is what is meant by the words "between your eyes"). Thus, the Tefillin symbolize that our thoughts, feelings and deeds should be dedicated to a life which is in accordance with the precepts of the Divine Torah.

The little boxes of the Head- and Hand-Tefillin contain scrolls of parchment upon which the words of the Shema are inscribed by hand by a Sofer (Scribe).

The Tefillin are a "sign"—the emblem of distinction, which we wear with pride, showing that we belong to the Jewish people. It is very much like the emblem or colors of a regiment by which it is distinguished and identified.[16]

Every day, except on the Sabbath and festivals, the Tefillin must be put on for the morning prayers. The exception is made because the Sabbath and the festivals are in themselves "signs" in the same sense.

And you shall write them upon the doorposts of your house and upon your gates.

This is the concluding verse of the first chapter of the Shema. Here the Mitzvah of *Mezuzah* is given. The words of the Shema are inscribed on a parchment (in the same way as the Torah and Tefillin are inscribed on parchment). The parchment is rolled up and placed in a case and then affixed to the right hand side (on entering) of the doorpost. Every Jewish home must have a Mezuzah affixed on every doorpost.

The Mezuzah is a sign that the entire house and all our possessions therein belong to G-d, are dedicated to G-d, and are to be used in a way that would please G-d. It is our way of expressing gratitude to G-d for our possessions. Without first

16 See *Tefillin*, by Alexander Cowen, M.L.Ch. (Brooklyn, N.Y. 1945).

acknowledging that G-d is the real owner of everything, we would
have no right to enjoy their use. This is also the thought behind
the Berachah which we make before eating and drinking anything.[17]

Every time we enter or leave the house, the Mezuzah is there
to remind us that we are Jews, and that both at home and outside
(at work, in business) we must live up to the great ideals of our
holy faith and to fulfill all the commandments of the Torah.

Finally, because the Mezuzah is a great and holy Mitzvah and
contains the sacred words of the Shema, it is regarded as the
ever watchful and faithful guardian of the Jewish home, blessing
it with peace and harmony, health and happiness.

3.

The second chapter of Shema begins with the words:

*And it will come to pass when you will hearken
diligently unto My commandments . . . to love G-d
your G-d and to serve Him with all your heart and
with all your soul. Then I will give the rain of your
land in its due season. . . .*

The first thing to note is that this chapter speaks in the second
person plural, not in the singular as in the first chapter. This
means that here G-d speaks to all of us together.

Secondly, this chapter contains everything that the first chapter
does, but in addition it has something else: a promise of reward
for following in the path of the Torah, and a warning of dire
consequences if we should neglect the laws of the Torah.

This chapter, like the first, is taken from the Torah.[18] There
are a few verses in the Torah immediately before this chapter
which are of interest to us. They speak of the holiness of our
Holy Land: It is different from all other lands; it is dependent

---

17 Berachoth 31a, b.
18 Deut. 11:13-21.

upon the rains from the sky; G-d loves this land and watches it
always. The welfare of this land is entirely bound up with the
people of Israel and their loyalty to the Torah. If the Jewish
people observe the commandments of the Torah, G-d will bless
the land: He will send down the rain at the right time, everything
will grow well and in abundance. But, G-d forbid, if the Jewish
people neglect the Torah, then the Holy Land cannot suffer to
hold them there. Famine, exile and suffering must follow, until
Jews again realize their mistakes, and return to G-d.

Thus, while the Jew must be a Jew always and everywhere,
and must observe all the Mitzvoth of the Torah no matter in
what land he lives, he must do so even more carefully in the
Holy Land, where he especially is in the constant presence of G-d
and under G-d's searching eyes.

After repeating the commandment of Tefillin, this chapter
goes on to say:

> *And you shall teach them (these words of the Shema)*
> *to your children, to speak of them, when you sit in*
> *your house. . . .*

"And you shall teach them"—"you" in the plural. Here it is
indicated that it is the duty of the community to see to it that all
Jewish children should receive a full Torah-true Jewish education.
It is a matter of Jewish law and custom that as soon as a child is
able to speak, he should be taught to recite the Hebrew words
Torah tzivah lanu, etc., meaning, "The Torah which Moses commanded us is the *inheritance of the congregation* of Jacob."[19]
The whole congregation of Jacob is responsible to keep and guard
this precious inheritance. To build and maintain Hebrew schools
and Yeshivoth to provide Hebrew education for all Jewish children—is both a communal and individual responsibility.

The commandment of Mezuzah is repeated, then come the
following words:

---

[19] Deut. 33:4.

*In order that your days and the days of your children
be many upon the land which G-d swore unto your
ancestors to give to them; like the days of the heaven
upon the earth.*

G-d promises us many happy days upon our land if we will
"hearken diligently" to His commands; not only for us but for
our children and the coming generations as well. "Like the days
of the heaven upon the earth" simply means "forever." But these
words mean something else. Heaven and earth are a pair. Just as
the earth cannot exist without the heavens, so would the heavens
have no meaning without the earth. In the same way are the
Jewish people and the Torah. By observing the Torah, the Jewish
people bring the heaven down upon earth: they combine the
holy and sublime with the earthly, and in this way lift up the
earth to high heaven.

4.

*And G-d spoke unto Moses, saying, Speak unto the
children of Israel, and bid them that they make them
a fringe* (tzitzith) *upon the corners of their garments
throughout their generations."*

The third chapter[20] of the Shema contains the commandment
of Tzitzith and, as we will see later, mentions the Redemption
from Egypt, when G-d redeemed Israel from Egyptian slavery
and gave them the Torah; that is, when Israel began its life as a
holy nation. When a king establishes a special regiment, a royal
regiment bearing the king's name, he gives the members of the
regiment a special uniform, or insignia to wear on their person
always. The insignia gives the members of the regiment distinction, and at the same time reminds them that their conduct must
always be of the highest, for by their conduct they bring either
credit or shame upon the king.

[20] Num. 15:37-41.

The fringes are like such an "insignia." G-d wished to make our people a holy nation, bearing G-d's Name. That is why G-d gave us the holy Torah, which teaches us what our conduct should be, and how we are to lead our lives. The *whole* life of the Jew has to be consecrated, from the time he rises in the morning, until he retires to sleep at night, and from the day of birth, when he first opens his baby eyes, until his last day of life on this earth, when he goes to "sleep." Just as the member of that royal regiment is expected to be on his best conduct not only during a parade before the king, but at all times, so the Jew is never "off duty." He is in the presence of G-d always; he is always "on parade" before G-d, the King of kings. Therefore it is not only in the synagogue, during prayer, that the Jew must remember G-d, nor only during the study of the holy Torah, but during all of the day's activities. There is no activity in the Jew's life that is exempt from precepts (*Mitzvoth*). Before he sits down to eat, he washes his hands; he says grace before and after eating. When he is engaged in business, he has to observe the laws of honesty and truthfulness. If he is a farmer in Israel, he has many laws to observe in connection with his working on the soil. In the community he has his obligations in giving charity and supporting its institutions. Before going to bed he recites his prayers, and rising in the morning he recites prayers again. His *house* is Jewish by the Mezuzah, and by the observance of the Sabbath and festivals. His *person* is Jewish by the Mitzvah of circumcision, and by observing the precepts connected with his person, such as rest on the Sabbath. And even his *clothes* are Jewish, by the Mitzvah of Tzitzith and Shaatnes.[21]

*And they shall put upon the fringe of each corner a
cord of blue.*

---

[21] *Shaatnes* is the prohibition against wearing garments of wool and linen mingled together (Deut. 22:11).

The fringes are white woolen threads, four on each corner, folded in two, making eight threads in all. One of them (longer than the rest) is used as the "Shamash" to wind around the others. When the threads are threaded through the hole in the corner of the garment, they are folded and knotted twice. Then the Shamash is wound around the other threads seven times; the threads are separated and knotted again twice. The winding is continued, this time—eight times, followed by a double knot, then eleven times, then thirteen times, with a double knot before and after. Thus we have five double knots in all.

In ancient days they also had a thread dyed with the color of sky-blue. This dye was obtained from the blood of a certain mollusc (called חילזון in Hebrew). Nowadays we do not know what kind of an animal it was, or where we can find it. Therefore we no longer have the thread of blue, but all the threads of the Tzitzith are white.

The purpose of the sky-blue thread or cord was to remind us of G-d. Said our Sages: "The blue cord of the Tzitzith resembles the sea, the sea reflects the heavens, and the heavens resemble the Throne of Glory."[22]

> *And it shall be unto you for a fringe, that you may*
> *look upon it, and remember all the commandments of*
> *G-d, and do them.*

The Hebrew word וראיתם also means "that you may understand." For the Hebrew verb which means "to see" does not refer only to seeing with the physical eye, but also seeing with our intellectual eye.

As already mentioned, the Tzitzith are like a uniform to remind us of our special obligations as members of that holy "regiment" of G-d, called the people of Israel. How do the Tzitzith remind us of *all* the commandments of G-d? Rashi explained it in this

---

22 Sotah 17a; Tanhuma, Shelach 15.

way: The numerical value of the Hebrew word ציצית adds up to
600 (צ—90; י—10; ת—400); then there are eight threads and
five knots in each of the fringes. The total is therefore 613, as
many as there are commandments in the Torah.[23]

But remembering is not enough. *And you shall do them,* says
the Torah. We cannot be good Jews in our hearts only; we must
practice Judaism in our everyday life. All our precepts are based
on *action,* for it is through action that the commands of G-d
are fulfilled.

> *And you shall not go about after your own heart and*
> *after your own eyes, after which you go astray.*

Our Sages called the eyes and heart "the two agents of evil,"
for the eyes see and the heart desires.[24] That is why we are warned
not to be led astray by the temptations of our eyes and heart.

There is an additional warning here not to rely upon our own
judgment when it comes to the practice of our precepts. For as
we said before, "seeing" in Hebrew means not only physical sight
but also "mental" sight—thought and understanding. So the
"eyes" and "heart" refer to external appearances and superficial
judgments. Those who do not understand the deep significance
of our holy Mitzvoth may think that the precepts have no meaning and no message for us in modern times. But they are led
astray by their ignorance; they judge superficially, and have no
idea of the deep inner meaning of each and every Mitzvah.

After warning us again to remember and *do* all the commands
of G-d, and thus be holy unto our G-d, this section of Shema goes
on to remind us of the Redemption of our people from Egypt.

This is not the first time in our prayers that we mention the
liberation from Egypt. As a matter of fact, we mention this event
many times in our prayers before reaching the Shema. And not

---

[23] Rashi on Num. 15:39. See also Nedarim 25a.
[24] Rashi on Num. 15:39. See also Sotah 8a.

only in our daily prayers, but also in Kiddush and in the prayers of the holy Sabbath day and of the holy festivals.

More than that. The first of our festivals—Passover—is dedicated to this event.

Why do we mention this event so many times and so frequently? Because the wonderful story of *Yetziath Mitzraim* (the liberation from Egypt) reminds us of at least five basic events and concepts relating to our early history which are always relevant to our existence and survival:

1. Our father Jacob came to Egypt with his family of 70 souls. Two centuries and ten years later a whole nation left Egypt. In a strange land and in suffering *our nation was born.*

2. G-d saw the terrible suffering of our people and kept His promise to our fathers Abraham, Isaac and Jacob, to free our people and set them up in the Promised Land. *G-d never forgets or forsakes us.*

3. In freeing our people from Egypt, G-d performed many wonderful miracles. G-d showed that *He is the Master of the world and of all Nations, and that nothing is impossible or too difficult for Him to do.*

4. G-d punished the Egyptians for their wickedness, and rewarded the children of Israel for their suffering. *G-d loves justice, punishes the oppressor and protects the oppressed.*

5. G-d liberated the children of Israel from Egypt *in order to give us the Torah* that we should become a *Kingdom of Priests and a Holy Nation,*[24a] so that we could teach the whole world the knowledge of G-d and His ways. And when all the peoples of the world will learn the ways of G-d, there will be no more oppressors and oppressed, no more bloodshed and war, but love and justice will reign everywhere, and mankind will enjoy the blessings of G-d.

[24a] Exod. 19:6.

אמת ויציב — גאל ישראל
BLESSING AFTER SHEMA

Following the (Morning) Shema, there is a prayer consisting of several sections, which begins with the words אמת ויציב ("True and firm") and concludes with the Blessing גאל ישראל ("Who redeems-[ed] Israel").

This prayer is the continuation of the theme of the blessing preceding the Shema (the everlasting love of G-d for the Jewish people), and also of the last section of the Shema itself (the liberation from Egypt).

The blessing after the Shema is already mentioned in the Mishnah,[25] while the Talmud[26] declares that anyone failing to say אמת ויציב after the Shema in the morning (and אמת ואמונה in the evening) has not fulfilled his duty, for it is written, "To declare Your kindness in the morning and Your faithfulness in the evening."[27] Rashi explains that the blessing אמת ויציב speaks of G-d's kindness to our ancestors whom He delivered from Egypt, and divided the sea for them, etc. (In the evening we say אמת ואמונה, "True and trustworthy," speaking of G-d's faithfulness to fulfill His promise of our redemption and salvation from cruel and tyrannical rulers, etc.)

In the Mishnah[28] it is further explained that the last two words of the third portion of the Shema should be joined with the word אמת, because it is written והי׳ אלקים אמת.[29]

25 Tamid 32b.
26 Berachoth 12a.
27 Ps. 92:3.
28 Berachoth 13a.
29 Jer. 10:10.

In the holy *Zohar*[30] it is stated that the words of the Shema number 245, three short of 248, which is the number of limbs in our body.[30a] Therefore the Chazzan repeats the three words (ה' אלקיכם אמת) to make up the number 248. Thus, the Zohar states, the person who reads the Shema carefully and with devotion purifies every limb of his body.

The word אמת (Truth) in this prayer begins a series of 16 words which are closely related to the concept of Truth. The sixteen expressions of truth are said to refer to the sixteen verses of the first two sections of the Shema, in which we proclaim G-d's Unity, our submission to the Heavenly rule, and our acceptance of G-d's commandments.

Of the said sixteen expressions of "truth," fifteen are preceded by a *vav*. The fifteen *vavs* equal the sum of 90 (15x6), which in turn equals three times the name of G-d (*yud-kei-vav-kei*: 10 plus 5 plus 6 plus 5, plus the four letters of the Name itself, i.e. 30).

Rabbi Chaim Vital,[31] the great exponent of the Kabbalah of the saintly Ari, points out that in the blessing אמת ויציב, the word אמת is repeated six times, alluding to the recurrence of אמת six times in the first portion of Bereishith, through combinations of the last letters of three-word groups.[31a] In this way we reaffirm that all that G-d created during the Six Days of Creation exists on Truth. (If we include also the word באמת in this prayer, the word Truth is here repeated seven times, alluding also to the seventh day, Shabbos.) Our Sages have already pointed out that "G-d's seal is Truth,"[32] because the word אמת consists of the first, middle, and last letter of the Hebrew alphabet, indicating that G-d was, is, and will be—eternal. Incidentally, the word אמת is the equi-

---

[30] Zohar Chadash, Midrash Hane'elam, quoted in Otzar Hatefiloth I, 290.
[30a] Tanhuma Hakadum Tetze; Makkoth 24a.
[31] Shaar Hakedushah, ch. 12.
[31a] (1) (בראשית) ברא אלקים את, (2) וירא אלקים את, (3) ויברא אלקים את, (4) ויברא אלקים את, (5) וירא אלקים את, (6) ברא אלקים לעשות.
[32] Sab. 55a.

valent of 9 (in "miniature" Gimatria—1 plus 4 plus 4)—the "eternal" number, since it always reappears in all multiples and combination of this number (9, 18, 27, etc.—in each case all digits adding up to 9, or multiples of 9).

The prayer אמת ויציב speaks of G-d's eternal faithfulness to the Jewish people, of the great love which He has shown toward us throughout the ages, since He liberated our ancestors from Egypt, and of being our "shield and salvation" in most difficult times. With Mosheh Rabbenu and the children of Israel, after the miraculous crossing of the Red Sea, we proclaim: "Who is like You, O G-d, among the mighty ones! Who is like You, glorious in holiness, revered in praises, doing marvels!"[33]

The prayer concludes with the prophetic assurance that G-d will once again redeem us from exile, whereupon we say the blessing: "Blessed are You, O G-d, Who redeems(ed) Israel."

The Talmud[34] rules that it is necessary לסמוך גאולה לתפלה—to make no interruption between this blessing and the Shemone Esrei. One of the thoughts behind this uninterrupted continuity is the need to bear in mind, as we are about to address our petitions to G-d, that He is indeed all-powerful and able and willing to accept and fulfill our petitions. At the same time it will put us in the proper confident and joyous frame of mind, in accordance with the requirement to "serve G-d with joy."

In a deeper sense, both *geulah* and *tefilah* are closely related to the same idea of our personal liberation in our daily life. *Yetziath Mitzraim,* the liberation from Egypt, is to us not merely a historical event, but a daily experience, trying to free ourselves from the limitations and shackles of the material life. The way we can realize this is primarily through *tefilah*, our daily prayers, as this subject is discussed at length in Chabad.[35]

---

[33] Exod. 15:11.
[34] Berachoth 4b.
[35] See Tanya chs. 31, 47 and elsewhere.

שמונה עשרה

SHEMONE ESREI

1.

In the order of our prayers, Shemone Esrei comes fourth. We have (1) the blessings upon rising from bed (*Birechoth Hashachar*); (2) the chapters of praise (*Pesukei d'Zimra*); (3) *Shema*; and (4) *Shemone Esrei*.

We can see how well arranged are our prayers.

(1) First, upon getting up in the morning we express our gratitude to G-d for the rest we had, for giving us back all our senses and restoring strength to our weary limbs. We thank G-d also for the great privilege of being a Jew and serving G-d, for having given us His holy Torah, and so on.

(2) We recite psalms of praise to G-d, describing His majesty and might, as the Creator of Heaven and Earth and all creatures, His loving kindness and goodness in taking care of all creatures.

(3) Having thus been inspired by G-d's goodness and love, we declare the Unity of G-d, and we take upon ourselves to love G-d and observe all His commands. This is contained in the *Shema*.

(4) After all the above, we come to the main part of the prayer—the *Shemone Esrei,* in which we put our requests before G-d.

172

This is one of the reasons why prayer has been likened to a ladder ("Jacob's Ladder") connecting earth and heaven, as mentioned above.[1] For the sections of our prayer are like the rungs of a ladder, one leading to the other.

Shemone Esrei means "eighteen," because originally this prayer had eighteen benedictions (blessings). It now has nineteen, as we shall see later.

The benedictions of the *Shemone Esrei* are as old as our people, and date back to the times of Abraham, Isaac and Jacob, although the final form of it, as we know it in our Prayer books, dates back to a later time, to the time of Ezra the Scribe and the Men of the Great Assembly (*Anshe Knesseth Hagedolah*) more than 2300 years ago. That was the time of the Babylonian Exile, when the Jews were driven from their land into Babylon. Many began to forget their holy tongue. It was then that the leaders and prophets of Israel at that time—the Men of the Great Assembly (numbering one hundred and twenty)—arranged the prayers in a certain order, and in Hebrew. Thus all the Jews, at all times and in all places would be reciting the same holy prayers, in the same language, and this would give them a feeling of unity and strength.

The Babylonian Exile lasted seventy years, and then the Second Beth Hamikdash was rebuilt by Ezra and Nehemiah, which stood for four hundred and twenty years. After the destruction of the Second Beth Hamikdash by the Romans, the Shemone Esrei was apparently partly forgotten and appeared in different variations. It again became most important to strengthen the idea of prayer among our people and to arrange the proper prayers for everybody. It was then that the head of the Jewish people, Rabban Gamliel of Yavneh, with the help of Rabbi Simeon the Flaxworker, arranged the form of the Shemone Esrei. Because the Jewish people suffered at that time (and through the ages afterwards) from the evils brought upon them by treacherous men who, for the sake of

[1] See pp. 3, 8 f.

money, or power, abandoned their own faith, these Sages included a new benediction into the Shemone Esrei, beginning with *"And for the slanderers let there be no hope."* It is a prayer for protection against all slanderers, informers and traitors. This benediction forms the twelfth in the Shemone Esrei, and increases the total number of benedictions to nineteen. Nevertheless the name Shemone Esrei remained as before.[2]

2.

Our Sages divided the Shemone Esrei into three sections:

I. The first three blessings—the salutation.

II. The next twelve (later, thirteen) blessings, containing all our requests, and

III. The last three blessings—the leave-taking.

Now, briefly, we will enumerate all the blessings:

I. (1) In the first blessing we salute G-d, as our G-d and the G-d of our forefathers. The blessing concludes with "Shield of Abraham."

(2) In the second blessing, which begins with the words, "You are mighty, O G-d," we speak of G-d as the giver of life, Who will restore life to the dead. The blessing is concluded with the words, "Reviver of the Dead."

(3) The third blessing begins with the words, "You are holy," and concludes with "The Holy G-d."

It is very important that we say these opening blessings with full understanding of what we are saying, for these blessings tell us why we come to Almighty G-d with our requests. We come to G-d not as "strangers," but as children of Abraham, who was first

---

2 Megillah 17a, 18a.

to recognize G-d, and with whom G-d made an ever-lasting covenant.

We, further, come to G-d Who is kind, Who supports the falling, heals the sick, Who has command over life and death.

G-d is holy, and we, His children, are holy, and G-d desires that we pray to Him.

After this introduction, we begin to state our requests:

II. (4) Our first request is for wisdom and understanding. This blessing concludes with "Blessed . . . Who Graciously Bestows Knowledge."

(5) Our next request is for increased devotion to G-d and His commands, and that He help us return to Him in true repentance. The blessing concludes with ". . . Who Accepts Repentance."

(6) Next we ask for forgiveness, that is, the healing of our soul, and we conclude with ". . . the Gracious One, Who Forgives Abundantly."

(7) In the seventh blessing we pray that our people be spared further suffering, and conclude with the words ". . . Redeemer of Israel."

(8) Our next petition is for healing of the sick. The blessing ends with the words ". . . Who Heals the Sick of His People Israel."

(9) Now we pray for our material needs, that G-d bless nature (during the winter we insert here a prayer for dew and rain). The blessing concludes with the words ". . . Who Blesses the Years."

(10) Our next request is for the return of our exiles to our Holy Land.

(11) We pray to G-d to restore our spiritual leaders, and that He reign over us with kindness and mercy.

(12) The twelfth blessing is the one that was added later, which brought the total of blessings to nineteen, although the name Shemone Esrei (eighteen) remained. This is a prayer that the slanderers of our people shall not succeed, and that the heretics and all our enemies should fail in their attempts to harm us. It concludes with the words, ". . . Who Breaks the Enemies and Subdues the Arrogant."

(13) We now pray for the righteous and pious, and conclude ". . . The Support and Trust of the Righteous."

(14) The rebuilding of Jerusalem is the subject of our next prayer.

(15) The fifteenth benediction is a prayer for the arrival of our Redeemer.

(16) The concluding request is that G-d accept and fulfill our prayers. This benediction concludes with the words, "Blessed . . . Who accepts Prayer."

Having thus concluded our requests, we now bring the Shemone Esrei to a close with the last three benedictions of the Shemone Esrei, containing expressions of gratitude. This is in the way a petitioner to a king would take leave and withdraw from his royal presence:

III. (17) The first of the last three benedictions is an expression of the ardent hope that "Our eyes may behold Your return unto Zion with mercy."

(18) The next benediction begins with "We thank You . . ." In it we thank G-d, "the Rock of our life, the Shield of our salvation," for our life and very breath, and for the miracles which G-d performs for us daily.

(19) The final benediction of the Shemone Esrei begins with "Grant peace . . ." It concludes with the words "Blessed . . . Who Blesses His People Israel With Peace."

3.

The Shemone Esrei is more than a collection of petitions or requests for ourselves, and our people. They also remind us of certain events in our history. According to our Sages, each blessing of the Shemone Esrei tells a story of some miracle that happened in the past, which was the first occasion when the blessing was said by the angels:

(1) G-d saved Abraham from the burning furnace, whereupon the angels praised G-d with the blessing of "Shield of Abraham."[3]

(2) When Isaac was taken off the altar, upon which his father Abraham had bound him by G-d's order, the angels praised G-d with the blessing of "Reviver of the Dead."[4]

(3) Jacob's sanctification of G-d's Name in Beth-el, after his dream, was the occasion for the angels to praise G-d with the blessing of "The Holy G-d."[5]

(4) When Joseph was about to appear before Pharaoh, an angel of G-d taught him seventy languages in one night. The angels then praised G-d with the blessing of "Gracious Giver of Knowledge."[6]

(5) When Reuben repented after he had offended his father, the angels sang "Who Accepts Repentance."[7]

(6) When Judah accepted the blame for Tamar, and G-d forgave him, the angels sang the blessing of "The Gracious One Who Forgives Abundantly."[8]

---

[3] Pirkei dR. Eliezer ch. 27 (on Abraham's victory over the four kings).
[4] Ibid. ch. 31.
[5] Ibid. ch. 35.
[6] Ibid. ch. 40 (when G-d revealed to Mosheh the mystery of the Divine Name).
[7] Ibid. ch. 43 (different version).
[8] Ibid. ch. 46.

(7) The Redemption of the children of Israel from Egypt inspired the angels to sing "Redeemer of Israel."[9]

(8) When Abraham recovered from his circumcision, the angels sang "Who Heals the Sick of His People Israel."[10]

(9) Isaac enjoyed G-d's blessing, and reaped a hundred-fold. The angels then praised G-d with the blessing of "Who Blesses the Years."[11]

(10) Upon the reunion of Jacob with all his sons in Egypt, the angels sang "Who Gathers the Exiles of His People Israel."[12]

(11) When the laws of justice were given to Israel through Moses, the angels sang "The King Who Loves Righteousness and Justice."[13]

(12) The death of the Egyptians in the Red Sea gave rise to the blessing of "Who Breaks the Enemies and Subdues the Arrogant."[14]

(13) When G-d's promise was fulfilled and Joseph was present at his father's bedside before he passed away, Joseph putting his hands on his father's eyes and weeping, the angels chanted "The Support and Trust of the Righteous."[15]

(14) The building of the Beth Hamikdash by King Solomon inspired the angels to sing "Builder of Jerusalem."[16]

(15) The song of praise which Israel sang at the Red Sea inspired the angels to sing the blessing of "Who Causes the Strength of Salvation to Flourish."[17]

(16) When G-d accepted the prayers of the enslaved children of Israel, the angels chanted "Who Accepts Prayer."[18]

---

9 Ibid. ch. 50.

10–21 Same as 3–9 The source of these historic associations is found in *Shibbalei Haleket,* Tefilah, ch. 18; quoted in Otzar Hatefiloth I, 307.

(17) After the Sanctuary was built in the desert, and G-d's *Shechinah* (Divine Presence) was felt there, the angels chanted "Who Restores His Shechinah to Zion."[19]

(18) After King Solomon completed the building of the Beth Hamikdash, and all Israel celebrated the occasion with songs and psalms in great joy, the angels joined with the blessing of "Your Name is Good and unto You it is Becoming to Sing Praises."[20]

(19) When the children of Israel finally settled in the Holy Land in peace and harmony, the angels chanted "Who Blesses His People Israel with Peace."[21]

Thus, according to tradition, all the nineteen blessings of the Shemone Esrei have their origin in the most ancient times. The Men of the Great Assembly merely arranged them and formed the full text of the Shemone Esrei, which we say three times a day, in our daily Morning, Afternoon and Evening services.

יעלה ויבוא

YAALE V'YAVO

On New Moons (*Rosh-Chodesh*) and all the Festivals, the prayer of *Yaale V'Yavo* is added in the first *Shemone Esrei* (*Amidah*). (The prayer is not said in *Musaf.*) *Yaale V'Yavo* is also said in the Grace after Meals on these festive days. It is likewise said during *Chol-Hamoed* (the weekdays of the festival).

Yaale V'Yavo means, "May it (our remembrance) go up and come" before G-d. It is a prayer that on the holy day of the festival G-d remember us and the whole House of Israel, as well as our holy city of Jerusalem, and bring us deliverance, much good, life, and peace.

The prayer begins with eight expressions of "going up" and "acceptance" of our prayer (go up, come, reach, be seen, accepted, heard, recalled and remembered), each expressing a step closer to the Almighty. According to the Gaon of Vilna, these eight expressions refer to eight stages through which our prayer must pass, before reaching G-d, for there are seven heavenly spheres and the Almighty is above them.[22] (The number eight has a special significance in Jewish life, as can be seen also from the Mitzvah of circumcision which is on the eighth day, the festivals of Shemini Atzereth and Chanukah.) There were times — in ancient days, when the Beth Hamikdash was in existence—when we were very close to G-d, and G-d was very close to us. But since we have wandered off the path of the Torah, our sins have created something like veils between us and G-d, and we must pray hard to pierce through these "veils."

According to Rashi,[23] *Yaale V'Yavo* is a prayer for the restitution of the Beth Hamikdash. During the festivals, it is natural that we should miss the Beth Hamikdash more than at any other time, for on these days in ancient times the service in the Beth Hamikdash was wonderfully impressive and inspiring. And so we pray to G-d to restore to us the Beth Hamikdash.

The prayer is introduced in a fitting place in our prayers. During the Three Festivals (Pesach, Shavuoth and Succoth), Rosh Hashanah, and Yom Kippur, *Yaale V'Yavo* is inserted in the *Shemone Esrei* after the prayer of "You have chosen us" (*Atta bechartanu*), in which the particular festival is mentioned. The prayer of *Yaale V'Yavo* follows, expressing our fervent plea that G-d remember us and our unfortunate loss, and bring back to us those happy and holy days of old.

During *Rosh-Chodesh* and *Chol-Hamoed, Yaale V'Yavo* is appropriately inserted in the prayer of *Retze* which is a petition for the restoration of the Service in the Sanctuary of old, in Jerusalem.

---

[22] Otzar Hatefiloth I, 355. See also Chagigah 12b, 13a.
[23] Sabbath 24a.

In Grace After Meals, *Yaale V'Yavo* is recited before the blessing of "And rebuild Jerusalem, the Holy City, speedily in our time. . . ."

In olden days, the service in the Beth Hamikdash included the sounding of the silver trumpets. The trumpet-calls during the offering of the sacrifices on the festival days and New Moons were like a call to repentance, similar to that of the Shofar on Rosh Hashanah. This is what the Torah says about it: "And on the day of your rejoicing, and on your appointed festivals, and on your New Moons, you shall blow with the trumpets over your burnt-offerings, and over your peace-offerings; and they shall be unto you a *remembrance* before G-d your G-d."[24]

Thus, the prayer of *Yaale V'Yavo* also substitutes for the sounding of the trumpets in the Beth Hamikdash of old.

In praying that G-d may remember us, we also refer to "the remembrance of our fathers, the remembrance of Mashiach the son of David Your servant, the remembrance of Jerusalem Your holy city, and the remembrance of all Your people the house of Israel." Thus, we refer to the past—our great ancestors, who spread G-d's Name throughout the world; to our future—when we will be redeemed by our Righteous Messiah, and the House of David will be restored; and to our present—when we are still in Galuth.

We conclude *Yaale V'Yavo* with the words:

> *Remember us, O G-d our G-d, on this day for our well-being* (here the congregation responds: *Amen*), *and be mindful of us for blessing* (Cong.: *Amen*), *and save us unto good life* (Cong.: *Amen*). *By the promise of salvation and mercy, spare us and be gracious unto us, have mercy upon us and save us; for our eyes are lifted towards You, because You are a gracious and merciful G-d and King.*

---

24 Num. 10:10.

א-להי נצור

MY G-D, GUARD MY TONGUE

The Shemone Esrei is actually concluded with the last of its blessings ("Grant peace"), but one must still remain in place and not step back three paces until after the prayer of *Elokai, netzor* ("My G-d, guard my tongue from evil"). This prayer was composed by the Sage Mar, the son of Ravina, who used to conclude his prayer with this petition.[24a] The text as it appears in the Siddur (with slight variations) is as follows:

> *My G-d, guard my tongue from evil and my lips from speaking falsehood. And to them that curse me, may my soul keep silent, and be like dust to all.*

> *Open my heart in Your Torah, and may my soul pursue Your Mitzvoth.*

> *And all who design evil upon me, speedily nullify their counsel and frustrate their design. May they be like chaff before the wind and an angel of G-d drive it. In order that Your beloved ones be delivered, may Your Right Hand save, and answer me. Do it for the sake of Your Right Hand; do it for the sake of Your Torah; do it for the sake of Your Holiness.*

> *May the words of my mouth and the meditation of my heart be acceptable to You, O G-d, my Rock and my Redeemer.*

> *May He Who makes peace in His high places, make peace upon us and all Israel, and say you, Amen.*

As can be seen, the prayer opens with a plea to G-d to help us

---

24a Berachoth 17a.

avoid the terrible sin of *Lashon hara,* slander and talebearing.[24b]
The seriousness of this sin is very frequently underscored in the
Talmud and Midrash. Indeed, it is placed in the same category
as bloodshed.[24c]

It is true that, as in the case of all sins and virtues in which
man has freedom of choice and action, we are expected to be in
full control of our language. It is up to us to speak good or evil.
However, the temptation, or provocation, as the case may be, is
sometimes so great, that people often find it hard to avoid the
pitfalls of *Lashon hara.* This is particularly true in regard to the
subtle kind of evil-speaking, such as insinuations, or veiled detrac-
tions, or belittling a person, or gossip, and the like. Our Sages of
the Talmud call all these forms of unworthy talk as the "dust" of
Lashon hara.[24d] That is why even so great a Sage as the author of
Elokai, netzor prayed for G-d's help to avoid any and all kinds of
evil-speaking and guile.

Actually, King David himself already prayed, "Set a watch,
O G-d, before my mouth; guard the door of my lips."[24e]

Therefore, we, too, pray for G-d's help to keep our mouth clean
from anything that smacks of evil-speaking. It is especially appropriate to say the prayer after Shemone Esrei, in view of the fact
that the *Zohar* states that "He who has an evil tongue, his prayers
will not come before the Holy One, blessed be He."[24f]

... *To them that curse me, may my soul keep silent.* This is to
say, that even in the face of strong provocation, may we have the
strength not only not to return the curse or insult, but to ignore it
completely, *and be like dust to all.* The earth is totally unaffected
by the proud and arrogant who tread upon it. Indeed, in the end
the earth will bury them all. As children of Abraham, who said,

---

24b Lev. 19:16.
24c Yerushalmi, Peah 1.
24d Baba Bathra 164b, 165a.
24e Ps. 141:3.
24f Zohar III, Vayikra 53a.

"I am but dust and ashes,"[24g] we should strive for the utmost degree of humility.

The way to succeed in this effort is through the Torah and Mitzvoth. Hence we continue, *Open my heart in Your Torah.* A Jewish heart is the treasure store of all good qualities, but sometimes, because of various circumstances, it is "locked." So we ask G-d to unlock our heart, in order to be receptive to G-d's Torah and Mitzvoth. Then we will not sit back and wait for an opportunity to do a Mitzvah, but we will actually *pursue* Mitzvoth as one eagerly and tirelessly pursues a most desirable thing.

It is to be expected that in the pursuit of Torah and Mitzvoth there will be all sorts of distractions and difficulties, internal as well as external. We therefore pray that G-d should nullify all such evil designs.

Since we do not claim any special merits or privileges, we pray that G-d should help us for the sake of His Name, His Right Hand (the quality of *chesed*), His Torah, and His Holiness, so that we could lead the pure and holy life which He expects of us.

The verse, *May the words of my mouth . . . be acceptable to You,* etc.,[24h] is like a sign-off, with which we take leave from the Divine Presence. In Nusach Ari it is also said after the last blessing of the Shemone Esrei, immediately before *Elokai, netzor,* at which point it is permitted to say Amen, Kedushah, etc. which cannot be said during the Shemone Esrei.

The prayer *Elokai, netzor,* like the Shemone Esrei itself, is concluded with a prayer for peace:

> *He Who makes peace in His high places. . . .*[24i]

Our Sages say that in the heavens there are hosts of angels, whose natures are as contrary as fire and water, yet they live and worship side by side in complete peace and harmony.[24j] The reason

---

24g Gen. 18:27.
24h Ps. 19:15.
24i Job 25:2.
24j Tana d'vei Eliyahu Rabba 17; Avoth dR. Nathan 12.

why there is such peace and harmony in heaven is that all the angels are so overwhelmed with awe and trembling in the presence of G-d that they are completely nullified in their individual identities, all being absorbed in the tremendous Divine Light.

A simple illustration will make it better understood: Two persons who are fighting will suddenly make peace with the approach of a police officer, because the fear of a higher authority which is stronger than both of them, will make them forget their differences.

Thus, we pray that "He Who makes peace in His high places, should bestow peace upon us and all Israel." First we are asking for our own peace—that we may achieve inner peace and harmony in the relentless struggle between our body and soul, our heart and mind. Only when both our heart and mind are permeated with fear of G-d and love of G-d will our inner conflicts be dissolved and inner peace and harmony be achieved. Such personal peace is the prelude to the collective peace among our people Israel. For only a person at peace with himself can be at peace with his fellow-man.

It is customary when reciting this last prayer for peace to step back three paces, bowing left, right, and center, in the manner of a person taking leave from his king.

With a short prayer for the speedy rebuilding of the Beth Hamikdash, the entire Shemone Esrei is finally concluded.

תחנון

TACHNUN

אשמנו

CONFESSIONAL PRAYER

After the Shemone Esrei, on ordinary weekdays, several prayers are recited which are called *Tachnun,* "supplication." The Hebrew word comes from the root *chen,* meaning "grace," for *Tachnun* is a special prayer for G-d's gracious forgiveness of our sins, even though we do not merit it.

According to Nusach Ari, the daily *Tachnun* includes the "confessional" prayer *Ashamnu*—"We are guilty." In some Sfardic congregations, however, this prayer is said only on Mondays and Thursdays, while in most *Ashkenazic* congregations this prayer is not included in the daily service (and is said only during *Selichoth* on Fast Days).

It is a commandment of the Torah that a person should acknowledge his sins before G-d and seek G-d's forgiveness. In a general way this is done in the Shemone Esrei, where the sixth benediction reads: "Forgive us, O our Father, for we have sinned; pardon us, O our King, for we have transgressed," etc. Nevertheless, the saintly Ari insisted that the prayer *Ashamnu* should be said on every weekday (both in Shacharith and Minchah), whenever *Tachnun* is said. This is based on the holy *Zohar,*[25] where the importance of reciting the confession *daily* is greatly emphasized. The Zohar declares that when a person acknowledges his sins, after Shemone Esrei, he places himself entirely at G-d's mercy, and averts stern judgment. It silences the Adversary, the Accuser

---

[25] Zohar II, 41a; III, 231a; Zohar Chadash 35a, etc.

186

in Heaven, who is none other than the Tempter on earth (the Yetzer Hara, alias Satan, etc.). This is good both for the person and for the world at large, because in this way the quality of Divine Mercy (*Rachamim*) is aroused, while the quality of stern Judgment (*Din*) is dispelled.

The prayer *Ashamnu* contains, in alphabetical order, 22 expressions of guilt, sin, transgression, etc. The first person *plural* is used ("*We* are guilty") to emphasize the common responsibility which we feel in every case of transgression. Hence, this prayer can truthfully be said even by a Tzaddik who has never actually committed any of the serious transgressions mentioned in *Ashamnu*. To be sure, each individual is accountable for his own misdeeds, and the community to which that individual belongs should not suffer *punishment* for the sins of one of its members—if the community was in no way involved in the act. On the other hand, it is also true that the Jewish people as a whole are like one body, where the failure of one part of it affects the whole body, and the benefit to one part, benefits the whole body. Thus, when any Jew sins, it casts a reflection on, and *hurts,* the entire Jewish people, and, conversely, when any Jew does a good deed, it benefits, also, the whole Jewish people.

The essential thing about reciting this confession of sin is to express sincere regret at having committed the wrongdoing, and to resolve most firmly not to repeat it again. Just to recite a list of possible sins without sincere regret for the past and with no resolution for the future, would be the height of impudence and shamelessness, for G-d looks into the heart and knows all our thoughts and feelings. It should be remembered that we make this acknowledgment directly before G-d (not to any intermediary, as in some religions), for it is only G-d Who can forgive and nullify our wrongdoing, and give us a fresh start.

The prayer *Ashamnu* is introduced by a short prayer:

Our G-d, and G-d of our Ancestors! May our prayer come before You, and do not turn away from our

supplication. For we are neither impudent nor ob-
stinate to declare before You, O G-d our G-d and G-d
of our Ancestors, 'We are righteous and have not
sinned', but we and our ancestors have sinned.

The reason for including our ancestors in our acknowledgment
of sin is that it is written, "And they shall acknowledge their sin
and their fathers' sin."[26] For, sometimes children may suffer additional hardships because of the sins of their fathers—if the children continue those sins. On the other hand, the fact that the
parents are partly to be blamed for the children's wrongdoing,
eases to some extent the latter's share of responsibility.

The prayer *Ashamnu* is followed by this further acknowledgment:

We did turn aside from Your commandments and
good statutes, and it was unworthy of us. But You are
righteous in all that has come upon us, for You did
act in truth, but we have been wicked.

The last verse is from Nehemiah.[27] Commenting on this verse,
our Sages declared: "G-d said to His Ministering Angels, 'Come
and I will show you the righteousness of My children. For though
I have burdened them so often with troubles and suffering in this
world, which overtake them in each generation and at frequent
intervals, yet they did not reject Me, calling themselves "wicked"
and Me—righteous.' "[28]

י״ג מידות

THE THIRTEEN ATTRIBUTES OF MERCY

When praying with the congregation (not individually), the
Thirteen Attributes of Mercy are said, following *Ashamnu*.

---

26 Lev. 26:40.
27 Nehemiah 9:33.
28 Pesikta Rabb. 36:3.

The Thirteen Attributes of Mercy were revealed to Mosheh Rabbenu when he prayed for G-d's forgiveness for the sin of the Golden Calf.[29] Our Sages say that on that occasion G-d, as it were, wrapped Himself in a Tallith, like a Chazzan stepping before the Ark, and said to Mosheh, "Thus shall you pray, saying, 'HaShem, HaShem, etc.'" Thus G-d showed to Mosheh how Jews can obtain G-d's forgiveness through Teshuvah (repentance and return to G-d) and reciting the Thirteen Attributes of G-d's Mercy.[30] For this reason, the Thirteen Attributes are said on all Fast Days, as well as during *Selichoth* before Rosh Hashanah (and in some congregations also during the Days of Repentance between Rosh Hashanah and Yom Kippur). But according to the saintly Ari, we are to say this on every weekday, at Shacharith and Minchah, except on days when Tachnun is not said.

The Thirteen Attributes are introduced by the prayer *Kel Erech Appayim* ("You, G-d, are forbearing [patient]"). In this prayer we appeal to G-d's forbearance and mercy, in accordance with the way of Teshuvah which G-d has taught us through Mosheh. Then we go on to recite the Thirteen Attributes aloud and in unison by all the congregation, with awe and concentration.

The Thirteen Attributes of Divine Mercy are:

(1) HaShem, (2) HaShem, (3) Kel, (4) Rachum, (5) v'Chanun, (6) Erech Appayim, (7) v'Rav Chesed, (8) ve'Emeth, (9) Notzer Chesed La'alafim, (10) Nosse Avon, (11) vaFesha, (12) v'Chata'ah, (13) v'Nakkeh.

The first two Attributes, symbolized by G-d's Name (HaShem, HaShem) indicate G-d's Mercy *before* and *after* a person has sinned. This means that before a person has sinned, G-d is merciful to him and helps him to avoid sin as long as the person is determined to remain free of sin. But if a person has failed, G-d is merciful to him and encourages him to do Teshuvah.

29 Exod. 34:6-7.
30 Rosh Hashanah 17a.

The third Attribute is indicated by G-d's Name "Kel" (*aleph-lamed*). It denotes "strength" in *mercy*, meaning that even when G-d shows His might in punishing a sinner, He does so mercifully, so that the sinner would not be overwhelmed.

The fourth Attribute, *Rachum* ("Merciful") represents G-d's mercy.

The fifth, *v'Chanun* ("Gracious") is the quality of granting favors even where they are not deserved.

The sixth, *Erech Appayim* ("Forbearing," or "Holding Back Anger"), is G-d's merciful quality of giving the sinner time to repent, and not punishing him at once.

The seventh, *v'Rav Chesed* ("Abundant in Lovingkindness"), is the Divine quality of tipping the scale toward leniency, where the good and bad deeds of a person balance.

The eighth, *ve'Emeth* ("Trustworthy"), is the quality of keeping His promise.

The ninth, *Notzer Chesed La'alafim* ("Preserving lovingkindness to a thousand generations"), refers to G-d's kindness in remembering the merits of our ancestors (*Zechuth Avoth*) and being kind to us for their sake.

The tenth, *Nosse Avon* ("Forgiving transgression"), refers to transgressions made knowingly as a result of temptation.

The eleventh, *vaFesha* ("Forgiving guilt"), refers to sins committed willfully in rebellion against G-d.

The twelfth, *v'Chata'ah* ("Forgiving carelessness"), that is, transgressions committed unknowingly, or carelessly.

The thirteenth Attribute *v'Nakkeh* ("Acquitting"), is the Divine quality of clearing away completely all sins of those who return to G-d with sincere repentance and love.

The number "thirteen" is significant, for it represents the twelve tribes of Israel together with the tribe of Levi (*Kohanim* and *Leviim*), and, in a sense, thirteen different types of people, each tribe with characteristics (or "attributes") of its own.

Thirteen is also the sum total of the Hebrew word אחד

("One"), the three letters of which add up to 13 (1, 8, 4). This would indicate that although there are thirteen Divine Attributes of Mercy, G-d's Unity is nevertheless perfect; He is One.

נפילת אפים

PSALM 25

After the Thirteen Attributes of Divine Mercy there follows— according to Nusach Ari and Nusach Sfard—Psalm 25—"To You, O G-d, I lift up my soul." It is preceded by a short confession: "O Merciful and Gracious One, we have sinned unto you; have mercy on us and save us."

This Psalm is said with the face down on the right arm—in the Morning Prayer, because the left arm has the Tefillin on it; at Minchah the face is lowered onto the left arm. Hence this is called *Nefilath Appayim* ("Falling on the Face"), a gesture expressing intense and devout prayer, as we find in the case of Mosheh and Aharon.[31] This is done also in remembrance of the Beth Hamikdash of old, where the worshippers used to fall down on their faces.

The famous commentator on the Torah, Rabbi Bahya, explained that this "falling on the face" has three meanings: (1) It expresses awe and reverence in the presence of the Shechinah; (2) it also expresses repentance and contrition; and (3) it symbolizes complete submission to G-d, to the point of complete self-effacement and self-sacrifice, as if all senses and feelings have ceased. In this way the person offers his life, as it were, for having rebelled against G-d. Indeed, there are sins, such as *chilul haShem* (desecration of G-d's Name) for which there is no forgiveness except through death. But G-d accepts the thought of self-sacrifice for the deed, and forgives all sins, including those which otherwise are redeemed only through death.

---

31 Num. 16:22.

The *Zohar* and Ari Hakadosh emphasize the importance of
this *kavanah* (intent), namely, that *nefilath appayim* expresses
one's readiness to offer one's soul for the Sanctification of G-d's
Name, in addition to the thought of atonement for sin. Says the
Zohar:

> Having recited the Prayer (i.e. Shemone Esrei)
> and confessed his sins (*Ashamnu*), he should now
> see himself as if he offered his life to his Master, with
> love, by saying, *"Unto You, O G-d, I lift up my
> soul . . ."* and G-d will also lovingly deem it as if He
> actually took his soul from him. Therefore he should
> fall on his face, like a dead person falling to the
> ground. For there are sins which only death redeems
> . . . and now that it will be deemed as if G-d took his
> soul, which he readily offered to G-d, he is at that
> moment forgiven for those sins. . . .[32]

Psalm 25 is an alphabetical psalm, in which each verse begins
with a letter of the Hebrew aleph-beth. In content it is close to
the idea of the Thirteen Attributes of Mercy which it follows.
For in this psalm, too, King David, the Sweet Singer of Israel,
calls upon G-d's infinite mercies and kindness (v. 6). He declares
that "G-d is good and upright" (v. 8), and that "All G-d's paths
are kindness and truth" (v. 10).

Expressing trust in G-d (v. 2), King David prays ardently for
understanding of G-d's ways: "Your ways, O G-d, make known
unto me; teach me Your paths. Make me walk in Your Truth . . ."
(4-5). But he knows that it is only through humility and fear of
G-d, and the observance of G-d's commandments, that a person
can partake of some hidden knowledge of G-d: "Who is this man
that fears G-d? Him will He guide in the way He will choose.
His soul shall dwell at ease, and his seed shall inherit the earth.

---

[32] Zohar Chadash 35a; see also Zohar III, 120b.

The secret of G-d is (revealed) to them that fear him, and He will show them His covenant" (12-14).

In this psalm King David expresses, in behalf of all Israel, sincere feelings of a repentant and yearning soul. It is fittingly concluded with the prayer, "Redeem Israel, O G-d, out of all its troubles." To this another verse is added: "And He will redeem Israel out of all its sins."[33]

According to Nusach Ashkenaz, *nefilath appayim* immediately follows the Shemone Esrei, and Psalm 6 (from v. 2) is said instead of Ps. 25. The psalm is preceded by a brief "confession": "O Merciful and Gracious One, I have sinned unto You; O G-d full of mercy, have mercy upon me and accept my supplication."

After the said Psalm there follows on Mondays and Thursdays the prayer of the "long" *Vehu Rachum*, and on other days—the prayer of *Va'anachnu lo neda*.

ואנחנו לא נדע

CONCLUSION OF *TACHNUN*

The prayer *Va'anachnu lo neda* consists of a collection of various Scripture verses. It is preceded by several verses from the prayer *Avinu Malkenu* (which is recited in its entirety on Fast Days, on Rosh Hashanah when it occurs during weekdays, on the Ten Days of Repentance, and at the conclusion of Ne'ilah on Yom Kippur). On Fast Days and the Ten Days of Repentance the entire *Avinu Malkenu* would be said here; on ordinary weekdays only the following four verses are said:

Our Father, our King, You are our Father;

Our Father, our King, we have no King but You;

Our Father, our King, have mercy upon us!

---

[33] Ps. 130:8.

*Our Father, our King, be gracious unto us and answer
us, for we have no good deeds; deal with us in
charity and lovingkindness, for the sake of Your
great Name, and save us!*

Then follow the Scriptural verses with which *Tachnun* is concluded. The first of these is, "And as for us, we know not what to
do, but our eyes are upon You."[34] According to authorities
(Abudraham, Tur, etc.) this verse expresses the thought that,
having followed the pattern of prayer of Mosheh Rabbenu,
namely, having prayed sitting, standing, and falling on our faces,
as he did on Mount Sinai,[35] we do not know what more to do,
except to rely on G-d's mercy. Therefore we pray, "Remember
Your mercies, O G-d, and Your kindness, for they are everlasting,"[36] and more in this vein.

We conclude this prayer, and *Tachnun*, with the verses:

For He knows our yetzer *(weak nature), and is mindful that we are dust.*[37]

*Help us, O G-d of our salvation, for the sake of the
glory of Your Name, and save us and forgive our
sins for the sake of Your Name.*[38]

והוא רחום
VEHU RACHUM

One of the principal prayers of Tachnun is *Vehu Rachum* ("But
He the Merciful"), often referred to as the "Long Vehu Rachum."
It is said only on Mondays and Thursdays.

---

34 II Chron. 20:12.
35 Deut. 9:9; 9:25; 10:10.
36 Ps. 25:6.
37 Ps. 103:14.
38 Ps. 79:9.

There are several versions regarding the authorship of *Vehu Rachum* and the time of its composition. According to one opinion mentioned in the literature of the Geonim, the prayer was composed in the days of Vespasian, father of Titus, who destroyed the Beth Hamikdash. According to this version, Vespasian had placed a number of Jews on three ships, from which the helms were removed. The ships thus began to drift helplessly. Divine Providence, however, saved the ships from being smashed by cliffs and storms. Each ship eventually landed in a different city in France: Lyons, Arles and Bordeau. At first, the poor refugees were kindly received by the governor of the province, and were given land and vineyards as a means of livelihood. However, when the governor died, his successor proved a cruel man. He robbed the refugees of whatever gifts they had received and threatened to drive them out. The Jews began a fast, praying to G-d for salvation. It was then that three leaders of the community, two of them brothers by the names of Joseph and Benjamin, and the third, Samuel, a cousin, all of them men of great piety and learning, composed the *Vehu Rachum,* each one a section of it.

According to another version, *Vehu Rachum* was composed by the Geonim, Rabbi Amittai, Rabbi Shefatiah and Rabbi Josephia, also in connection with a grave danger that threatened their community.

The reason *Vehu Rachum* was introduced into the Morning Service of Monday and Thursday only, is that on these days in ancient Israel the courts (Beth Din) were held. It is considered that also On High these are Days of Judgment. Therefore, *Vehu Rachum* is said on these days as a special plea for mercy, since we know that according to the standards of strict justice none of us could face judgment.

Another reason for saying *Vehu Rachum* only on Mondays and Thursdays is that these days were often observed as fast days by many Jews.

Anyone who understands the meaning of the words will see

at a glance that *Vehu Rachum* is a very moving prayer, coming from the depths of the suffering Jewish heart. It is full of cries of sorrow and pain which our people have suffered since the destruction of our Beth Hamikdash to this day. We know that we were driven from our Holy Land because we did not keep it holy enough, and that we are suffering so much because we nave not been faithful enough to G-d, and to our Torah and Mitzvoth. Therefore, our first thought is to pray for forgiveness and mercy, and then we pour out our hearts, appealing to G-d for help and protection. This *motif* is repeated over and over again throughout the long prayer of *Vehu Rachum,* for, indeed, there is no end to our tale of woe.

Vehu Rachum contains seven chapters, a hymn, and a concluding portion. The latter is also said on other days when *Tachnun* is said.

The first chapter, as well as the second, consists mostly of Biblical verses (from the Psalms, Jeremiah, Daniel, Isaiah, Joel, etc.) which express confession of our sins and an acknowledgment that our suffering is due to our having drifted from G-d. The first chapter concludes with a moving prayer (from Daniel) that G-d turn away His anger from Jerusalem and cause His face to shine upon the Sanctuary which is in ruins, and that He do so not for the sake of our good deeds which are few, but for G-d's sake.[39]

The second chapter begins with a continuation of Daniel's prayer, which is almost like a repetition:

> *Incline Your ear, O G-d, and hear; open Your eyes and see our desolation, and the city which is called by Your Name; for we do not lay our supplications before You because of our righteous acts but because of Your abundant mercies.*[40]

It continues in this vein with quotations from Isaiah and Joel.

---

[39] Daniel 9:15-17.
[40] Dan. 9:17-20.

The third and fourth chapters are also of similar content. They do not contain Biblical quotations, but the style is very similar.

In the fifth chapter we call upon G-d by His many qualities: He is our Father, King, Rock, Redeemer; He is Everlasting, Mighty, Loving, Slow to Anger, and Full of Mercy. We appeal to Him to deal with us according to these Divine qualities, and deliver us from our enemies and from all manner of sorrow and hurt.

In the sixth chapter we cry to G-d to remember our ancestors, Abraham, Isaac and Jacob, and spare us for their sake, "for such is Your way — showing lovingkindness *freely* (undeservedly) in every generation." Promising to search our ways and to turn back to G-d, we cry: "O G-d, save us! O G-d, send us good fortune! O G-d, answer us on the day we call!" While the nations of the world say about us, "Their hope is lost," we still cling to G-d and trust in Him alone.

In the last chapter we appeal to G-d, Who is always ready to receive those who sincerely return to Him: "You, Who opens Your hand to repentance, to receive transgressors and sinners . . . forget us not." Again we pray to G-d to look upon our terrible suffering in the lands of our exile. We have been shamed and disgraced and insulted; we have been defenseless against violence, injury and murder. "How long shall Your strength remain in captivity, and Your glory in the hand of the foe?!" we exclaim in anguish. Nevertheless, we have remained loyal to G-d and have continually proclaimed G-d's glory and unity. Therefore, we appeal to G-d: "Be gracious unto the people who in constant love proclaim the unity of Your Name twice every day, saying: 'Hear, O Israel, G-d is our G-d, G-d is One!' "

Then follows a hymn with a refrain in which the whole of the *Vehu Rachum* is mirrored, praying to G-d something like this:

*Look down from heaven and see how we have become
a scorn among the nations; we are regarded as sheep
brought to the slaughter; the nations of the world say,
"There is no hope for you!"; others say with scorn,
"Where now is your G-d?" They have killed many of
us and now we are left a few out of many. Yet, despite
all this, we have not forgotten Your Name; forget us
not also!*

This stirring hymn is followed by three beautiful stanzas:
"O Guardian of Israel!" "O Guardian of an Only Nation!" and
"O Guardian of a Holy Nation!" in which we pray for G-d's love,
mercy and protection, since Israel is the only people in the world
who believe in G-d's Unity and Holiness, and have given their
lives for the sanctification of G-d's Name throughout the ages.

Finally comes the concluding portion of *Tachnun*, the prayer
Va'anachnu lo neda, which has already been discussed.

Tachnun is not said on Shabbos, Yom Tov, Rosh-Chodesh, and
certain other days of festive importance. For example, it is not
said during the whole month of Nissan, on Pesach-sheni (Iyar
14th), Lag B'Omer, from Rosh-Chodesh Sivan until the 12th
(inclusive), Tisha-B'Av, the 15th of Av, Erev Rosh Hashanah,
from Erev Yom Kippur to the end of Tishrei, the 15th of Shevat,
Purim-Kattan (14th and 15th of Adar I), etc. Neither is Tachnun
said in the house of a mourner, or on the celebration of a marriage.

After *Tachnun,* or when *Tachnun* is omitted, after the *Shemone
Esrei, Ashrei* is said again, followed by Psalm 20 and the prayer of
Uva l'Zion. We have already discussed the significance of *Ashrei,*
and why it is said three times daily (twice in the Morning Service
and once in Minchah).[40a] So we may proceed with Psalm 20.

40a See p. 125 f. above.

למנצח – יענך

PSALM 20

For the Chief Musician, a Psalm of David:
*G-d answer you in the day of distress; the Name of
the G-d of Jacob lift you up;*
*May He send you help from the Sanctuary and sustain
you out of Zion;*
*May He remember all your offerings, and accept your
sacrifices forever (Selah);*
*May He grant your heart's desire, and fulfill all your
counsel.*
*We will rejoice in Your salvation, and in the Name of
our G-d we will raise banners; G-d fulfill all your
petitions.*
*Now I know that G-d has saved His anointed; He will
answer him from His holy heavens with the mighty
saving acts of His right hand.*
*Some (trust) in chariots and some in horses, but we
will make mention in the Name of G-d our G-d.*
*They are bowed down and fallen, but we are risen
and stand upright.*
*Save, O G-d; the King will answer us on the day we
call.*

Psalm 20 has been introduced into the Morning Prayer, just
before the prayer of *Uva l'Zion,* for several reasons.

According to our Sages,[41] this psalm has a special significance
in that it follows the first eighteen psalms[42] with which King
David praised G-d before he prayed, "G-d answer you in the day

----

[41] Abudraham, based on Midrash Tehillim.
[42] According to Berachoth 9b, the first two psalms are counted as one.

of distress." It is fitting therefore that we should also recite this psalm after we say the *Shemone Esrei,* containing eighteen benedictions.

Moreover, although this psalm was composed in connection with certain events that happened to King David, as we will see presently, it is also a prophecy of the time when Mashiach, the anointed descendant of David, will bring about the complete Geulah of the Jewish people. This is why this psalm has been placed directly before the prayer of *Uva l'Zion* ("May the Redeemer come unto Zion").

The distress in which King David found himself, in connection with which this psalm was composed (as mentioned above), had to do with the wars which King David had to wage against the enemies of the young Jewish kingdom. Our Sages said[43] that when David sent his general Yoav (Joab) into the battlefield, he recited the prayer "G-d answer you in the day of distress . . . send you help from the Sanctuary and sustain you out of Zion," etc. For while the enemy relied on his iron chariots and trained horses, we, the Jewish people, must rely on G-d to give us victory against overwhelmingly powerful foes.

According to another tradition, this psalm was originally composed in connection with the danger which faced David when he and a handful of men were nearly overwhelmed by the Philistines.[44] At that time, Avishai the son of Tzeruyah (Yoav's brother) came to David's rescue, reciting the prayer, "G-d answer you in the day of distress."[45]

As explained in the Zohar[46] and other sources, Psalm 20 is very significant in many ways. It contains *nine* verses (apart from the first, which is like a caption), *seventy* words, and *three hundred*

---

43 Sanhedrin 49a; see also Sotah 49a.
44 II Sam. 21:15-17.
45 Sanhedrin 95a.
46 Zohar III, 241b.

and ten letters—all very meaningful numbers in Kabbalah and in Torah generally. We have already had occasion to mention that the number *nine* represents the word אמת (truth), the gimatria (numerical equivalent [במספר קטן]) of which is nine. Seventy recalls, among other things, the number of Yaakov's children who came into Egypt. Three hundred and ten is the number of worlds in the hereafter awaiting a Tzaddik.[47]

In the writings of the saintly Ari the whole of Psalm 20 is interpreted as alluding to the "distress" of the Divine Shechinah in "exile," which parallels the distress of the Divine soul being confined in a body and dragged into material things; the battle it has to wage against physical temptations, and so forth. It is only by calling upon the Name of G-d and living according to G-d's will that the soul can be saved with the help of G-d.

The *Rokeach*[48] notes that the letter ט (the ninth letter of the Hebrew alphabet) is omitted from this psalm. The reason for this, he writes, is that there are nine things that prevent a prayer from ascending to heaven, and the omission of this letter signifies that none of them will hinder the acceptance of this prayer, which begins with the words, "G-d answer you in the day of distress," and ends with, "Save, O G-d; the King will answer us on the day we call."

Because of the deep meaningfulness of this psalm, it is the custom to recite it (with other psalms and prayers) in a case of some distress or danger, G-d forbid, whether of a personal nature, or threatening the community at large.

For the same reason it is *not* included in our daily prayers on Shabbos, Yom Tov, Rosh-Chodesh, and on certain other days on which no *Tachnun* is said. According to Nusach Ari, Psalm 20 is never recited (as part of our daily prayer) on *any* day when Tachnun is omitted.[48a]

---

47 Sanhedrin 100a.
48 Rokeach, ch. 28.
48a See p. 198 above.

וּבָא לְצִיּוֹן

UVA L'ZION

Towards the end of the Morning Prayers there is a prayer beginning with the words "Uva l'Zion Goel," meaning, "A Redeemer shall come unto Zion." The prayer consists of various Biblical verses, some of them also translated into Aramaic, which was the language spoken by most of the people during the days of the Talmud. For only the scholars spoke Hebrew in those days.

This prayer contains, in a few words, most of the important messages mentioned earlier in the prayers. It also contains the Kedushah ("Holy, holy, holy is the L-rd of Hosts"), which is said twice before, during the Morning Services. The first time the Kedushah is said is before the *Shema* and the second time during the repetition of the *Shemone Esrei.* In the prayer of Uva l'Zion, as before the Shema, the Kedushah is not said congregationally (in the presence of at least ten worshippers), but by each worshipper for himself, as it is merely said as a quotation from the prophet.[49]

The prayer of *Uva l'Zion* is said to have been arranged for the benefit of latecomers to the Morning Service. For this reason it is like a digest of the whole Morning Service and contains also the Kedushah. For this reason also it is not said in the Morning Service of the Sabbath and Festivals, when people usually come early.

---

[49] Isaiah 6:3.

202

On these Holy days the prayer of *Uva l'Zion* is said in the Afternoon Service instead.

It does not mean, however, that by saying the prayer of Uva l'Zion one need not say the rest of the prayers, for this prayer is only an addition to the service and not a substitute.

At this point we might mention that the Tefillin may be removed *after* the Kedushah of Uva l'Zion, though many worshippers remove the Tefillin after completing all the prayers, including those following after Uva l'Zion.

As for the prayer itself, it can be seen that the first two verses are taken from Isaiah.[50] The first of these contains a promise of the Redemption, which is linked with repentance. The second contains G-d's assurance of the everlasting covenant between G-d and Israel, and that G-d's spirit and the Torah shall never depart from Israel.

The next verse is taken from the Psalms, "You are Holy, You Who abides amid the people of Israel." The Hebrew word *yoshev* (abides), has the meaning of "waiting" (as in the words "biding time"), for G-d "sits and waits for the praises of Israel." In other words, G-d looks forward to our prayers and welcomes them in the same way as a loving father waits for greetings from his beloved children.

Next comes the Kedushah, with a translation in Aramaic, which has already been discussed.[50a]

The Kedushah is followed by a verse from the Prophet Ezekiel. "Blessed be the Glory of G-d from His place."[51] The Prophet, in a heavenly vision, heard the angels praise G-d with these words.

---

[50] Isaiah 59:20-21.
[50a] See pp. 145-148 above.
[51] Ezekiel 3:12.

Then comes the exclamation, "G-d shall reign for ever and ever!" which the Jews sang in the Song of Moses after crossing the Red Sea.[52] Here again comes the Aramaic translation.

To underline the importance of the Kedushah and subsequent quotations from the prophets, there follows a prayer, first said by King David, "O G-d, the G-d of Abraham, of Isaac, and of Israel, our Fathers, keep this forever as the inward thought in the heart of Your people, and direct their heart unto You."[53] Next come Biblical quotations, mostly from the Psalms, and one from the Prophet Micah, which speak of G-d's mercy, forgiveness and truth. We praise G-d for having created us to bring Glory to Him, by living a way of life according to the Torah which He gave us, an everlasting life. "He gave us a Torah of truth and planted everlasting life in our midst." The Torah is called a "Tree of Life" which G-d *planted* in our midst, and it is up to us to cultivate it and allow it to grow and bring G-dly fruits.

We pray that G-d open our hearts and place love and fear of Him in our hearts, that we may do His will and serve Him with a perfect heart; that we may not lead an empty and fruitless life. We pray for love and fear of G-d, even though it is mostly up to us to be G-d-fearing and to love G-d, for we have a free will to do as we please. Therefore, we pray to G-d to help us observe His laws and statutes with love and reverence.

The prayer's last verses are: "Blessed is the man who trusts in G-d.[54] . . . It pleased G-d for his righteousness' sake to magnify the Torah and glorify it."[55] The last verse speaks of the greatness of the Torah and its many commandments which G-d gave us to observe, and that we Jews are very fortunate and privileged that G-d gave us these wonderful laws and truths.

---

[52] Exod. 15:8.
[53] I Chron. 29:18.
[54] Jeremiah 17:7.
[55] Isaiah 42:21.

שיר של יום

SONG OF THE DAY

1.

In the days of old, when the Beth Hamikdash was in existence, the Leviim (Levites) had an important part in the holy service conducted there daily. Their task was to sing hymns of praise to G-d, which they also accompanied on musical instruments.

Song and music are the manifestations of a great inner joy that cannot be contained inwardly. A person, overcome with joy, breaks out in song. Song and music are also infectious; they call forth a response in the listener, and often touch upon the innermost feelings of a person, making him want to join in the singing. This is especially so in the case of sacred music, which inspires higher feelings, and often touches upon the very heartstrings of the soul. Our Sages say[56] that the angels in heaven express their devotion and love to their Creator through song. Indeed, the song and music of the Levites in the Beth Hamikdash of old was something of the same order; it expressed love of G-d and the joy of serving G-d.

One of the highlights of the service of the Levites was the singing of the "Song of the Day" (*Shir-shel-Yom*) after the daily sacrifice of the *Tamid*. It consisted of a special Psalm from the Book of Tehillim for each day of the seven days of the week.

Inasmuch as our daily prayers take the place of the daily sacrifices in the Beth Hamikdash, the *Shir-shel-Yom* which the

---

[56] Hulin 91b.

Levites used to sing in the Sanctuary has been made a part of our Morning Service. Its place in the Siddur is towards the end of the Morning Services, after *Uva l'Zion*—according to Nusach Ari, or at the very end of the service—according to Nusach Ashkenaz. In either case, it corresponds to the order of the service in the Beth Hamikdash and has the additional significance of finishing the Morning prayer on a note of song, to inspire us with the joy of Mitzvoth for the rest of the day. The first of the Mitzvoth following the prayer should, of course, be an immediate period of Torah learning.

According to Nusach Ari, the *Shir-shel-Yom* is preceded by Psalm 86, followed by selected Biblical verses, and Psalm 124. On days when no *Tachnun* is said, Psalm 86 is omitted.

תפלה לדוד

PSALM 86

Psalm 86 in many respects parallels Psalm 25, which is part of *Tachnun,* and which has already been discussed.[56a]

> *A Prayer of David. Turn Your ear, O G-d, and answer me, for I am poor and needy.* (v. 1)

Poverty and riches in the Psalms, as our Sages note, do not necessarily refer to worldly goods, but to poverty and riches in good deeds and merits. The pious and humble person always considers himself "poor" in good deeds, for he always feels he ought to have done more and better. And he considers himself "needy"—of G-d's love and nearness, for which he has an insatiable desire. (The Hebrew word *evyon,* from the verb *avah,* implies "desire.") And as the poor man depends upon the kindness and charity of his benefactor, so does King David, speaking for all of

---

[56a] P. 191 above.

us, appeal to G-d's infinite kindness and grace to bestow favors even upon the unworthy.

Compare this opening verse with Psalm 25:16: "Turn unto me and have mercy upon me, for I am desolate and poor."

Rejoice the soul of Your servant, for unto You, O G-d, I lift up my soul. (v. 4)

Compare with the opening verse of Ps. 25: "Unto You, O G-d, I lift up my soul." We have already explained that these words express complete readiness to give our life and soul for the Sanctification of G-d's Name (*Kiddush Hashem*), as the saintly Ari points out, and should therefore be said with deep sincerity and devotion.

Teach me Your ways, O G-d, that I may walk in Your truth; unify my heart to fear Your Name. (v. 11)

Compare: "Show me Your ways, O G-d, teach me Your paths. Lead me in Your truth, and teach me . . ." (Ps. 25:4, 5).

Teach me Your ways . . . that I may walk in Your truth. G-d's ways and G-d's truth are to be found in the Torah. But there is a possibility that one may misunderstand and misinterpret the Torah. As in everything else, one needs G-d's blessing also in order to understand the Torah well, and be successful in Torah learning. Referring to this verse, our Sages make the following commentary: "King David said, 'Master of the World, when I study Your statutes, let the Yetzer Hara have no power to distract me, nor to lead me into error, that I might not be shamed, nor discouraged from learning Torah; but make my heart one, that I may study Your statutes *wholeheartedly.*' "[57]

Unify (unite) my heart to fear Your Name. These are very meaningful words. For the heart is the "seat" of desire, and quite often there could be conflicting desires. Rabbi Schneur Zalman of Liadi, author of the *Tanya* and *Shulchan Aruch,* and founder of

---
[57] Shemoth Rabba 19:2.

Chabad Chasiduth, explains it as follows: There are two kinds of heart's desires, "inner" ones and "external" ones. *External* desires are those that are not born in the heart; they are aroused there by the mind. These, in turn, can also be of two kinds. When the mind dwells on G-dliness and heavenly matters, the heart is roused to a deep feeling of reverence for G-d, and the heart is filled with fear of G-d and love of G-d. But there is also another "mind," a mind that dwells on earthly things, creating a desire and love for earthly pleasures and material things. In such a case, a person's heart is "split," as it were, sometimes desiring that which is good and holy, and sometimes desiring that which is really worthless, or even bad. It is almost as if the man had two hearts instead of one, which are in conflict with each other, at times one gaining the upper hand, at other times the other.

However, in the Jewish heart there is also an innermost point or core, that knows only one love and one desire—the love of G-d and the desire to be attached to G-d alone. It is sometimes called "dos pintele yid." It is a *gift from G-d,* by virtue of the Divine soul which a Jew possesses. It could be "asleep" and inactive, but it is always there, and always ready to be "awakened" and come to life; and when it does, even the most estranged Jew can be transformed and become most closely attached to G-d. This *inner* heart is beyond reason and comprehension; it has a mystical quality of its own. When this great love for G-d is aroused in the inner heart, it easily overcomes all "external" desires, for it floods the entire heart, and the heart becomes truly *one.*[58]

There is, of course, quite a difference between the love of G-d that is aroused by the mind in the "external" heart, and that which springs from the innermost core of the heart. The first is limited to the degree and measure of one's mind and comprehension; the second is unlimited.

This is what King David meant when he prayed, "Unite my

---

[58] Lik. Torah, Balak 67b, f.

heart," and "make my heart one." He prayed that he should achieve unity of heart not only "externally," so that there would be no outside distractions and conflicts, but that he should achieve a completely perfect heart, from which all evil has been eradicated, and which is filled with the fear and love of G-d which are boundless.

And with King David we also pray for this "unity" of heart— not only when we recite this Psalm, but each and every morning in the blessing immediately preceding the Shema, where we pray: "And unite our heart to love and fear Your Name."[59]

> *O G-d, arrogant men are risen against me and a band*
> *of violent men have sought after my soul.... (v. 14)*

Compare: "See mine enemies for they are many," etc. (Ps. 25:19). As already noted, the forces of evil that pose a grave danger to a person are not surrounding enemies, but frequently also enemies "within"—the Yetzer Hara and all sorts of temptations. Together with a constant personal effort to overcome them, one needs also G-d's help. That is why King David prays, "Give Your strength unto Your servant" (v. 16).

Psalm 86 concludes with the verse:

> *Show me a sign for good, that they that hate me may*
> *see and be ashamed, because You, O G-d, have helped*
> *me and comforted me. (v. 17)*

It is not for himself that King David asked for a sign of G-d's benevolence. He asked for a clear and obvious sign that even his enemies would acknowledge. According to Rashi, this request was not granted him in his lifetime, but only in the time of his son and successor, King Solomon. For when the Beth Hamikdash was completed and King Solomon was about to dedicate it, the gates of the Sanctuary locked themselves and did not open until he prayed, "O G-d, turn not away the face of Your anointed; remem-

---
[59] Ibid.

ber the mercies of Your servant David."[60] At the mention of
David's merits, the gates opened wide.[61]

2.

*O, House of Jacob, come let us walk in the light of
G-d.*[62]

*For, all the nations will walk each in the name of
its god, but we will walk in the Name of G-d, our
G-d, for ever.*[63]

*May G-d, our G-d, be with us as He was with our
Fathers; may He not leave us, nor forsake us; to turn
our heart unto Him, to walk in all His ways, and to
keep His commandments and statutes and judgments
which He commanded our Fathers. And may these
words, which I have implored before G-d, be near
unto G-d our G-d day and night, that He uphold the
cause of His servant, and the cause of His people
Israel, as each day requires. That all the nations of the
world shall know that G-d (Y-H-V-H) is G-d
(Elokim), there is none else.*[64]

The above selected verses from the books of Isaiah, Micah and
I Kings speak for themselves and are clearly connected.

The first verse is from a famous prophecy by Isaiah about the
"last of days,"[65] namely, the days of Mashiach. At that time there
will be peace on earth, "nation shall not lift up sword against
nation,"[66] and many of the nations of the world will turn to

---

60 II Chron. 6:42.
61 Sabbath 30a; Shemoth Rabba 44:2.
62 Isaiah 2:5.
63 Micah 4:5.
64 I Kings 8:57-60.
65 Isaiah 2:2.
66 Ibid. v. 4.

Jerusalem for guidance and inspiration, "for out of Zion shall go forth the Torah ('guidance,' 'instruction'), and the word of G-d from Jerusalem."[67] But we Jews do not have to wait for that ideal time to live up to G-d's will. The prophet calls upon the Jewish people ("House of Jacob") to walk *now* in the light of G-d.

The next verse above is from an almost identical prophecy of Micah. It adds a note to Isaiah's prophecy, to the effect that although the nations of the world will turn to Jerusalem for guidance, this does not mean that they will embrace the Jewish faith. Indeed, our Sages declare that in the days of Mashiach no would-be converts to the Jewish faith would be accepted,[68] because they might be swayed by the glory of Israel rather than by wholehearted conviction. Unlike certain other faiths which dream of converting the whole world to their religion, the Jewish religion has no such ambition, and Jews have not engaged in missionary work. We only look forward to the time when the nations of the world will live up to the basic laws of justice and morality which G-d has made obligatory upon them since the covenant which He made with Noah and his descendants after the Flood.

The third passage (from I Kings) is taken from the moving prayer by young King Solomon at the dedication of the Beth Hamikdash. Here we find an explanation of what is meant by the words "to walk in the light of G-d," or "in the Name of G-d." It simply means to keep His commandments—the Torah and Mitzvoth. King Solomon, too, prophesied that eventually all the nations of the world will recognize that there is truly but *one* G-d: that G-d the Creator (Y-H-V-H) Who is unknown and unknowable, is the G-d Whose presence can be seen in Nature (Elokim); the G-d of mercy is the same G-d that dispenses stern judgment— "there is none else" (*ein od*).

---

[67] Ibid. v. 3.
[68] Yevamoth 24b; Avodah Zarah 3b.

In a deeper sense, the words *ein od* mean "there is *nothing* else." When we realize that G-d is the Creator, and that everything exists only because G-d wills it to exist, it becomes clear that in actual reality there is nothing but G-d.[69]

שיר המעלות לדוד, לולי ה׳
PSALM 124

In this short psalm, King David speaks of Israel's dependence on G-d at all times, especially when facing a vicious enemy "who would swallow us alive" (which is the case most of the time).

There is also the danger of the "arrogant waters sweeping our soul," that is to say, not only physical danger, but also spiritual danger. There are many temptations and pitfalls in the daily life, both outside (in the environment) and within ourselves, which threaten to ensnare and trap us. And while we must always be on the alert, we must be thankful to G-d that we do not fall prey to our enemies, for it is thanks to G-d that "our soul escapes like a bird from the snare of the fowlers; the snare is broken, and we escape." With all our personal effort and determination, we realize that "Our help is in the Name of G-d, the Creator of heaven and earth."

שיר של יום ליום א׳
FIRST DAY: PSALM 24

This day is the first day of Shabbos (week) on which the Leviim used to say in the Beth Hamikdash. . . .

The Daily Psalm, or Song of the Day (*Shir-shel-Yom*) is introduced by the declaration, "This day is the first (second, third,

---

[69] This concept stems from the doctrine of *continuous creation*, briefly discussed above (p. 142 f.). It is explained at length in *Shaar Hayichud vehaEmunah*, by Rabbi Schneur Zalman.

etc.) of Shabbos," etc. In our holy tongue (*Lashon ha-Kodesh*) the days of the week are called "First Day," "Second Day," etc., as we find in the very first chapter of Bereishith. The proper names of the days of the week in other languages (e.g. Sunday, Monday, etc.) are really left-overs from the pagan cults, when each day of the week was dedicated to a different diety, such as the sun (Sunday), moon (Moon-day), and so forth. These pagan names of the days have no place in our holy tongue.[70]

Furthermore, in Jewish life the days of the week are connected with the holy Shabbos day which is dedicated to G-d. It is from the holy Shabbos day that each day of the week derives a measure of holiness and inspiration. It is stated in the Zohar that Shabbos is the source of blessings for all the days of the week. In the Talmud the entire week is often called "Shabbos." Our Sages further say that the fourth of the Ten Commandments—"Remember the Shabbos day to keep it holy"—indicates that we should remember the Shabbos on each day of the week. Accordingly, the declaration introducing the daily psalm is worded: "This day is the ... day of *Shabbos* (i.e. of the week)"—instead of *ha-Shavua* ("of the week").[71]

In the Talmud[72] we find the origin of the custom of the Daily Song, the particular psalms recited by the Levites on the seven days of the week, as well as the connection between the particular psalm and the particular day of the week.

On the first day of the week the Levites used to recite Psalm 24, which begins:

> *A psalm by David. Unto G-d belongs the earth and all that is in it; the world and all that dwell in it* (v. 1).

---

[70] See Ramban on Exod. 20:8.
[71] Mechilta, comp. Pesikta Rabb. 63.
[72] Rosh Hashanah 31a; Tamid 6:4; Sofrim 8:1.

The connection between this psalm and the first day of the week is obvious. On the first day G-d created heaven and earth.

After the first two verses which speak of Creation, the psalm goes on to refer to the holiest place on earth, the "Mountain of G-d" and the Beth Hamikdash, as well as of man, the end purpose of Creation:

> *Who will ascend the mountain of G-d, and who will stand in His holy place? He that has clean hands and a pure heart, who has not lifted up My Name in vain and has not sworn falsely* (vs. 3-4).

To be clean of hand means, of course, that one's acts and deeds are good, and no wrongful act has been committed. To be pure of heart means that one's feelings and thoughts are likewise good, having no ill-feeling or prejudice towards anyone. Not to "lift up G-d's Name in vain" means not to swear by G-d on something which is obviously true. Not to "swear falsely" (the Hebrew word used here actually means "cunningly") refers to an oath which, on the face of it, is true, yet it is dishonest. By way of illustration, our Sages cite a case, as where a person was sued for a certain amount of money. The defendant put the money in the hollow of his walking stick, and before taking the oath handed his staff to the plaintiff to hold, while he swore that he had returned the money to the plaintiff.[73] Unfortunately we often hear of even highly-placed persons who make "shady" deals, claiming they did nothing wrong "legally," but whose actions are nevertheless morally wrong.

Man is the "end purpose of Creation," it was stated earlier. But it is only the *good* man—the man whose actions, feelings and thoughts are good, both in his duties to G-d and fellow-man— that truly completes and justifies the entire Creation.

---

[73] Pesikta Rabb. 22:6; Vayyikra Rab. 6:3.

The second half of the psalm is dedicated to the Kingship of G-d:

> *Lift up your heads, O gates, and be lifted up, O everlasting doors, that the King of Glory may come in* (v. 7).

With the creation of man, G-d became King, for one is no king who has no subjects over whom to rule. Adam became G-d's first subject and he immediately proclaimed the sovereignty of the Creator as the "King of the Universe." For this reason Psalm 24 has been made an important part of the Rosh Hashanah prayers, both in the Evening prayer and in the section of *Malchuyoth* (kingship) of the Musaf prayer. For Rosh Hashanah, as we all know, is the anniversary of the creation of man, and of the "Coronation" of the King of kings.

According to Ibn Ezra and other commentaries, King David composed this psalm after he bought the site of the Beth Hamikdash (Mount Moriah) from Arunah the Jebusite. This psalm reflects David's joy and inspiration when he brought the Holy Ark to the City of David and placed it in a tent.[74] In his prophetic vision David could see the magnificent edifice, the Beth Hamikdash, which would be the permanent home of the Holy Ark; the gates of the Sanctuary would be opened to admit the Ark, and G-d's Glory would appear for all to behold.[75]

The verse "Lift up your heads, O gates," etc., is repeated again (v. 9). Ibn Ezra explains the repetition as a reference to the third Beth Hamikdash, which will be built when Mashiach will come, and which will never be destroyed again. According to Targum, the first refers to the gates of the Beth Hamikdash, while the second refers to the gates of Gan Eden. According to other Sages, the reference is to the gates of heaven. Actually, all these interpre-

---

[74] II Sam. ch. 6.
[75] Chron. 6:42; Sabbath 30a.

tations are in harmony, for the Beth Hamikdash itself is called the Gates of Heaven, and our Sages also said that the Sanctuary on earth is directly situated "below" its completely spiritual counterpart in Heaven.[75a]

שיר של יום ליום ב'
SECOND DAY: PSALM 48

On the second day of the week the Song of the Day was Psalm 48, composed by the descendants of Korah.

The connection between this psalm and the second day of the week, as stated in the Talmud,[76] is to be found in the verse *Great is G-d and praised exceedingly in the city of our G-d, in His holy Mountain* (v. 2). The reason is that on the second day of Creation G-d "divided His creation (into the Upper and Lower worlds) and extended His reign over them." To this, Rashi adds the commentary that, by making the firmament which divided between the Upper and Lower Worlds, G-d became great in heaven above as He became great on earth below, namely, in His city and holy mountain, where the Divine Presence was felt most.

The nature of this "division" will be better understood in the light of the explanation given by Rabbi Schneur Zalman, founder of Chabad[77]: Before G-d "made the firmament and divided between the water under the firmament and the water above the firmament"[78] and "called the firmament heaven,"[79] there was no division between heaven and earth, or, the spiritual and material. Both were mixed together; the spiritual was not purely spiritual, and the material was not concretely material. By way of illustra-

---

[75a] Yalkut Tehillim, 713.
[76] Rosh Hashanah 31a.
[77] Lik. Torah, Shelach 42a.
[78] Gen. 1:7.
[79] Gen. 1:8.

tion: A barrel of wine, in which the wine and the sediments are mixed together; when the sediments are separated and fall to the bottom, the wine above becomes clear, while the sediments below become thick. Similarly, when G-d first created heaven and earth, the two were not separated. The separation between the spiritual world and material world took place on the second day of Creation, and that is when G-d became great. But why did G-d become great only after this division?

Again, in Chabad,[80] we will find the answer. The Alter Rebbe explains it as follows: A king is no king without a people. In other words, a king is no king to his immediate family and close relatives; a king is king to unrelated subjects, to his people who are not his relatives. The angels in heaven are closer to G-d than the humans on earth. But the angels are like G-d's immediate "family"; it is not so remarkable that they love and respect G-d and are obedient to Him. It is more remarkable when people on earth acknowledge G-d's kingship and obey His will. It is therefore here on earth that G-d's sovereignty becomes a reality. All the more so, since man has been given freedom of choice to accept it, or reject it.

Our physical world — the Alter Rebbe further explains — is likened to a city.[81] A city consists of many different dwellings, and is inhabited by many different people. And so is our world full of many different and separated material and physical things. It is in a city ruled by a king that the king's sovereignty is felt, not in the king's own home with his family.

This, therefore, is the inner meaning of the opening verse of Psalm 48: "Great is G-d and praised exceedingly . . . (where?) . . . in the city of our G-d, in His holy mountain."

Rashi, in his commentary on this verse in Tehillim, states that it refers to the future, that is, to the days of Mashiach, when

---

[80] Shaar Hayichud vehaEmunah, ch. 7; Torah Or 53d; Lik. Torah Bamidbar 6a; Balak 68a, etc.

[81] Torah Or 56b.

Jerusalem and the Beth Hamikdash will attain their fullest glory. Indeed, the entire psalm is a hymn to Jerusalem and the Beth Hamikdash. But, of course, there is no contradiction between Rashi's commentaries on the same verse in the Talmud[82] and in Scripture. Both are true, for it will be in those future days of Mashiach that G-ds kingship will be truly felt and acknowledged by all men in the highest possible degree, and the destiny of Creation will be fulfilled.

שיר של יום ליום ג'
THIRD DAY: PSALM 82

On the third day of the week, the Song of the Day recited by the Leviim in the Beth Hamikdash was Psalm 82, composed by Asaph.

The reason for this selection, the Talmud[83] states, is that on the third day of Creation G-d made dry land appear, and thus prepared the earth for habitation, in readiness for His congregation, the Jewish people. This is alluded to in the first verse of the psalm: "G-d stands in the G-dly congregation; He judges in the midst of judges."

"G-d stands" is to be understood in the sense of "G-d reveals Himself."

He judges in the midst of judges (elohim). In the Torah,[84] judges are called "elohim," because they dispense justice, which is a Divine quality, and pronounce judgment in the Name of G-d.

The entire psalm is devoted to the theme of justice. The psalmist condemns those judges who judge unjustly: *They know not, nor do they understand; they walk in darkness; all the foundations of the earth are shaken* (v. 5). Without justice, the world cannot

---

[82] Rosh Hashanah 31a.
[83] Ibid.
[84] E.g. Exod. 21:6; 22:80.

exist, as our Sages of the Mishnah said, "On three things the world exists: on truth, justice and peace."[85] If there is no justice, there is no truth and there is no peace; *the foundations of the earth are shaken.*

שיר של יום ליום ד'
FOURTH DAY: PSALM 94

The Song of the Day for the fourth day of the week was Psalm 94, beginning with the verse, *"O G-d, G-d of retribution; O G-d of retribution, shine forth."*

On the fourth day of Creation, the great luminaries, the sun, the moon and the stars, were placed in their orbits in the sky. Soon people began to worship them, thinking they had a power of their own, and could benefit or harm them. They did not know that there was really only one G-d, Who loved only goodness and justice. They thought there were many gods, and imagined them to be like themselves, some good, some evil; some stronger, some weaker. In the eyes of the people there was no justice among the gods, and therefore there need be no justice among men. The strong oppressed the weak, without fear of punishment.

In the Torah G-d has often warned that He would not tolerate injustice; that He was a G-d of retribution, punishing the wicked and rewarding the good.

The Psalmist, seeing so much injustice and cruelty in the world, calls upon G-d, G-d of retribution, to appear and punish the wicked. *Arise, O Judge of the earth, render to the proud their desserts* (v. 2).

To those fools who think that G-d does not see their evil deeds, or does not hear the cry of the oppressed, the Psalmist says:

[85] Avoth 1:18.

Consider, you brutes among people, and you fools,
when will you be wise? He that planted the ear, shall
He not hear? He that formed the eye, shall He not
see? (vs. 8-9).

But the Psalmist also has a word of consolation for the oppressed. A person does not suffer in vain; there is always a purpose
in suffering, for it purifies and strengthens one's moral character.
The one who inflicts suffering will surely be punished for his
wickedness, but the victim should realize that G-d is good, and
that there is hidden good even in suffering, which is only temporary and could be nothing but a test of faith in G-d, and a means
to bring one closer to G-d. Thus the Psalmist says, *Happy is the*
man whom You, O G-d, chastise, and teach out of Your Torah
(v. 12). Whether the suffering comes at the hand of a wicked
man, or by the hand of G-d, a person must realize that the Judge
of the earth will not do anything unjust. In the darkest moments,
"G-d is my help," and "Your lovingkindness, O G-d, holds me up"
(vs. 17-8). As for the evildoers, (*G-d*) *brings back upon them*
their own iniquity, and in their own evil shall He cut them off....

To finish on a happy note, the first verses of the following
Psalm (95) are added, namely, *Come, let us rejoice unto G-d; let*
us shout for joy to the Rock of our salvation, etc.

As we can see, the theme of Psalm 94 is in some respects a
continuation of Psalm 82, the Song of the Day for Tuesday.

שיר של יום ליום ה׳
FIFTH DAY: PSALM 81

On the fifth day of the week the Leviim recited Psalm 81 as the
Shir-shel-Yom (Song of the Day). It begins with the words (after
the caption identifies it as a Psalm of Asaph):

*Sing aloud unto G-d our strength, shout for joy unto
the G-d of Jacob. Raise a song, and strike the timbrel,
the pleasant lyre with the harp* (vs. 2-3).

It is a jubilant psalm of praise to G-d. The connection of this
psalm with the fifth day of the week, our Sages say, is the fact that
on the fifth day of Creation the water, land and air were filled with
living creatures. Until that day, it was a silent world, but when the
fields and meadows, mountains and valleys were populated with
lively, colorful creatures, each kind in its own way singing praise
to its Maker, the world became a symphony of praise to the
Creator.

Since we observe the anniversary of the Creation every year,
there follows immediately a reference to the festival of Rosh
Hashanah:

*Blow the Shofar on the New Moon, in the time ap-
pointed for the day of our festival. For it is a statute
for Israel, a (day of) judgment by the G-d of Jacob*
(vs. 4-5).

Then follows a reference to Joseph (v. 6). It was on Rosh
Hashanah, our Sages tell us,[86] that Joseph was freed from prison
and elevated to the highest position in the land of Egypt, second
only to Pharaoh.

In this vein the Psalmist goes on to mention the deliverance
from Egypt and the Revelation at Sinai. Here is a further connection with the fifth day of the week, for it was on a Thursday
that the children of Israel departed from Egypt.[87]

We are reminded of G-d's readiness to answer prayer and to
reward trust in Him. For, as in the case of the waters of Merivah,[88]
when G-d tested Israel's faith in Him, so is every crisis a test of

---

[86] Rosh Hashanah 11a.
[87] Seder Olam.
[88] Ex. 17:7; Num. 20:13.

our loyalty to G-d (v. 8). The Jewish people is sternly warned against disobedience to G-d, for it is only by keeping faith with G-d that Israel can prosper. Indeed, G-d appeals to us:

> O that My people would listen to me; that Israel
> would walk in My ways. I would soon subdue their
> enemies, and turn My hand against their adversaries
> (vs. 14-15).

The concluding verse speaks of the miraculous way in which G-d took care of the Jewish people during their wandering in the desert on the way to the Promised Land, when G-d sustained them with manna from heaven and water from a rock.

שיר של יום ליום ו'
SIXTH DAY: PSALM 93

On the sixth day of Creation G-d completed the "work of Creation" when He formed the first human beings and "breathed" into them a soul. Adam, the first man, was an intelligent being, endowed with the gift of speech. Our Sages tell us[89] that the first thing Adam did was to proclaim the Creator as King of the Universe, dedicating himself and the world around him to the service of G-d. This is the reason why Psalm 93 was the selection for the Song of the Day for the sixth day in the week. It begins:

> G-d has become King; He has robed Himself in ma-
> jesty; G-d has robed Himself; He has girded Himself
> with strength; the world also is set firm, it shall not
> fall. Your Throne is set firm from old; You are from
> everlasting (vs. 1-2).

---

[89] Zohar III, end of Emor (p. 214) ; see also Pirkei dR, Eliezer, ch. 11.

The Psalmist goes on to speak of the roar of the rivers and oceans—the mighty nations threatening to engulf the world—but G-d above is mightier:

Than the voices of many waters, mighty waters,
breakers of the sea—more mighty is G-d on High
(v. 4).

The last verse speaks of G-d's testimonies through His prophets, who had prophesied about the glory of G-d and His Holy House (the Beth Hamikdash):

Your testimonies are very sure; holiness becomes
Your house. O G-d, for evermore.

Just as in the time when Adam was created, all mankind (for there were no other human beings) proclaimed G-d's sovereignty, so will it be when Mashiach will come, when all mankind will again recognize G-d's kingship.

שיר של יום ליום השבת
SHABBOS: PSALM 92

Although the present volume deals with the *daily* prayers (recited on weekdays only), the Song of the Day for the Sabbath is included here for the sake of completion, and also because it has an obvious bearing on the weekdays.

The *Shir-shel-Yom* (Song of the Day) which the Levites used to chant in the Beth Hamikdash of old on the day of Shabbos was Psalm 92 of Tehillim (*Mizmor Shir l'Yom haShabbos*).

On the seventh day of Creation, all "work" of creation had ceased, and G-d "rested" and made this day a holy day, a day of rest.

Needless to say, "work" and "rest," insofar as G-d is concerned, are not to be understood in the plain sense of the words as used in regard to human beings. For when a human being does any kind of work or activity, he uses up some of his energy, and after a day's work he gets tired and has to rest. But it was no effort at all for G-d to create the world, as it is written, "By the word of G-d the heavens were made, and by the breath of His mouth—all their hosts."[90] Everything was created by G-d's "word," and the whole of Creation did not make any change in G-d, just as, by way of example, a spoken word does not cause a change in a human being. On the seventh day, G-d did not create anything new, except the Shabbos itself as a day of rest and holiness.

We, Jews, have been commanded to "imitate" G-d in all His ways. So we were commanded to work during the six days of the week and to rest on the seventh day and keep it holy. Since we consist of a body and soul, the commandment to work and to rest applies to both the body and the soul. In other words, Shabbos has a two-fold meaning: a physical and a spiritual. The first simply means that we are commanded to stop all and any of the 39 kinds of *creative* physical activities and their offshoots, as are clearly spelled out in Jewish Law, before sunset of the sixth day, Friday, and to dedicate the seventh day, Shabbos, entirely to G-d, to *holy* pursuits. There is a complete change-over in our routine; even our physical needs: our food, clothes, our walking and talking, everything is different and *special—Shabbos'dik* (Shabbos-like). (We emphasized the word "creative" in describing physical work which is prohibited on Shabbos, because the important thing here is not the actual physical exertion itself. For example, it is easier to strike a match, or turn an electric switch than moving a heavy chair from place to place inside the house; yet striking a match or turning on the light is prohibited, while moving the chair is permitted.)

---

90 Ps. 33:6.

The second aspect of Shabbos has to do purely with our *soul,* which also enjoys a "rest" on Shabbos. By this we mean that during the six days of the week the soul has something of a struggle in carrying out its purpose of bringing holiness into our every-day activities. For we Jews are a holy people not only on Shabbos and Yom Tov, but every day of the year. Not only do we pray and have Mitzvoth every day, but all our activities, including our eating and drinking and business affairs, have to be done according to G-d's will, as required by the Torah, the Jewish Law. Yet during the six days of the week this entails an effort, also because of many distractions. On Shabbos, however, our soul receives from Heaven a special measure of holiness and inspiration (called "Neshamah Yetheirah"—an "Extra Soul"), so that the holiness comes without effort, and we enjoy a special spiritual joy and restfulness, called *Oneg Shabbos.*

Thus, Shabbos is a day when "it is good to give thanks unto G-d, and to sing praises unto Your Most High Name" (v. 2).

In a broader sense, our life on earth is likened to the "working days," of the week, while our after-life is likened to Shabbos, when we truly enjoy the fruits of our labors here on earth, in the highest spiritual degree of the soul's release from her earthly chains and her immediate nearness to G-d.

Shabbos and the week-days are, in a sense, like day and night. In a similar sense our present life in the Galuth is likened to the dark night, while our redemption when Mashiach will come, and the change which will then be brought about, is likened to the dawn of a new day. This is expressed in the next verse, "To declare Your lovingkindness in the morning, and Your faithfulness in the night" (v. 3). In the "morning" we can see G-d's lovingkindness; in the "night" we have to have *faith* in G-d's kindness, because it often comes as a "blessing in disguise."

Shabbos is the day when we can reflect upon G-d's works and derive extraordinary joy in appreciating them, as we read on:

For You, O G-d, have made me rejoice with Your work; in the works of Your hand I will exult. How great are Your works, O G-d; Your thoughts are very deep (vs. 5-6).

The Shabbos gives us a better appreciation of, and deeper insights into, the whole order of the world which G-d has created.

G-d created man so that he would have free choice to do as he pleases. It is inevitable that there should be wicked men who rebel against G-d. But G-d reigns supreme, and He is a G-d of justice. If the wicked appear to prosper, it is only because they are to perish, but the righteous will triumph. This is the thought in the following verses:

A brutish man will not know, neither will the fool understand this: When the wicked spring up as grass, all doers of iniquity bloom forth—it is that they might be destroyed for ever. But You, O G-d, are On High for evermore. . . . The righteous man shall flourish like a palm-tree; he shall grow like a cedar in Lebanon. Planted in the house of G-d, they shall blossom in the courts of our G-d. They shall still produce fruit in old age; they shall be full of sap and freshness. To declare that G-d is upright; He is my Rock, and there is no unrighteousness in Him. (7-16).

"The righteous (*Tzaddik*) shall flourish like a palm-tree, like a cedar in Lebanon," the Psalmist says. Our Sages mention[91] various reasons why the righteous man has been likened to the above mentioned trees. The date-palm is highly valued for its fruit and usefulness. Every part of the tree serves a good purpose; nothing of it is wasted. Its fruit, the date, is a nourishing food and

---

[91] Taanith 25b; Ber. Rabba, beg. ch. 41.

the source of date-honey. Its branches are used for shade, for baskets, and other useful purposes. A branch of the palm serves as a *Lulav,* one (and the "outstanding" one) of the "Four Kinds" taken during the festival of Succoth, over which a special Berachah is made. Unlike branches of other trees, the branches of the palm are undivided and symbolize oneness with G-d; it also symbolizes victory over the inner adversary, the *Yetzer Hara.*

The cedar of Lebanon is famed for its uprightness, strength and durability. Cedars are evergreen trees, stately in appearance, with a sweet and fresh odor. The wonderful Beth Hamikdash built by King Solomon was made from cedars of Lebanon.

For these, and other, reasons, the Tzaddik is aptly compared to the date-palm and the cedar of Lebanon.

What the Tzaddik is among men, the Shabbos is among the days of the week. The Tzaddik is the perfectly righteous man; there is no evil in him at all; he is a completely holy man. Other men, who have not reached that level, are mostly good, but still have certain traits which have to be improved and perfected. The Tzaddik is called the "foundation of the world,"[92] for it is in the merit of the Tzaddik that the world exists, and through him other men are blessed, in addition to their own merits.[93]

Similarly, the days of the week have both the holy and the profane. Through our daily conduct in accordance with the holy Torah and Mitzvoth, we bring holiness into the profane, and "elevate" the ordinary, mundane matters to the level of holiness. But Shabbos is *all* holiness, and through Shabbos all the other days of the week are blessed.[94]

Furthermore, Shabbos gives us a "taste" of the World to Come,[95] when all of us will attain the level of Tzaddik.

---

[92] Prov. 10:25.
[93] Yoma 38b.
[94] Zohar II, 63b.
[95] Berachoth 56b.

Finally, it should be mentioned that according to our Sages, this Hymn to the Shabbos (Psalm 92) was composed by none other than Adam himself.[96] Indeed, who could better appreciate the spirit of Shabbos and the spirit of holiness than the first man, the creature of G-d's own hands?

Thus, it is significant and meaningful that the hymn to Shabbos is also a hymn to the Tzaddik.

לדוד אורי

PSALM 27: "G-D IS MY LIGHT"

Psalm 27—"G-d is my light and my salvation"—has been included in the Siddur as a special prayer which is said twice daily during the month of Elul and the greater part of Tishrei (until Shemini Atzereth). It is said immediately after the Daily Psalm (*Shir-shel-Yom*) in the morning, and before *Alenu* of Minchah. (According to Nusach Ashkenaz, it is said at Maariv instead of Minchah.)

This psalm expresses intense faith in G-d, as well as a fervent longing to be with G-d, and to experience the joy of being close to Him. It also speaks of G-d's loving care and protection. These are sentiments which are particularly fitting for said season of the year, when we part with the old year and usher in the new.

The significance of the month of Elul as a time of especial Divine grace and mercy in preparation for the new year, has been explained by the Alter Rebbe, founder of Chabad, by the illustration of "a king in the field," when the king is easily accessible, and particularly gracious.[97]

The period of the Ten Days of Return, from Rosh Hashanah through Yom Kippur, is, of course, also a time of exceptional

---

[96] See note 89, above.
[97] Lik. Torah, Re'eh 32b.

Divine closeness and forgiveness. It is to this period, our Sages say,[98] that the prophet referred when he said, "Seek G-d when He is to be found; call unto Him when He is near."[99]

Finally, Succoth, as one of the Three Pilgrimage Festivals, is also a most auspicious time for coming closer to G-d.

In the light of the above, and as we take a closer look at some of the verses of this psalm, we shall better appreciate some of the reasons why it has been included in our daily prayer during the said season of the year.

> *G-d is my light and my salvation; whom shall I fear?*
> *G-d is the stronghold of my life; of whom shall I be*
> *afraid?* (v. 1)

Some people have a feeling of loneliness, anxiety, or fear, without really knowing why, since there appears to be no external reason to be afraid. Such a feeling is something internal, and quite often it comes from the soul. The soul naturally craves to be close to G-d, for it is a part of G-dliness. This craving is satisfied only if the Jew lives his daily life in accordance with G-d's will, a life of Torah and Mitzvoth. If this way of life is lacking, and the person knows about it, he feels a sense of guilt, which makes him afraid of the consequences. If he does not know what he is missing, his soul nevertheless feels it, and the result is a general feeling of disquiet, or even fear, "without knowing why."

In order to get rid of such feelings, one must return to G-d with the full certainty that G-d will not spurn or reject His wayward child. On the contrary, G-d is always ready to bring close to Him anyone who seeks Him and calls unto Him, particularly during the period of especial Divine grace and forgiveness. The realization that G-d is the Creator and Master of the world, Whose benevolent Providence extends to each and every individual, him-

98 Rosh Hashanah 18a.
99 Isaiah 55:6.

self included, and putting his trust in G-d's infinite goodness, will dispel the darkness of loneliness and fear.

This, then, is the meaning of "G-d is my light and my salvation; whom shall I fear," etc.

Our Sages of blessed memory explained[100] that "G-d is my light" refers to Rosh Hashanah, and "my salvation" refers to Yom Kippur. Rosh Hashanah and Yom Kippur are the great G-d-given opportunities for us to bring light and salvation into our daily life throughout the year.

> *When evildoers draw near against me to devour my flesh, even my oppressors and enemies—they stumbled and fell . . . though war should rise against me— in this I trust.* (vs. 2-3)

Here King David (speaking, as usual, for each and every Jew, and for the Jewish people as a whole) declares that his trust in G-d does not waver even if the danger seems real and imminent; even when he is actually surrounded by enemies, or even if they began a war against him.

In a deeper sense, the "enemies" and "war" mentioned here mean also, and especially, the *inner* enemy—the *Yetzer Hara,* the evil inclination within man. This is a cunning and dangerous enemy who often appears as a friend (מרעים—"evildoers"—may mean also "friends"). He tempts the flesh, and besieges a person constantly, first to lead him astray, and then to prevent him from returning to G-d. When facing such a situation, David declares, "in *this* I trust," that is to say, in the knowledge that G-d is my light and my salvation.

In the Midrash [101] it is explained that "in this" (בזאת) refers to any and all of ten things, each of which is alluded to in the Torah by the word זאת. Included are: the Torah, the Covenant,

---

100 Vayyikra Rabba 21:3.
101 Ibid. 21:5.

Shabbos, Jerusalem, etc. For the sake of any of these things G-d will never forsake His people in the hour of need.

However, King David fervently hopes that he will be left in peace by all enemies, within and without, so that he could dedicate himself to the service of G-d without distraction. Thus he continues:

> One thing I ask of G-d, this alone I seek; That I may dwell in the house of G-d all the days of my life; to behold the pleasantness of G-d, and to visit in His sanctuary. (v. 4)

King David declares that if he had but one request to ask of G-d, he would ask only that he may "dwell in the house of G-d and behold the pleasantness of G-d."

This reminds us of the one request which was made by David's son, young Solomon, when he succeeded his father to the throne. When G-d appeared to him in a dream and said, "Ask what I should grant you," the wise young king replied, "Give Your servant an understanding heart."[102] He did not ask for riches, power, honor, and the like, but for an "understanding heart." G-d gave him that and everything else with it.

Similarly, when King David asked "to dwell in the house of G-d" he meant to gain the wisdom of G-d, only he wished more: "to behold the pleasantness of G-d," which means to gain even deeper insights into G-d's wisdom. This is possible, of course, only through the study of G-d's Torah and the fulfillment of His Mitzvoth. At the same time, this is the surest way to secure G-d's protection and to triumph over all enemies (vs. 5-6). Therefore he appeals to G-d to hear his voice and answer him graciously (v. 7).

---

[102] I Kings 3:9.

For You my heart said, "Seek My face"; Your face,
O G-d, I will seek. (v. 8)

Rashi explains the words "For You my heart said" to mean:
My heart speaking for G-d, says: "Seek My face." In other words,
the Jewish heart echoes G-d's constant call, "Seek My face," which
brings the response, "Indeed, I will seek Your face, O G-d."

The Hebrew word for "face"—*Panim* (פנים)—also means
"inwardness." This is no coincidence, for the face usually reflects
the inner feelings and qualities of a person. When a person is
happy, inspired, enthused, and the like, you can see it in his face.
Kindness and benevolence similarly show up in the face.

Also wisdom is reflected in the face, as King Solomon said,
"A man's wisdom lights up his face."[103]

Thus when G-d says, "Seek My face," it means "seek My inwardness," and the inward, or essential, qualities of G-d are
holiness, wisdom, benevolence, and other Divine qualities, which
we must strive to emulate. This we can achieve only by immersing
ourselves deeply in G-d's holiness and wisdom, and following in
G-d's ways with all our heart and soul. Learning the Torah superficially, or doing the Mitzvoth mechanically, or by force of habit,
will not give us the full benefit of G-d's "face."

Benevolence and holiness are particularly associated with G-d's
"face." Thus we find in the familiar Priestly Blessing: "May G-d
cause His face to shine unto you and be gracious unto you," and
"May G-d lift up His face towards you and grant you peace."[104]
And in connection with the Three Pilgrimage Festivals we find
the commandment in the Torah: "Three times in the year shall
all your males be seen unto the face of G-d, your G-d."[105] In the
Beth Hamikdash the Jews came "face to face" with G-d and saw
with their own eyes the holiness and benevolence of G-d's Presence.

[103] Eccl. 8:1.
[104] Num. 6:24, 25.
[105] Deut. 16:16.

It is interesting to note that when Mosheh Rabbenu begged G-d, "Show me Your Glory," G-d told him, "You cannot see My face."[106] Mosheh's wish to see, that is, to understand, the inner being and essence of G-d, could not be granted, because no creature can understand the Creator. But what is not given to the created mind to *understand* is given to be *felt*. During the time of the Beth Hamikdash, G-d's Presence was deeply felt by all those who attended the Avodah there. Nowadays, in the absence of the Beth Hamikdash, a similar experience can be had through sincere prayer permeated with love and fear of G-d, especially on the holy and joyous days of Yom Tov. It can also be experienced through the study of the Torah and the observance of the Mitzvoth which bring a person very close to G-d. Indeed, the Torah and Mitzvoth bridge the gulf between the Creator and created, since G-d's wisdom and His inner will are contained in His Torah and commandments.

"Seek My face" is therefore the central theme of this psalm, and it is particularly timely for Elul and Tishrei, as mentioned earlier.

While seeking G-d's face, David hopes that he would be worthy of G-d's favor to show His face to him, so he prays:

> *Hide not Your face from me . . . forsake me not . . .*
> *O G-d of my salvation.* (v. 9)

"Hiding the face" is the opposite of "showing a friendly face." We have been warned in the Torah[107] that if we turn away from G-d, G-d will "hide His face" and temporarily withhold His benevolent watchfulness and protection, letting the natural elements and forces take over. In such a case the distress is two-fold: spiritual—being removed from G-d, and material—being at the mercy of the hostile forces in the surrounding world. We therefore

---

106 Exod. 33:18, 20.
107 Deut. 32:20.

pray to G-d not to hide His face from us, for He is our only salvation.

> *For even if my father and mother have left me, G-d will gather me up.* (v. 10)

There comes a time when parents leave their children to care for themselves, or when they pass on and leave their children behind. But G-d, our real Father, never forsakes us. G-d is always there to take care of everyone, and this is very comforting.

King David is not content with merely feeling secure under G-d's loving care. He prays,

> *Teach me, O G-d, Your way, and lead me on an even path. . . . Do not give me up to the will of my adversaries. . . .* (vs. 11-12)

Here, undoubtedly, King David has in mind not only his enemies in human form, but also his *inner* adversaries, to which he referred earlier (v. 2).

After expressing (v. 13) his unshakable belief "to see the goodness of G-d in the land of the living"—the everlasting happiness of eternal life in the Hereafter, King David concludes this meaningful psalm, speaking to himself and to each and every one of us:

> *Hope unto G-d; be strong and let your heart take courage, and hope to G-d.* (v. 14)

אֵין כֵּאלֹקֵינוּ

THERE IS NONE LIKE OUR G-D

According to Sfardic custom, as well as Nusach Ari, the hymn "Ein Kelokeinu," followed by a Talmudic section on *Ketoreth* (Incense), is recited in the daily Morning Prayer, after the Song of the Day, and before *Aleinu*. The latter concludes the Morning Prayer. According to Ashkenazi custom, *Ein Kelokeinu* is recited in the Morning Prayer of Shabbos and Yom Tov only.

The hymn consists of five stanzas. The first reads:

> *There is none like our G-d;*
> *There is none like our L-rd;*
> *There is none like our King;*
> *There is none like our Savior.*

The second stanza has the variation "Who is": "Who is like our G-d," etc.

The third reads: "Let us acknowledge our G-d," etc.

The fourth: "Blessed be our G-d," etc.

The fifth: "You are our G-d."

The first three stanzas form an acrostic אמן: the *aleph* of *Ein kelokeinu*, *mem* of *Mi kelokeinu*, and *nun* of *Nodeh lelokeinu*.

235

The Divine Name *elokim* ("G-d") usually refers to the Hidden G-d in Nature, the life-force that sustains everything that exists. It has been pointed out[108] that the numerical equivalent (*gimatria*) of *elokim* is the same as that of *hateva* (*Nature*), namely 86. *Elokim* also means "strength," thus *elokeinu* means not only "our G-d," but also "our strength."

The Divine Name formed by the four Hebrew letters *aleph, daleth, nun* and *yud,* means "my Lord," or "my Master." It usually refers to G-d as He is *revealed* in Nature—in the orderliness and so-called "laws" of Nature. He is the Lord and Master of the world. In addressing G-d by this Name we affirm our master-servant relationship with G-d.

"King" is often applied to G-d in the sense that we are His willing and fortunate subjects, enjoying the benefit of His benevolent and gracious Kingship over us, for which we owe Him undivided loyalty. The king-subject relationship is a closer one than the master-servant relationship.

Finally we refer to G-d as our Savior, for to Him we always turn in times of trouble, confident that He will save us, whether we deserve it or not, as He has so often saved us in the past, during the long history of our people in exile.

The above Names, or "attributes," of G-d are only some aspects of G-d as our "personal" G-d, with Whom we have an intimate relationship. Beyond these there are various Divine Names indicating G-d's qualities which are above and beyond our human understanding, for we can never understand the nature and essence of G-d our Creator.

Having declared that there is none like our G-d, L-rd, King and Savior, and that no one and no thing can be compared to Him,

---

108 Shaar Hayichud vehaEmunah, ch. 22.

we go on to say, "Let us acknowledge (also, Let us give thanks to) our G-d," etc., which is obviously the right thing to do.

Finally we say, "You are He Who is our G-d," etc. We have already had occasion to point out that sometimes we address G-d in the second person singular (You), and sometimes in the third person singular (He), and very often we use both forms together (You are He). The first indicates a direct appeal to G-d, in a familiar form, as though we are standing directly in the Presence of G-d. However, as we come closer to G-d we also realize that G-d is hidden from us, and this is expressed in the third person, as when we speak of a person who is not in our immediate presence. Thus, our relationship to G-d combines both the "You" relationship and the "He" relationship. When we feel that G-d is near to us, we must realize that He is yet very far; and when we feel that G-d is far from us, we must realize that He is yet very near. This is also the explanation why most blessings that we make contain both forms; they begin, "Blessed are You," etc.—in the second person, and then change to the third person. (In English translation this important and meaningful distinction is often lost.)

The hymn "Ein kelokeinu" is followed by a Talmudic section[109] on the composition of the Incense (*Ketoreth*) which used to be offered in the Beth Hamikdash of old twice daily, morning and evening. We have already discussed this.[110]

Next follows another passage from the Talmud:[111]

> *The school of Elijah taught: He who studies Jewish laws every day is assured of future life, as it is written, "His are the eternal paths"[112]; read not "paths" (halichoth) but "laws" (halachoth).*

---

109 Kerithoth 6a.
110 See p. 85 f.
111 Megillah 28b.
112 Habakkuk 3:6.

The play on the word *halichoth-halachoth* is a pointed reminder that following the ways of Judaism according to the Halachah leads to eternal life.

Studying the Torah makes one a Torah scholar, and Torah scholars increase peace in the world, both in their own world (inner harmony and peace of mind) as well as in the world at large. This is the subject of the following Talmudic passage,[113] which comes next:

> *Rabbi Elazar quoted Rabbi Chanina: Students of the*
> *Torah increase peace in the world, as it is written,*
> *And all your children are taught of G-d, and great is*
> *the peace of your children."*[114] *Read not "your chil-*
> *dren" (banayich) but "your builders" (bonayich).*

Here again we are reminded by the play on the word *banayich-bonayich* that children taught to know, love, and fear G-d, are the true builders of world peace. For it is only after a person attains true harmony and peace with himself—which is attained through the knowledge of G-d—that he can contribute to world peace.

Several selected verses from the Psalms conclude this part of the Siddur on the theme of peace, and how peace is intimately connected with Torah:

> *Great peace have they who love Your Torah,*
> *and for them there is no stumbling.*[115]
> *Peace be within your walls,*
> *Security within your mansions.*
> *For the sake of my brethren and friends*
> *I will speak: Peace be within you.*

---

113 End of tractate Berachoth.
114 Isaiah 54:13.
115 Ps. 119:165.

For the sake of the house of G-d, our G-d,
I will seek good for you.[116]
G-d will give strength to His people,
G-d will bless His people with peace.[117]

The "strength" which G-d gives His people—our Sages explain[118]—is the strength of the Torah, which is also the source of peace.

A prayer for peace is the last of the Eighteen Benedictions (Shemone Esrei), and on the theme of peace, also, the prayers following Shemone Esrei are concluded. When recited in the synagogue with the congregation, *Kaddish d'Rabbanan* is said after these selected Talmudic passages and verses. The hymn *Aleinu* concludes the Morning service.

---

116 Ps. 122:7-9.
117 Ps. 29:11.
118 Shir Hashirim Rabba 2:10; Zohar I1, 58a; III, 269a. Cf. Zevachim 116a. See also Tanya ch. 36.

עלינו לשבח

ALEINU

1.

The last prayer of all the daily prayers, *Shacharith* (Morning), *Minchah* (Afternoon) and *Maariv* (Evening)—as well as of the Shabbos and Festival prayers, is the well-known prayer of *Aleinu l'shabe'ach*—"It is our duty to praise." The prayer begins with the words:

> *It is our duty to praise the Master of all things ... to Him Who created the world in the beginning, for He has not made us like the nations of other lands, and has not placed us like other families of the earth....*

This is a very, very old prayer. The famous Rav Hay Gaon, the last of the Babylonian Geonim, states[119] that this prayer was composed by Joshua, as he led the children of Israel into the Promised Land. (The initials of the first sentences, read backwards, form his name "Hoshua"). Thus, when Joshua was about to settle the Jewish people in the Holy Land, he made them remember, through this hymn, that they were different from the Canaanite peoples and other nations and tribes of the earth, who "worship vain things and emptiness."

> *But we kneel, worship and offer thanks before the Supreme King of kings, the Holy One, blessed be He,*

---

[119] Shaarei Teshuvah, 43.

240

*Who stretched forth (created) the heavens and laid
the foundations of the earth.*

That this is a very old prayer is also evident from the text,
which does not mention anything about our return to Zion, or
the rebuilding of the Beth Hamikdash. Had this prayer been
composed after the destruction of the Beth Hamikdash there
certainly would have been included in it a prayer for our return
to our Holy Land.

The great Amora Rav, who lived at the same time as Shemuel,
made this prayer part of the Musaf service of Rosh Hashanah
and Yom Kippur.[120] It is then recited in a very solemn manner,
and the Chazzan, as well as the congregation, actually kneel in
the synagogue. (This, as well as during certain portions of the
Avodah service on Yom Kippur, describing the service by the
High Priest in the Beth Hamikdash, are the only times when we
kneel during our prayers.)

It is a very important prayer, and everyone should be familiar
with it. Jewish Law requires that when it is recited in the synagogue, everyone join in it, even if one has already said it, or just
happened to walk into the synagogue at that time. It is known
that for the last 600 or 700 years, this prayer was the concluding
prayer of all congregational services, though, as already mentioned, it was known and recited much earlier.

All through the dark Middle Ages, when Jews were persecuted
and often burnt at the stake, many Jewish martyrs recited *Aleinu*
with their dying lips. For in it they proclaimed their undying
faith in the One and only G-d, and their hope that one day all the
nations of the earth will recognize G-d. Though they died for
their faith, they proclaimed their gratitude to G-d that He had
not made them like their persecutors—"that He has not made our
portion like them, nor our lot (fate) as all their multitude."

---

[120] Talm. Yerushalmi, Rosh Hashanah 1:5; Avodah Zara 1:2; Vayyikra Rabba 29:1;
Tanhuma, Haazinu 4.

Rabbi Joseph Ha-Cohen, author of *Emek Habacha* (*"Valley of Weeping"*), where he describes the persecution of the Jews in his time and before his time, tells the story of many Jewish martyrs who died at the stake in the city of Blois, in France, in the year 1171. As the fire was consuming them, the saintly martyrs were singing a strange song. The churchmen who had assembled to witness the death of the Jews wondered at the strange singing of the dying Jews, and learned later that they were singing *Aleinu l'shabe'ach*.

No wonder that the Christian masters in the various lands did not like this prayer. Miserable Jewish traitors who for the love of money, honor, or power, became converts to Christianity, often slandered this holy prayer and accused it of being directed against the Church. They pointed to the words (taken originally from Isaiah) "they worship vain things and emptiness and pray to a god that cannot save,"[121] (following the first paragraph quoted above, and followed by the words "but we kneel"), and claimed that this was an attack on the Church. Actually, as already mentioned, this prayer was already part of the Musaf service of Rosh Hashanah during the days of Rav, long before there ever was a Christian church in Babylon; and it clearly referred to the idol worshippers of that time, or even of the time of Joshua. But this did not matter, as long as it could serve as an excuse to make trouble for the Jews. And so the censors ordered that those words be taken out of the prayer, or they prohibited the whole prayer. Many learned Rabbis tried to prove how wrong the accusations against this prayer were, among them Rabbi Manasseh ben Israel, who wrote a whole chapter on it in his book *In Defense of the Jews*. This great scholar also relates an interesting story about *Aleinu*. The Sultan Selim happened to read the prayer of *Aleinu* in a Turkish translation of the Jewish Prayer Book. He was so impressed by it that he said, "Truly this prayer can serve for all

---

[121] Isaiah 45:20.

purposes; there is no need of any other prayer." However, for many centuries the prayer was censured and the "offensive" words were removed from the text. Now, however, when we live in a free country, the words can be included again.

After expressing our gratitude to G-d for having given us the privilege of serving Him, we go on to declare:

He is our G-d; there is none else. In truth He is our King; there is nothing beside Him, as it is written in His Torah, "And you shall know this day, and consider in your heart, that G-d is the G-d in heaven above and upon earth beneath; there is nothing else."

This concludes the first part of *Aleinu*. It is well to sum up the message it contains: It is our duty to praise G-d the Master of all things and to proclaim Him as the Creator of the world. We are happy that He has chosen us from among all nations of the world to give us His Torah, for otherwise we should have remained as ignorant and as cruel as the heathen. We proclaim and declare that G-d is One in heaven and on earth, and that truly there is nothing beside Him. Everything we see around us, the whole of Nature, is nothing separate from G-d, but just the way in which G-d makes Himself known to us; everything that exists, exists because G-d keeps everything in existence. This is a thought we must remember this day and every day; we must always reflect upon it in our heart, and never for a moment forget it.

2.

The second part of *Aleinu* reads:

Therefore we hope unto You, O G-d our G-d, that we may soon behold the glory of Your might, the removal of the abominations from the earth, and the

complete annihilation of the idols, in order to estab-
lish the world under the kingdom of the Almighty;
and all mankind will call upon Your Name, to turn
unto You all the wicked (men) of the earth. All the
inhabitants of the world will recognize and know that
unto You must bend every knee, avow every tongue;
before You, O G-d our G-d, they will kneel and fall
down, and unto Your glorious Name give honor; and
they all will accept upon themselves the yoke of Your
kingdom, and You shall reign over them for ever and
ever. For the kingdom is Yours, and to all eternity
You will reign in glory, as it is written in Your
Torah: "G-d will reign for ever and ever."[122] *And it is*
said, "And G-d shall be King upon all the earth; in
that day shall G-d be One, and His Name One."[123]

In this beautiful prayer we express our fervent hope for that Great Day, when all idolatry and wickedness will be no more, and all mankind, even the lowliest of men ("children of flesh") will acknowledge the sovereignty of G-d. Even the wicked ones will submit to G-d's rule; and while they may not do it as willingly and joyously as the Jewish people (compare with the prayer before the *Shemone Esrei,* where we say: "And his kingdom they [the children of Israel] *willingly* accepted upon themselves; unto You they responded with song, with great joy; and said all together, 'Who is like You,' " etc.), they will nevertheless accept the "yoke" of G-d's kingdom, with complete submission. And G-d will accept everyone, and reign upon *all* the earth.

Then "G-d will be One, and His Name will be One," or "G-d and His Name will be One." For at the present time many people accept G-d's rule "in name only." Most people generally do not see and do not realize, and certainly do not *feel* deeply, that G-d,

---

[122] Exod. 15:18.
[123] Zechariah 14:9.

"personally," as it were, rules the world and the affairs of men. People do not realize that G-d's Providence extends to everyone individually, and to the minutest detail of the daily life. If they did, people would feel a greater sense of security and contentment. Some people even say that "G-d has abandoned the world," while others say that He watches it "from a distance," seldom intervening in the history of nations, or in the life of individuals. These erroneous thoughts create a "division" between G-d the Creator of the Universe and G-d the King and Master of the world, as if He and His Name were two separate things.

The distinction between G-d and His Name can be better understood by means of the following illustration from a human monarch. The person of the king, and the majesty of his kingdom, can be seen and felt in the royal court and in the city of his residence, where the king's immediate presence is often seen and felt. But in the rest of the country the king rules "in name only," by "remote control" as it were, through his officials and through his decrees and ordinances. Some people, living far away from the king, may become completely unaware of the king, thinking that the officials rule in their own right.

In a somewhat similar way, G-d's "personal" rule over the world at large, and over the small "world" of the individual, is often overlooked because people seem to be under the immediate rule of the forces of Nature. Indeed, this is how idolatry started. Instead of realizing that there is only One G-d, the Creator and Master of *all* the forces of Nature, people began to worship the many different forces of Nature. Others recognized them as "servants" of the King, but with a will and power of their own, which should be appeased now and again. And even those who were wise enough to realize that behind every "official" there was the authority of the king, they were, for the most part, ignorant of the true majesty of the king; they only knew him by his name, by his authority. But then, one day, the king decides to visit even the remotest parts of his realm, and to appear before all his subjects, so that they would know him personally, and see him in all his majesty.[124]

In the *Aleinu* prayer, we express our fervent hope for the day when G-d will "appear" in all His majesty before the whole world, so that all will see and recognize Him, and submit to His rule. "That Day" is the day of which our prophets prophesied, the day when our righteous Mashiach will come, sent by G-d to establish His rule on earth. Then *all* people will recognize the absolute unity of G-d.

Following *Aleinu*, *Kaddish* is said. If there is a mourner, he recites the Kaddish, but in any case it is well to have Kaddish recited (in congregation, of course), as it is quite appropriate to follow up *Aleinu* with the words, "May G-d's great Name be magnified and sanctified . . .," etc., which also speaks of the Messianic Era.

It is customary to recite after *Aleinu* the following three meaningful verses:

> *Be not afraid of sudden fear; neither of the desolation of the wicked when it comes.*[125]

> *Take counsel together, and it shall be frustrated; speak a word, and it shall not stand; for G-d is with us.*[126]

> *And even to (your) old age, I am He; and even to (your) hoary days, I will carry you; I have made, and I will bear; and I will carry and deliver you.*[127]

The first of the above verses tells us not to be afraid of fear, for fear is paralyzing and harmful in itself. Even when the wicked

---

124 Lik. Torah, Shir Hashirim 40c.
125 Prov. 3:25.
126 Isaiah 8:10.
127 Isaiah 46:4.

are there, and planning to destroy the world, we should not be afraid.

The second verse tells us why we should not be afraid. For we say to our enemies: "You may make your wicked plans, and utter your wicked threats, but nothing will come of them, *for G-d is with us.*"

In the third verse the prophet assures us that no matter how long the exile may be, G-d will always "carry" us. We are G-d's "burden" and responsibility, and G-d will never drop this burden, for our exile and dispersion among the nations of the world is also of G-d's making. He will therefore surely deliver us from our enemies and from the Exile.

The origin of this custom, or, at any rate, the significance of these verses, is to be found in the Midrash on the Book of Esther. There, our Sages tell us that when Mordechai learned of the wicked decree which Haman obtained to murder all the Jews, Mordechai went out into the street and met three small Jewish boys. He asked each of them to tell him what he had learned in *Cheder* that morning. The first one quoted the verse "Be not afraid," etc.; the second boy—the second verse, mentioned above; and the third—the third verse. Mordechai then knew that the Jewish people should fear no enemy; that Haman's plans would come to naught; and that G-d would deliver them from all danger. His confidence was strengthened because he knew that so long as Jewish children go to Cheder and study the Torah and observe its Mitzvoth, G-d will never forsake His people. We are told further that Mordechai then went and gathered all the Jewish children and inspired them to even greater devotion to the Torah, and at that very moment the evil decree of Haman was nullified in Heaven.[128]

It is customary, finally, to add the following verse:

---

[128] Esther Rabba, ch. 7.

Surely the righteous shall give thanks to Your Name;
the upright shall dwell in Your presence.[129]

We, the Jewish people, of whom the prophet said, "And Your people are all righteous,"[130] etc., shall always give thanks to G-d, especially when the Exile will come to an end, and we shall dwell in G-d's manifest presence.

The above verse, which concludes a very moving Psalm of David,[131] in which he prays for deliverance from wicked men, and declares that "G-d is the strength of my salvation," is also a fitting conclusion of each of our three daily prayers.

---

129 Ps. 140:14.
130 Isaiah 60:21.
131 Ps. 140.

תפלת מנחה

∙

AFTERNOON PRAYER

תפלת מנחה

MINCHAH

AFTERNOON PRAYER

It has already been mentioned[1] that the three daily prayers—
Shacharith, Minchah, Maariv (or *Arvith*)—were originally instituted by our three Patriarchs, Abraham, Isaac and Jacob, respectively. Abraham introduced the Morning Prayer (*Shacharith*),
Isaac—the Afternoon Prayer (*Minchah*), and Jacob—the Evening Prayer (*Maariv*).

Each of these prayers therefore reflected the particular nature,
or personality, of the Patriarch who instituted it.

What were the particular qualities that characterized the
Patriarchs?

Abraham was a man of *chesed* (kindness).[2] Throughout his
life he practised the Divine quality of kindness, being extraor-
dinarily kind even to total strangers, helping them materially as
well as spiritually. His hospitality was proverbial, and everywhere
he went he spread the knowledge of G-d.

Divine kindness also characterized his personal life. G-d was
very good to him. Abraham was a great prince,[3] revered and
respected by all the people and tribes with whom he came in

---

[1] See Introduction, p. 8 f. above.
[2] Micah, last verse.
[3] Gen. 23:6.

contact. Abraham's life was likened to the rising sun, growing stronger and brighter in the morning hours.

The Morning Prayer, Shacharith (literally, "Dawn Prayer") is likewise characterized by G-d's kindness, with the word *chesed* appearing often in the text of the Morning blessings and prayers, as we had occasion to note.

In the character and life of Isaac—*din* (strict justice) was the predominant feature. If *love* was the underlying quality of Abraham's Divine service, *fear* (reverence) was the underlying quality of Isaac's Divine service; love and fear being the counterparts of *chesed* and *din*. If Abraham's life was likened to the rising sun in the morning, Isaac's was like the declining sun in the afternoon. The "four hundred years of exile"[4] began when Isaac was born. Isaac had to deal with enemies who envied his wealth, contested his water rights. He became blind in his old age, had a troublesome son, Esau, and was irked by the latter's heathen wives. Isaac represented "twilight," and the quality of stern justice.

Thus the Zohar says:

> It is written, "Woe unto us, for the day is waning, the evening shadows are falling."[5] What are the "evening shadows?" These are the accusing angels and the quality of judgment prevailing at that time [of the day]. Therefore we have been taught that a man should attune his mind during the Minchah prayer. During all prayers a man should attune his mind, but more so during the prayer of Minchah, because at that time the quality of stern judgment prevails in the world. For this reason Yitzchak (Isaac) instituted the Minchah prayer at this time.[6]

---

4 Gen. 15:13, Rashi.
5 Jeremiah 6:4.
6 Zohar I, 230a; II, 36b.

Why is the Divine quality of judgment aroused towards the evening? Abudraham mentions the fact that Adam, the first man, committed his sin in the tenth hour of the day. (Reckoning the day from 6 a.m. to 6 p.m., the tenth hour would be about 4 p.m.) Adam was then judged by G-d. Indeed, according to Abudraham, the word *Minchah* is derived from the Targum interpretation on Gen. 3:8, indicating the "decline of the day."[7]

It is also understandable why Divine judgment comes towards the end of the day. In the morning a person rises with a clean slate, free from sin. But towards the end of the day his actions come up for Divine scrutiny, to see if they were all in accordance with G-d's Will.

Elsewhere, the Zohar[8] also emphasizes that it was towards the evening that the Beth Hamikdash was set on fire, because that time of the day is the time of stern judgment. Also the saintly Ari and other authorities emphasize the special importance of the Minchah prayer.

On the other hand, our Sages also point out that the time of Minchah is especially favorable for prayer. Thus, they point out that Elijah was answered at Mount Carmel during the time of Minchah.[9]

It is also understandable, as the Tur[10] points out, why the Minchah prayer is particularly acceptable to G-d. The Morning prayer is said first thing in the morning, before one has become involved with the day's activities. But Minchah has to be said in the afternoon, when a person is already engaged in, and often at the height of, his daily affairs. This means that the person must interrupt his work or business, disengage his mind from mundane

---

[7] See also Rashi's Commentary on Gen. 3:8.
[8] Zohar I, 132b.
[9] I Kings 18:36.
[10] Tur, Orach Chaim, par. 232.

affairs and concentrate on his prayer despite all distractions. That is why G-d especially appreciates the Minchah prayer when it is recited with devotion and sincerity.

As for the Minchah prayer itself, it consists of the following sections: *Ashrei, Shemone Esrei, Tachnun* (on days when Tachnun is said), and *Aleinu.* It is customary to recite the section of *Korbanoth* and *Ketoreth* before *Ashrei,* because, as already mentioned, the prayers are the present substitutes for the daily sacrifices in the Beth Hamikdash of old. Minchah corresponds to the *Korban Tamid*[11] of the afternoon.

When Minchah is recited in the congregation (with a *Minyan* of ten adults, i.e., from age of Bar Mitzvah and on), the half Kaddish is recited after *Ashrei,* and the *Shemone Esrei* is repeated aloud by the *sheliach tzibbur* (Reader, or Chazzan). In that case the *Kedushah* is recited, and *Modim dRabbanan,* as in the morning, and the complete Kaddish is recited after the *Shemone Esrei* (or after *Tachnun,* as the case may be), and the Mourner's Kaddish after *Aleinu.*

All the above mentioned prayers have already been discussed in connection with the Morning Prayer.

---

11 Exod. 29:38-42; Num. 28:1-8.

תפלת ערבית

◦

EVENING PRAYER

תפלת ערבית

MAARIV

INTRODUCTORY READINGS

The Evening Prayer—*Maariv,* or *Arvith*—basically consists of
the *Shema*, with two benedictions before, and two after it, the
Shemone Esrei, and *Aleinu.*

However, the prayer is introduced by a selection of verses from
the Book of Psalms (*Tehillim*), including Psalm 134. In regard
to these introductory passages there are certain differences between
Nusach Ari, Nusach Ashkenaz, and Nusach Sfard.

In Nusach Ari (according to the Chabad custom) the arrangement of the introductory passages is as follows: First come the
verses *Vehu rachum*[1] and *HaShem hoshia.*[2] These are followed by
Ps. 134, and two additional selections of three verses, each of the
latter three being repeated three times.

If the prayer is said in congregation, the *Half Kaddish* is recited
by the Reader and *Barechu* is said—just as in the Morning Prayer
before the blessing of *Yotzer.*

We shall now discuss the introductory passages.

---

1 Ps. 78:38.
2 Ps. 20:10.

והוא רחום

VEHU RACHUM

*And He is merciful, forgives sin, and will not destroy;
many a time He turns back His anger and does not
arouse all His wrath.*[3]

*Save, O G-d; the King will answer us on the day
we call.*[4]

The holy *Zohar* explains the significance of the opening verse,
"And He is merciful," in the light of the fact that the night is
associated with perils, fears, and Divine judgment, in contrast with
the daytime, which is associated with Divine *chesed,* benevolence,
as we had occasion to note earlier. Accordingly, the *Zohar*[5] declares that the verse, *Vehu rachum,* is a prayer for protection from
the fear of the night and all that is associated with it.

The Abudraham explains further why this verse is particularly
suited to open the Evening Prayer. Inasmuch as the Morning
Prayer and the Afternoon Prayer substitute for the daily sacrifices
(*Tamid*)[6] which were offered in the Beth Hamikdash of old in
the morning and afternoon, these prayers bring atonement for
sins committed during the day. But the Evening Prayer has no
corresponding sacrifice to bring forgiveness for sins committed
after sundown. For this reason the Evening Prayer begins with
the verse, "And He is merciful, forgives sins," etc., by which we

---

3 Ps. 78:38.
4 Ps. 20:10.
5 Zohar II, 130a.
6 Exod. 29:38-42; Num. 28:1-8.

express our faith in G-d's forgiveness at all times—provided, of course, there is sincere repentance.

On Shabbos and Yom-Tov, with their special qualities of holiness and joy, there is no Divine judgment (*din*), and therefore there is no mention of sin, or prayer for forgiveness. Consequently, the above two verses are omitted from the Evening Prayer of Shabbos and Yom-Tov.

As can be seen, the verse *Vehu rachum* speaks of G-d's abundant mercies. It will be noted that the Hebrew text of this verse consists of thirteen words, corresponding to the Thirteen Attributes of Divine Mercy.[6a] The verse further emphasizes G-d's infinite patience with a sinner. G-d does not wish to destroy the sinner, but gives him a chance, again and again, to repent and turn away from evil. But when a person fails to repent, and G-d finds it necessary—for the benefit of the sinner—to punish him, He does it sparingly—"He will not arouse *all* His wrath." The purpose of the punishment is not to destroy, but to make the sinner stop and think and consider his ways, with a view to turn away from evil, and do good. Therefore G-d metes out punishment to the extent that the individual can bear, for G-d is merciful even as He punishes. Our Sages gave the following illustration: A creditor had two persons who owed him money; one was a friend, the other was not. From the friend, the creditor collected his debt in easy installments; while he made the other pay in full at once. So G-d, Who is our friend, collects His "debt" in easy payments.[7] However, the wise person will not wait until the time of payment comes. G-d, in His mercy, has made it possible for everyone to obtain His prompt forgiveness through sincere repentance. This is the meaning of the second verse, "O G-d, help; the King will answer us on the day we call."

6a See p. 188 f. above.

7 Avodah Zara 4a.

שיר המעלות הנה ברכו

PSALM 134

The short (three-verse) Psalm 134 is particularly suitable as an introduction to Maariv, because it contains the words, "servants of G-d, who stand in the House of G-d *at night*."[8]

The psalm reads:

> *A Song of Degrees. Now bless G-d, all you servants of G-d who stand in the House of G-d at night. Lift up your hands in holiness and bless G-d. May G-d bless you out of Zion; He Who is the Maker of heaven and earth.*

This psalm has been included in the Evening Prayer in accordance with the Talmudic saying that when a person returns from work at night and goes into the house of prayer, he should first read some Scripture, or study the Talmud, according to his habit, and then say the *Shema* and the *Tefilah*.[9] Indeed, in many if not most synagogues there is a regular *shiur* (study period) of Torah between Minchah and Maariv. At any rate, the said short Psalm has been made part of the introductory Scriptural passages because it helps to induce the proper mood for the Evening Prayer.

The three-verse Psalm 134 is followed by two selections of three verses each from the same source (*Tehillim*). The first of these consists of the following verses:

> *By day G-d ordains His kindness, and in the night — His song with me; a prayer unto the G-d of my life.*[10]

---

8 Ps. 134:1.
9 Berachoth 4b.
10 Ps. 42:9.

The deliverance of the righteous is from G-d, their stronghold in time of trouble. G-d helps them and delivers them from the wicked and saves them, because they take refuge in Him.[11]

The appropriateness of the first of the above three verses is self-evident: "Because of G-d's kindness (*chesed*) during the day, I sing His praises at night, for He is the G-d of my very life." Our Sages, interpreting "His song" to mean His Torah, gave a deeper insight into the significance of this verse. Thus they declared, "He who engages in the Torah at night, the Holy One blessed be He bestows upon him a ray of kindness in the day, as it is written, 'By day G-d ordains His kindness—[because] His song [the Torah] is with me at night.' "[12] According to another version, the "night" refers to this world, while the "day"—to the next world. Accordingly, the meaning of the verse would be: He who studies the Torah in this world, enjoys special Divine illumination in the world to come.

The latter two verses are the conclusion of Psalm 37, in which David draws a distinction between the wicked and the righteous. The wicked may prosper for a time, but they are doomed to be cut off and perish like straw and grass, having no future in this world, and certainly not in the world to come, but the righteous will triumph both in this world and in the Hereafter. Thus, while we may have encountered wicked, proud, and arrogant people during the day, all seemingly having their way, our faith in G-d and in His justice is not diminished thereby, for we are certain that ultimately the wicked will pay for their wickedness, while the righteous will reap their reward.

The next group of three verses follow in logical sequence to the above, as an expression of complete trust in G-d:

---

[11] Ps. 37:39-40.
[12] Chagigah 12b.

The G-d of Hosts is with us; the G-d of Jacob is our high refuge, Selah.[13]

O, G-d of Hosts, happy is the man who trusts in You.[14]

O, G-d, save us; the King will answer us on the day we call.[15]

The "G-d of Hosts" is the Creator of the "hosts" of heaven and earth. He is also the G-d of Israel, called the "hosts of G-d."[16]

These three verses are repeated three times each to emphasize their significance. The great Sage Rabbi Akiva declared that he who recites these three verses is assured that no harm will befall him.[17]

The selection of the passages from *Tehillim* as an introduction to the *Shema* of the Evening Prayer corresponds to the *Pesukei d'Zimra* of the Morning Prayer. In both cases, the purpose is to attune our minds and hearts to the highlights of our prayers, the *Shema* and *Shemone Esrei*. As already noted, the central theme in the morning is G-d's *chesed*, while in the evening the emphasis is on *emunah* and *bitachon* (faith and trust) in G-d.

---

13 Ps. 46:8, 12.
14 Ps. 84:13.
15 Ps. 20:10.
16 Exod. 12:41, etc.
17 Quoted in Otzar Hatefiloth, p. 450.

המעריב ערבים

FIRST BLESSING BEFORE SHEMA

The first blessing before the Shema of the Evening Prayer is similar in content to the first blessing preceding the Morning Shema, except that in the morning the blessing speaks of G-d's wonder in creating light (*yotzer or*), while in the evening the blessing speaks of G-d's wonder in creating twilight. Thus it begins, *Blessed . . . Who by His word, brings on evenings (maariv aravim)*. The plural is used, because there are actually two stages of twilight. The first is brought on when the sun sets beyond the horizon, but its light is still reflected in the clouds; the second is the deeper twilight when this reflected light also disappears, and the stars begin to appear—this stage marks the beginning of night.

The Hebrew word *erev* ("evening") comes from the verb meaning "to mix," because as soon as the sun passes the meridian and begins to decline towards the west, the evening begins to mingle with the day, until the day finally gives way to the night. Thus, the whole afternoon is already called *bein ha'arbayim*, "between the evenings," or, literally, "between the mixtures," which is the expression used in the Torah to denote the time of the evening sacrifice (*Tamid*), and also of the paschal lamb.[18]

The opening words of this blessing refer, of course, to the first evening which G-d created, as it is written, "And it was evening (*erev*), and it was morning, one day."[19]

---

18 Exod. 12:6; 29:29, etc.
19 Gen. 1:5.

... With wisdom He opens the gates (of the heavens). There are many references in T'NaCh to the "gates" of heaven.

... And with understanding He changes the times and varies the seasons. What appears as a "natural" and "ordinary" change in time, from day to night, and from night to day; from summer to winter and from winter to summer, and so on, is really a wonderful act of Creation through which G-d continuously displays His infinite wisdom and will.

... He creates day and night; rolls away the light from before the darkness, and the darkness from before the light. G-d could have created the day and night so that one would displace the other suddenly and abruptly. Life would be much more difficult in such a case. But in His wisdom G-d "rolls away" the light slowly, to give His creatures a chance to prepare for the night.

... And He makes the day pass, and He brings the night, and He separates the day from the night, the G-d of Hosts is His Name. G-d has made a distinction between light and darkness, between the day and the night, for they are two distinct creations, which differ not merely in the quantity of light, but in their very nature. We have already had occasion to note that in the day G-d rules through His attribute of *chesed* (kindness), and during the night—through His attribute of *din* (stern justice). We also know that certain Divine commandments apply during the daytime, while others have to be fulfilled at night. Here are deep mysteries which are linked with the mysteries of the Creation itself.

Mention of the distinction between day and night may be considered as a link with the next blessing, which speaks of G-d's everlasting love for His people Israel. Here, too, there is a distinction between the Jewish people and the rest of humanity, for it is the Jewish people that G-d has chosen, to give them the Torah and Mitzvoth, as will be discussed further.

The first blessing concludes with the blessing, *Blessed ... Who brings on* (literally, *Who mixes*) *evenings.*

אהבת עולם

SECOND BLESSING

With an everlasting love have You loved the
House of Israel, Your people....

These are the opening words of the second blessing preceding
the Shema of the Evening Prayer. They are based on G-d's declaration, through the prophet Jeremiah, "With an everlasting love
I love you."[20]

It can be seen that the opening words אהבת עולם, as well as
the theme of this blessing, are similar to those of the second
benediction preceding the Morning Shema. It is a particularly
fitting introduction and preparation for the Shema, the first section
of which begins with the words, "And you shall love G-d, your
G-d, with all your heart," etc.[21]

G-d's love for our people expresses itself, first of all, in the fact
that He has chosen us from among all nations of the world to give
us the Torah and Mitzvoth, to serve Him and be always near to
Him, as the prayer continues:

...Torah and Mitzvoth, statutes and laws, You have taught us.

G-d has not only *given* us the Torah and Mitzvoth, but He has
also *taught* and *trained* us to observe them in our daily life. The
Hebrew verb *lamad* (in the transitive *piel*) means both "to teach"
and "to train." Ever since G-d gave us the Torah at Sinai, He has
made certain that it should not depart from us. It has been a
recurring experience throughout our long history that whenever
the Torah was neglected by our people and in danger of being
forsaken, G-d compelled us to return to it, even if it was necessary

---

20 Jeremiah 3:3.
21 See p. 156 f. above.

to do so by means of an Amalek, or a Haman, and the like. But, of course, it is better that we should keep the Torah and Mitzvoth willingly and with joy. Divine Providence has also seen to it that before a Torah center was destroyed in one place, a new Torah center began to flourish in another.

. . . *For they* [the Torah and Mitzvoth] *are our life and the length of our days.* This is a reference to the verse, "To love G-d, your G-d, to obey His voice and to cleave to Him—for this is your life and the length of your days."[22]

The Torah and Mitzvoth are not something added to our life, but our life itself. Jewish life without Torah and Mitzvoth is simply unthinkable.

The prayer ends, as it began, on the note of "everlasting love": *"And may Your love not depart from us for ever,"* and concludes with the blessing: "Blessed are You, O G-d, Who loves His people Israel."

---

[22] Deut. 30:20.

אמת ואמונה

FIRST BLESSING AFTER SHEMA

True and trustworthy is all this. . . .

"All this" refers to all that is contained in the three sections of the Shema: Our declaration of G-d's Unity and our acceptance of His Kingship (*ol malchuth shamayim*)—in the first; our acceptance of unswerving obedience to His commandments (*ol Mitzvoth*)—in the second; the Mitzvah of Tzitzith, symbol of all the Mitzvoth, and the event of the Liberation from Egypt—in the third.

In the Talmud[23] we find the following statement in the name of Rav:

> He who has not said אמת ויציב in the morning and אמת ואמונה in the evening, has not fulfilled his duty, for it is written, *"To relate Your kindness in the morning, and your faithfulness in the nights."*[24]

Rashi explains that, although the theme is similar in the morning and evening versions, there is this difference: The morning version speaks of G-d's kindness to our ancestors, whom He brought out of Egypt and for whom He split the sea asunder, etc. In other words, it speaks of G-d's wonders and miracles for our people in the past. The evening version, on the other hand, speaks of G-d's care and love for our people also in the present and, especially, in the future.

---

23 Berachoth 12a.
24 Ps. 92:3.

In this connection the prayer also includes two verses which are the highlight of the Song at the Sea, namely, "Who is like unto You among the mighty, O G-d," etc., and "G-d will reign for ever and ever."[25]

Since the main theme of this prayer, as of the corresponding morning version, is the redemption of Israel—*Geulah*—both in the past and in the future, it appropriately concludes with the blessing, "Blessed are You, O G-d, Who redeems Israel."

The inclusion of this prayer, with its central thought of *Yetziath Mitzrayim,* in both the Morning and Evening prayers, is in fulfillment of the ruling of our Sages that the liberation from Egypt must be remembered daily and nightly. It is based on the interpretation of the commandment in the Torah: "That you remember the days of your going out of Egypt *all the days of your life.*"[26] The emphasis on the word *all* provided the following deduction, according to Ben Zoma: Had it said only "the days of your life," it would have implied the daytime only; now that it says "*all* the days of your life," the nights are included.[27]

As we had occasion to note, the "night" often serves as a metaphor for the Exile. It is, therefore, particularly important that in the very darkness of the Exile we should reaffirm our trust in G-d, that, just as He delivered our people from bondage in Egypt, so will He again redeem us from the present Exile.

Needless to say, our reciting the event of *Yetziath Mitzrayim,*[28] the miraculous crossing of the sea, and the joyous song which Mosheh and all the people sang on that occasion—all this is not simply for the purpose of recalling an important event in the history of our people. The real purpose is that we should relive this experience daily, as if it happened to us personally. If we can visualize ourselves standing on the shores of the Red Sea, having

25 Exod. 15:11; 19.
26 Deut. 16:3.
27 Mishnah, Ber. 12b.
28 See also p. 171 above.

just witnessed our wonderful salvation, attended by obvious miracles wrought for us by the "Great Hand" of G-d—we, too, as our ancestors of old, must willingly and joyously accept G-d's Kingship, and be filled with a tremendous sense of awe and love for G-d.

השכיבנו

SECOND BLESSING AFTER SHEMA

In Nusach Ari (with some variations in Nusach Ashkenaz) the second blessing after the Shema begins as follows:

*Cause us, O our Father, to lie down in peace, and
raise us up, O our King, unto good life and peace. . . .*

It is significant that in praying to G-d for a peaceful night, we address Him as "our Father," but on getting up in the morning, we address Him as "our King."

We have already had occasion to note in connection with *Modeh ani*[28a]—our first prayer on waking up in the morning, that our first thought of G-d in the morning is that of a Ruler (King) to Whom we owe our life, and Whom we must, therefore, obey without question, as a subject obeys his king.

At night, however, we think of G-d more in terms of a Father than a King. For, in the course of the day we have learned from all that has happened to us that G-d has been more than a King to us; He has shown us many kindnesses and has taken care of us like a loving father. And so, when we are about to retire for the night, we feel confident and secure in G-d, as a child feels secure in the arms of his father.

In terms of *our* relationship to G-d, "King" and "Father" signify two forms of serving G-d. A king is obeyed primarily out of fear of displeasing him; a father is obeyed primarily out of love. Each

---

28a See p. 16 above.

of these attitudes has a preeminence over the other. Obedience to a royal command must be carried out without question, with self-surrender (*kabbalath ol*); this is the first condition of true obedience, the kind of obedience that is required in the army, for instance. Personal feelings or motivations have no part in it. On the other hand, a fatherly request is carried out by a loving son with enthusiasm and joy, and often beyond the "call of duty."[29]

Our first obligation in our service to G-d should be that of subject to his king, or a servant to his master. But as we get to know G-d better, and as we more fully appreciate the vital importance of G-d's commandments for our own good, we can develop also that higher attitude of serving G-d out of love. The highest form of Divine service is that which combines the two, *yirah* and *ahavah* (reverence and love), and that is why we sometimes address G-d as both "Our Father, our King."

. . . Direct us aright with good counsel from You. . . .

At night, when a person goes to bed, his mind begins to wonder and is filled with all sorts of thoughts. He may review the events of the day, and make decisions for the next. It is a good time to make good resolutions. We therefore pray to G-d for His guidance that our decisions should be right and that we should be able to carry out our good resolutions, for only such thoughts and ideas as are inspired by G-d are truly good and of lasting value.

. . . and spread over us the tabernacle of Your peace . . . and shelter us in the shadow of Your wings.

"Peace" and "protection" are the main themes of this prayer, for we realize that these great blessings come from G-d alone.

One of the reasons for the inclusion of this prayer in the Evening Service is to be found in *Midrash Tehillim,* where we find the following saying by Rabbi Eliezer: "He who puts on

---

[29] Lik. Torah, Balak 70c; Re'eh 20b; Berachah 94b.

Tefillin on his head and arm, Tzitzith on his garment, and a Mezuzah on his door, is guarded against sin."[30] At night, two of these protectors are missing, since the Mitzvoth of Tefillin and Tzitzith apply only in the daytime. Therefore, our Sages have included this special prayer for Divine protection.

The prayer concludes with the blessing: "Blessed are You, O G-d, Who guards His people Israel for ever."

This is in reference to the verse, "Behold, the Guardian of Israel slumbers not, nor sleeps."[31]

While we go to sleep, we can rest assured that G-d will not fall asleep on His "guard duty," but will be constantly watchful over us. Our Sages pointedly commented:

> G-d is not like a human being. Among humans, the master sleeps, while his servant stands watch over him. But of G-d it is said, "Behold, the Guardian of Israel slumbers not, nor sleeps." Here is a case where the servant sleeps, and the master keeps guard over him.[32]

In Nusach Ari, the *Shemone Esrei* follows immediately after the prayer of השכיבנו, and is concluded with *Aleinu,* both of which have already been discussed in the Morning Service.

In congregation the *Half-Kaddish* precedes the *Shemone Esrei,* and *Kaddish-Tithkabel* is recited after the *Shemone Esrei.* There is no repetition of the *Shemone Esrei* by the Reader (*Chazzan*) because the *Kedushah* is not recited at night.

---

[30] Midrash Tehillim on Ps. 6.
[31] Ps. 121:4.
[32] Ber. Rabbah 25:42.

ברכת המזון

∘

GRACE AFTER MEALS

FOREWORD

Every living thing—plant, animal, or human being—must have food to live. The Creator has provided food for all living things: Sunshine and rain make plants grow from the soil; the plants provide food for animals; and human beings feed on both plants and animals.

Nature as a whole is divided into four orders, or "worlds": minerals, vegetables, animals and man. The lower order supports the higher order.

The fact that food sustains life is such a "natural" thing, that most people take it for granted. People eat and drink when they are hungry and thirsty, without giving a thought to the wonder of nutrition. It is not very often, if at all, that people ask themselves: How is it that bread, water, milk, eggs, meat and similar foods—which *have no life* in themselves—give life to the living? Can anyone give anything which one does not possess?

We Jews have been taught to look at the daily routine of eating quite differently; we have been taught not to take it for granted.

First of all, any right-thinking person can understand that there must be a difference between the way animals eat and the way humans should eat. The difference is not in "table manners"; nor in the fact that people use forks and knives, while animals do not; nor in the fact that people generally cook their food, or add salt and pepper to make their food tastier, while animals eat raw food.

People generally recognize that they must go about getting their food in a decent and honest way. Many people, especially

275

farmers, realize their dependence on G-d for their daily bread. Nevertheless, if people eat for the sake of eating, simply to satisfy a bodily need, they are basically no different from the dumb animals. In this case, as a matter of fact, the animals have an advantage: animals do not overeat, while human beings often over-indulge in food, much to their own harm.

We Jews have been taught quite a different attitude towards food. We have been taught to consider food not an end in itself, but a means to an end. Our purpose in life is to serve our Creator, and for this it is necessary that we have a healthy body and mind. Needless to say, serving G-d includes also serving our fellow-man, for our duties to fellow-man are part of our duties to G-d.

Therefore, before we eat anything we must make a blessing thanking G-d for our food, each kind of food having its particular blessing. The blessing reminds us that we are not only dependent upon G-d for our food, but that our eating is part of our Divine service. For the same reason we make a blessing *after* eating, again not only to express our gratitude to G-d, but to remind us to use the energy of the food for Divine service.

But beyond all this—and we now come to the second point— is yet a deeper and more meaningful attitude to food, which teaches us to consider food with a sense of reverence, so much so, that wasting food is considered a sin, almost like the desecration of ? holy thing. This will be better understood if we consider the question posed earlier: "How is it that food, which is *lifeless,* gives life?"

Our Holy Torah, called *Torath Emeth,* the Law of Truth, because it was given by the G-d of Truth, provides the answer: "Not on bread alone does man live, but by all that comes from the Mouth of G-d does man live."[1]

----

[1] Deut. 8:3.

The meaning of these profound words (as explained at length in the teachings of Chasiduth)[2] is as follows:

When G-d created the world and all that is in it *out of nothing,* all things came into being by the word of G-d; by G-d's command, "Let there be!"

Now, creation by G-d is not the same as "creation" by man. When a human being makes a thing, say, a table or chair, he does not have to give that thing any further attention; the thing will not fall apart when he leaves it. The reason for this is simple: A human being does not *create* anything *out of nothing.* He uses materials, in this case wood, which existed independently of him. He merely *changes* things.

But G-d created things *out of nothing;* they came into being by G-d's command, and it is G-d's command which gives them existence. Consequently, they are *constantly* dependent upon G-d's command. Should G-d withdraw His command ("Let there be"), all things would turn to nothing—to the state of not-being as before G-d created them; they could not exist on their own for a single instant. In other words, G-d's creation of the world was not a one-time act after which everything was left to exist on its own, but it is a *continuous* process. To use a simple illustration: If you lean a stepladder against a wall, the ladder could remain in that inclined position only so long as the force of the wall supports it. Should that wall be removed, the ladder must topple to the ground, because it is not "natural" for a ladder to remain in a leaning position without support. In the same way, nothing could exist without a special Divine force keeping it in existence. This is what is meant when we say in our daily morning prayers: "[G-d] in His goodness renews *every day continuously* the work of creation."[2a]

This Divine "force" which is in everything that exists, is something like a "soul." From what has been said above, it is clear that

[2] Shaar Hayichud vehaEmunah, and elsewhere.
[2a] See also p. 142 f. above.

even the so-called inanimate ("dead") objects, like a stone, have a "soul," namely, the Divine "spark" or force which is the *real* existence of the thing. We cannot, of course, see that "soul," just as we cannot see the soul of a living creature, for we cannot see spiritual things with our eyes of flesh. But we do know without a doubt that without such a soul, nothing could live or exist.

The above is true, of course, also of the food we eat.

The food we eat is not a simple material thing. It has a "spark" of G-dliness in it, and it is this Divine force within the food that gives us life. The material part of the food becomes "bone of our bones and flesh of our flesh," but it is the *spiritual* part of the food—*"that which comes out of the Mouth of G-d"*—that feeds the spiritual part of our being, giving us life and spiritual powers to think, speak and do good and holy things.

OUR TABLE — A MIZBE'ACH

In the light of what has been explained above, it is clear why the Jewish attitude towards eating is so radically different from the attitude of other peoples. We consider eating as a means of attaching ourselves to our Creator through the Divine "spark" in our food, somewhat similar to the manner of our attaching ourselves to G-d as when we fulfill the commandment of putting on Tefillin, or wearing Tzitzith, and the like. For in the leather boxes and straps of Tefillin, as in the wool of the Tzitzith, or the fruit of the Ethrog, etc., there are Divine "sparks" by means of which we derive "food" and sustenance for our Divine soul.

It will now be more clearly understood why the Jewish people is a holy people. We are a *holy* people in that we bring holiness into our daily life, not only by the observance of the holy religious precepts which G-d commanded us, but also in our eating and drinking, and in whatever we do. Our guideline is "Know Him (attach yourself to Him) in all your ways,"[3] as our great teacher, the Rambam, has ruled in his famous Code.[4]

There is thus no split in our daily activities between our experience when engaged in eating and drinking, etc., and our experience when engaged in prayer, Torah-study, or doing any other Mitzvah. We truly come to appreciate the feeling of "You are children of G-d, your G-d." Children are *always* children, not occasionally so. Likewise, we have to act as G-d's children not merely when we are engaged in G-dly matters, but in whatever we are engaged— in the totality of our daily life. This is the only way to achieve complete unity and harmony with ourselves, with G-d, and with the surrounding world. This is why the Jewish people has been described as "*One* people on earth,"[5] for they experience oneness and harmony not only in "G-dly" matters but also in "earthly" matters.

It goes without saying that all the above is conditioned upon eating *Kosher* food, the kind of food which G-d has permitted us to eat. A Jew who is not careful about Kosher food, G-d forbid, places himself in a category lower than an animal or beast, for the latter do not break G-d's laws when feeding. But even eating Kosher food, if it is done without the sanctity which the Torah requires of the Jew as outlined above, could reduce such eating to the level of animal-feeding.

There is yet a further important point. When the Jew eats Kosher food, and Kosher food only, carefully making the Berachoth before and after, etc., he is not only elevating his own life to the level of holiness, but he is also "elevating" his share in Nature. The minerals, vegetables and animals, which constitute his food, are transformed into his own flesh and blood, that is to say, into energy and vitality wherewith to serve the Creator of all things.

On the other hand, if a person misuses the energy and vitality

---

[3] Prov. 3:6.
[4] Hil. Deoth 3:3.
[5] II Sam. 7:23.

derived from his nourishment, he degrades not only himself, but Nature around him.

To put it very simply: When a Jew has a Kosher chicken-dinner in the proper manner, he has enabled the chicken to serve G-d through him; and not only the chicken, but also the chicken-feed upon which the chicken was reared. But if he uses the energy from his chicken-dinner to cheat or steal, the chicken can justly demand, "By what right have you taken my life, and involved me in crime, which I could never have committed otherwise?!"

Our Sages[5a] taught us to regard our table as our altar, and our eating as a Divine service. Indeed, it is written, "This is the table before G-d."[6] Our washing the hands before eating, our reciting the blessing for washing the hands (including the words, "Who has sanctified us with His commandments"), our making a blessing over the bread, dipping it in salt—all these reflect the Divine service in the Beth Hamikdash of old.

For in the Beth Hamikdash of old, the Kohanim had to sanctify their hands (and feet) by washing, and had to recite certain Berachoth before their *Avodah* (Divine Service); only *Kosher* animals could be offered on the Mizbe'ach, after they were slaughtered in the prescribed manner, and prepared ("Kashered") as required by Jewish Law. Each sacrifice was accompanied by a dose of salt. The offerings in the Beth Hamikdash included not only Kosher animals, but also offerings from the world of plants and minerals—thus "elevating" the lower "worlds" of Nature to the level of holiness. In this way *all* of Nature, which at first glance appears to consist of separate things, "separate" from G-d—is brought into one and the same world of holiness; man and his world are re-united in and with G-d.

5a Berachoth 55a.
6 Ezekiel 41:22.

This, then, is the "other side of the coin" of the Jew's characterization as "one people on earth": By living his daily life as prescribed by the Torah, the Jew brings out the *unity* even in earthly things.

From the above, it will become self-evident why we must approach *Birkath Hamazon* with especial reverence. The saintly Sheloh[7] writes that it is a good custom to put on one's jacket before *bentching* (saying *Birkath Hamazon*), in the same way as one would do before reciting the daily prayers; similarly to put on one's hat (not merely keeping the yarmulka on). Many other holy sources emphasize the importance of reciting Birkath Hamazon with joy and devoutness and concentration, and not to run through it mechanically.

Besides, in Birkath Hamazon we express our gratitude to G-d for our daily bread. It would be most unbecoming to express our thanks in an absent-minded or casual way. By expressing our *sincere* thanks to G-d for our daily bread, we can be confident that G-d would continue to provide for our needs in a generous measure. The author of the famous *Sefer haChinuch* makes a special point of this, saying, he who is careful in reciting Birkath Hamazon will be blessed with sustenance in an honorable and gracious manner.[8]

---

[7] Isaiah Hurwitz, *Shenei Luchoth Haberith,* p. 82.
[8] Sefer Hachinuch, Mitzvah 428, beg. of Ekev.

סדר ברכת המזון

INTRODUCTORY PSALMS

על נהרות בבל

PSALM 137

Several introductory psalms precede the Grace After Meals.

On weekdays it is customary to recite Psalm 137 and Psalm 67.

Psalm 137—"By the rivers of Babylon"—is a reminder of the destruction of the Beth Hamikdash. As the saintly Shaloh observes, the loss of the Beth Hamikdash should be particularly felt at our dining table, because, as already noted, our table in many respects represents the "altar" of the Sanctuary of old. This is, therefore, the time to remember the saying, "Woe unto the children who have been banished from their Father's table."[9]

It is to be noted that this Psalm refers to the destruction of both the First Beth Hamikdash (by the Babylonians—v. 1) and of the Second (by "Edom," i.e. Rome—v. 7). This is the basis of the Talmudic statement, by Rav Yehudah in the name of Rav, that G-d had shown King David in a prophetic vision the two destructions.[10]

Commenting on the first verse of this Psalm—*By the rivers of Babylon, there we sat and also wept, when we remembered Zion*—the Midrash relates the following episode:

---

[9] Shenei Luchoth Haberith 82a.
[10] Gittin 5a; 57b.

282

When the exiles reached the river Euphrates, Nebuzaradan (the victorious commander of the Babylonian army) offered the Prophet Jeremiah the option of either settling in Babylon or returning to his homeland. Jeremiah decided that his presence was needed more by the remnants of Jews who had been left in the Holy Land. As he turned to go, the exiles sat down by the river and began to weep, crying, "Jeremiah, our Master, how can you leave us!" Whereupon Jeremiah answered them, "Heaven and earth are my witnesses that had you wept (i.e. repented) but once when you were still in Zion, you would not have been exiled!"[11]

It is in this Psalm that we read the moving pledge, first made by those exiles but later re-echoed by Jews throughout our long exile: "If I forget you, Jerusalem, may my right hand forget [to function]; let my tongue cleave to the roof of my mouth, if I do not remember you, if I raise not Jerusalem above my joy."[12]

למנצח בנגינות

PSALM 67

Since Psalm 137 recalls all the tragedy and bitterness of the destruction and exile, it is followed by the more cheerful Psalm 67 —*To the chief musician . . . G-d be merciful unto us and bless us, and cause His face to shine upon us, Selah.*[13]

The theme of this Psalm centers on the ultimate triumph of our people, when even the nations of the earth will recognize the justice and righteousness of the Supreme Judge.

---

[11] Midrash Tehillim on Ps. 137:1.

[12] Ps. 137:5-6.

[13] Ps. 67:1-2.

According to the saintly Rabbi Mosheh Alshich, this Psalm speaks of the Messianic Era which will be ushered in by the appearance of our righteous Mashiach, when G-d will bestow an abundance of blessing on Israel, and His Name will be sanctified by all the nations of the world.[14]

In this context the following verse assumes special significance:

To make known Your way upon the earth.[15] . . .

At present, when our people is in exile, suffering untold persecution and misery, it is difficult, indeed impossible, to know G-d's ways. Even Mosheh Rabbenu found it difficult to understand why the wicked prosper and the righteous suffer, and pleaded with G-d, "Show me, I beg you, Your ways."[16] But when Mashiach will come and G-d's ultimate judgment will be revealed to all—then G-d's way will be known and understood.

In view of the fact that we do not dwell on the destruction or similar sad events in our Sabbath and Yom Tov prayers, the above two Psalms are omitted, as also on days when no Tachnun is said (such as Rosh Chodesh, Chol Hamoed, etc.). Instead, we say two inspiring Psalms, in which we remember Zion in a happier setting, namely, the Geulah and Return to Zion (Ps. 126), and Zion's ultimate glory (Ps. 87).

שיר המעלות בשוב

PSALM 126

A song of degrees. When G-d returned the captivity of Zion we were like dreamers.

According to Rashi, this Psalm, or Song, was sung by the Jews

---

14 Rabbi Menachem Mendel of Lubavitch, *Yahel Or*, p. 230.
15 Ps. 67:3.
16 Exod. 33:13.

returning from the Babylonian Exile to rebuild the Beth Hamik-dash in Jerusalem.

Certain other commentaries[17] see in this Psalm (also) a prophecy about the future return to the Land of Israel with the coming of Mashiach and the Geulah Shlemah.

"We were like dreamers" does not refer to the return, as the first impression might indicate, but rather to the past exile. What this phrase means is that, because of the abundant good that G-d will bestow upon Israel at the time of the return, all the suffering during the long years of exile will be like a dream—unreal and illusory.

In Chabad[18] the concept of "dream" as applied to the Galuth is explained as follows: In a dream anything is possible. The most far-fetched and unthinkable paradoxes and contradictions do not seem irrational. This is so because when a person sleeps, his essential spiritual and rational powers are in a state of suspension; while the powers of illusion and imagination take over and have free play, making illusions and images appear quite real and true. On awakening, when the person regains possession of his full intellectual faculties, he realizes that it was only a dream.

Similarly, the Galuth is like a dream. For the Galuth is a time of "concealment of the Divine Countenance" (hester Panim).[19] During this time, G-d's rule in the world operates in a hidden way. We cannot clearly see the Divine Providence as it extends to each and all particulars in the world around us. Our concept of G-d-liness is clouded, as our judgment of what is true and real. What we see around us is a world turned "upside down": the wicked triumph, the righteous suffer; worthless concepts are accepted as real values, while real values are discarded as worthless.

Moreover, in a dream it is possible for two opposites that are mutually exclusive to appear in perfect harmony, and no contra-

---

17 Notably *Metzudath David*.
18 E.g. *Torah Or* 28c, f.
19 Deut. 31:18; 32:20.

diction is seen. Similarly in the daily life during the Galuth the Jew often fails to see the contradiction between the pursuits of the soul striving after G-dliness and those of the body seeking physical pleasures. Thus, during the time of prayer and Torah study, he divests himself of all mundane affairs and gives himself fully to the love of G-d. Yet after prayer, the great love of G-d, which surpasses all other loves, seems to evaporate easily, and he sees no contradiction in spending the greater part of his time and energy in the pursuit of ephemeral mundane illusions. The reason for this dream-like inconsistency is that the Divine "spark" in his soul is "asleep" and "dreaming" during the time of the Galuth, when it is itself in exile and captivity, as it were.[20]

However, when Mashiach will come, and there will be a Divine revelation exceeding anything in the past, and "all the earth will be filled with the knowledge of G-d as the waters cover the sea,"[21] then there will be a real awakening, and we will see that we had been living in a state of "dream." Furthermore, what is equally significant, we shall then be able to "interpret" our dream, as everything will be seen clearly in the brilliant light of the new Divine revelation.

It should be noted that while, as mentioned, Chabad discusses the entire subject at great length, it is basically also the view of our great thinkers and philosophers, from Maimonides to Albo. Thus, Joseph Albo, commenting on the opening of this Psalm, declares that our present-day concept and intellectual grasp as compared with those of the future, stand in relation to each other as "dreaming" and "awakening."[22]

> *Then our mouth will be filled with laughter, and our tongue with singing. . . .*[23]

---

[20] See also *Yahel Or*, pp. 490, 492.
[21] Isaiah 11:9.
[22] Joseph Albo, *Ikkarim* IV:ch. 33.
[23] Ps. 126:2.

"Then"—in the new world order that will be ushered in by the Messianic Era—"our mouth will be filled with laughter," i.e. joy and singing. Most joys at present are neither true nor lasting joys. Indeed, we find a statement in the Talmud, in the name of Rabbi Shimon ben Yochai, that "a person should not fill his mouth with laughter in this world,"[24] since no joy can now be complete. True joy is only that which is derived from the knowledge of G-dliness.

Rabbi Menachem Mendel of Lubavitch, famed author of the monumental Halachic work *Tzemach Tzedek,* and third generation of Chabad leaders, points out that the Hebrew word שחוק ("laughter" as an expression of true joy) is the numerical equivalent of twice אור ("light"), and the same as the Hebrew word ואהבת ("and you shall love" G-d, your G-d).[25] Here is an allusion to the double measure of Divine light that will be revealed in the future, and that the joy resulting from it will be identified with our true love for G-d.

They that sow in tears will reap in joy. He that goes forth and weeps while scattering the seed, will surely come back carrying his sheaves.[26]

The farmer that sows his field, makes a certain sacrifice, for he must part with good seed and put in a great deal of effort in planting them. But he knows that he will reap a good harvest that will compensate him many times over.

Good deeds and Mitzvoth are likened to the planting of seeds. They entail a certain immediate sacrifice, but the reward is sure to come, even if it takes some time.

Seldom does the farmer stop to reflect on the wonder of a small seed giving birth to a new plant with many seeds. Equally

24 Berachoth 30a.
25 Yahel Or, p. 493.
26 Ps. 126:5-6.

seldom do we stop to reflect how a small act in the performance of G-d's command can bring results beyond our knowledge and imagination. But the truth is that in both cases it is the will of G-d that brings about the results. For it is G-d's will that has given the soil its infinite power of growth, just as it is G-d's will that the performance of a Mitzvah on our part should have infinite results. So great is the reward of a Mitzvah that, as our Sages declare, there is nothing in this world that can fully reward for even a relatively small effort and sacrifice put into a Mitzvah, and most, if not all, of it is reserved for the world to come. And while G-d's commandments must be fulfilled for their own sake, without thought of reward, G-d has let it be known that reward is sure to come, and "they who sow in tears will reap in joy."

לבני קורח

PSALM 87

Psalm 87 is, in many respects, a continuation of Psalm 127. It speaks of the glory of Zion, and how every Jew has a share in it.

G-d loves the gates of Zion more than all the dwellings of Jacob.[27]

"The Gates of Zion," our Sages say, refer to "the gates that are distinguished (*metzuyanim*, a play on the word *tzion*) in Halachah."[28] It is as a center of Torah-study that G-d particularly loves Zion, and it is this that makes it "the city of G-d."[29] We are all familiar with the verse, "For out of Zion comes forth Torah, and the word of G-d out of Jerusalem."[30]

---

27 Ps. 87:2.
28 Berachoth 8a.
29 Ps. 87:3.
30 Isaiah 2:3.

And the singers like the players (on flutes) will say:
All my thoughts are of You.[31]

In the future, we shall sing G-d's praises and declare "All our thoughts are of You," i.e. of G-d, being completely absorbed in the great salvation which He will bring to us.

Rabbenu Bahya, however, in his commentary on the verse, "A land which G-d, your G-d cares for; the eyes of G-d, your G-d, are always upon it, from the beginning of the year to the end of the year,"[32] renders the concluding words of Psalm 87 as G-d saying to the City of Zion, "All My thoughts are of you." In other words, while G-d's Providence extends to the whole world, it is particularly concentrated on the Land of Israel, and from there it extends to the rest of the world. Thus, the Psalm concludes on the note it began—"G-d loves the gates of Zion."

---

[31] Ps. 87:7.
[32] Deut. 11:12.

מים אחרונים

MAYIM ACHRONIM

After the recital of the introductory Psalms and verses follows the custom of *Mayim Achronim*—the *second* washing of our hands, this time our finger tips, prior to our actual saying of the Birkath Hamazon. (The *first* washing — *Mayim Rishonim* — is done *before* the meal, in connection with which the blessing *Al Netilath Yadayim* is said.)

Before *Mayim Achronim* the following verse is recited: "This is the portion of a wicked man from G-d; and the heritage appointed unto him by G-d."[33] After *Mayim Achronim* the following verse is said: "And he spoke unto me, This is the table that is before G-d."[34]

The custom of *Mayim Achronim* and the relevance of the two verses quoted above have an interesting explanation.

Our Sages of blessed memory gave a hygienic explanation for the custom of washing the finger tips at the conclusion of the meal, namely, in order to wash off *Melach Sedomith* ("Sodomite Salt") which might have clung to the finger tips, and which would be harmful to the eyes if this (or other impurity) would come in contact with them.

---

33 Job 20:29.
34 Ezekiel 41:22.

290

Needless to say, this "hygienic" reason is but one reason for this custom. All our customs and precepts come from the Torah— and that includes both the Written Torah and the Oral Torah (the Mishnah and Talmud, etc.). The Torah is endless and inexhaustible, and so are its commandments and precepts which have an infinite number of reasons and explanations. Some are simple and known; some are deep and hidden. From time to time our great and saintly Sages reveal new insights into the Divine commandments. But, in any case, the explanations are of secondary importance when it comes to the fulfillment of the precepts, which are, first and foremost, Divine commandments to us, to be fulfilled without question, and to be studied later.

The same is true of "Mayim Achronim." The hygienic basis for this custom, mentioned earlier, is but one reason. There is a deeper significance in this custom which arises from the symbolic meaning of *Melach Sedomith.*

It is well known that only a person who has suffered pain can truly understand another person in pain. Only a person who has known starvation can truly understand another starving person. There is a saying, "The sated man does not understand the hungry man."

Now, the rich man as he sits down to his meal, that is to say, when he is hungry, would feel more kindly toward a poor man, should one knock at his door and ask for a meal. Being hungry himself at that moment, the rich man would better understand how the hungry pauper feels. But after the rich man has had his meal, he might not feel so sympathetic towards the poor man. The rich man might even be annoyed at having his rest disturbed. He might blame the poor man for bothering him, instead of going out to earn his own living in order to avoid being a burden on others. A full stomach often goes with a dull head, and an insensitive heart. Thus, there is the danger of a special kind of "Sodomite Salt"—a Sodomite thought—coming with the meal.

We know what the Sodomite attitude was towards strangers and beggars. Even Lot's wife was infected with this kind of *Melach Sedomith,* and it was no mere coincidence that she turned into a pillar of salt.[34a]

Therefore, when our Sages said that *Melach Sedomith* is "harmful for the eyes," they might well have meant also that with a meal there is yet another danger, perhaps even more serious, namely, the danger of entertaining a Sodomite thought which might sneak in on a full stomach; the danger of becoming "blind" to the needs and sufferings of the poor.

In this connection, it is well to remember the interpretation which our Sages give to the verse, "And you shall sanctify yourselves and you shall be holy; for I, your G-d, am holy."[35] Why the repetition? they ask. Surely, "and you shall sanctify yourselves means "and you shall be holy." And they answer: "You shall sanctify yourselves"—by washing your hands before the meal, and "you shall be holy"—by washing your hands after the meal— with *Mayim Achronim.*[35a]

It is not enough to sit down at the table with pure hands and pure thoughts; we must see to it that we remain pure and holy also after the meal, and not permit "Sodomite Salt" to cling to us and to contaminate our thoughts and insights, as the Sodomites permitted themselves to turn into beasts by their gluttony and wealth.

When the Jew has eaten in accordance with the Torah—"you shall eat and be satisfied and you shall bless G-d, your G-d" . . .— he recalls the words of Job's friend Tzophar, in which the indulgencies of the wicked man, especially gluttony, are forcefully condemned and the inevitable punishment is vividly described:

34a See Rashi on Gen. 19:26; Ber. Rabba and Yalkut on same.
35 Lev. 20:7.
35a Berachoth 53b; Chulin 105a.

The joy of the hypocrite is but for a moment . . .
he shall fly away like a dream and shall not be found
. . . his food is turned in his bowels . . . he swallows
riches and vomits them up again . . . nothing is left
of his eating . . . in the fullness of his sufficiency he
suffers. . . .[36]

Recalling these words, and recoiling from such an attitude, the
Jew quotes the last sentence of that chapter: "This is the portion
of a wicked man from G-d; and the heritage appointed unto him
by G-d."[36a] Thereupon he proceeds with *Mayim Achronim*, sym-
bolically washing off his hands any "impurities" that contaminate
the table of the wicked man.

Having done so, he says: "And he spoke unto me: This is the
table that is before G-d,"[36b] for the Jew's table is comparable to
the altar of sacrifice, as our Sages said.[37] Hence also the custom
of dipping bread in salt, as all sacrifices in the Sanctuary of old
had to be accompanied by a salt offering,[38] as mentioned earlier.

Thus, though we may be many miles away from Sodom, the
danger of "Sodomite Salt" is ever present. Washing our finger tips
with *Mayim Achronim* at the end of our meal reminds us that we
are children of a holy nation—holy not only during "holy days"
in the year, or on holy occasions, but in all our ways, even when
we are eating and drinking. This is the meaning of the commandment of the Torah: "And you shall sanctify yourselves, and you
shall be holy; for I, your G-d, am holy."[39] Just as G-d is *always*
holy, so must we try to be.

---

36 Job 20:4, 8; 14-22.
36a Ibid. 20:29.
36b Ezek. 41:22.
37 Berachoth 55a.
38 Lev. 2:13.
39 Lev. 11:44; 20:7.

ברכת המזון

BIRKATH HAMAZON

(GRACE AFTER MEALS)

הזן

FIRST BENEDICTION

Birkath Hamazon (Grace After Meals) consists of four sections, or benedictions. The first begins and concludes with a blessing; the second and third conclude with a blessing; and the fourth begins with a blessing.

The first section begins with the blessing: "Blessed are You, O G-d, our G-d, King of the Universe, Who feeds the whole world. . . ."

In the Talmud[40] it is stated that Mosheh Rabbenu instituted this blessing when the manna began to come down from heaven to feed the children of Israel during their wanderings in the desert, on their way from Egypt to the Promised Land. The manna first came down on the 15th of Iyar, in the year 2448 after Creation, that is, one month after the children of Israel left Egypt. Later, when the Torah was given, it contained the commandment: "And you shall eat and be satisfied, and bless G-d, your G-d. . . ."[41]

---

40 Berachoth 48b.
41 Deut. 8:10.

294

Although the Torah says "and be satisfied," implying that the blessing should be said after one has eaten enough bread to satisfy one's hunger, our Sages have ruled that the obligation to say Grace applies when one has eaten bread of the size of an olive (*k'zayith*) or more. The commandment to say Grace applies to bread made of any one of the five species of grain: wheat, barley, spelt, oats, and rye.

The first benediction of Grace expresses praise to G-d, Who in His goodness feeds and sustains the whole world, providing all creatures with their daily food. Two verses from *Tehillim* are quoted to this effect.[42] (The second one is omitted in Nusach Ashkenaz.)

The section concludes with the blessing: "Blessed are You, O G-d, Who feeds all."

נודה לך

SECOND BENEDICTION

According to the same Talmudic source,[43] the second benediction was introduced by Joshua, when he led the children of Israel into the Promised Land. It begins with the words: "We thank You, O G-d, our G-d, for giving as an inheritance to our ancestors a desirable, good, and ample land. . . ."

The benediction expresses our thanks to G-d particularly for those things with which G-d has distinguished us as a unique nation: for our liberation from Egyptian bondage, for the covenant (*Brith*) sealed in our flesh, and for the Torah and Mitzvoth revealed to us. Our gratitude to G-d is expressed also for our life and sustenance "every day, at all times, and every hour." The

---

42 Ps. 136:25 and Ps. 145:16.
43 Berachoth 48b.

benediction continues with a specific reference to the verse containing the commandment to say Grace, mentioned above: "And you shall eat, and be satisfied, and bless G-d, your G-d, for the good land which He has given you." It concludes with the blessing: "Blessed are You, O G-d, our G-d, for the land and for the food."

The mention of food (*mazon*) in the second benediction may seem a repetition at first glance, since this is the main theme of the first benediction. The explanation, however, is that the first benediction was instituted in gratitude for the manna, the "bread from heaven," as mentioned above. The second benediction was introduced when the Jews entered their land and began to eat of its produce, grown from the soil—bread from the earth. Thus, whether a person's bread comes to him easily, as the manna from heaven, or he has to work hard for it, he must thank G-d for his daily bread. For, ultimately, it is G-d Who makes the grain grow in the field and enables man to harvest it. Furthermore, it is G-d Who has endowed bread with the nutrients to sustain man physically and mentally, as discussed at some length earlier on.[43a]

On Chanukah and Purim, the prayer *V'Al Hanissim*—thanking G-d for the miracles of those days—is introduced into the middle of the second benediction, as also in the *Shemone Esrei* the place of this prayer is in the prayer of thanks, after *Modim*.

רחם

THIRD BENEDICTION

The Talmudic source mentioned above states that the third benediction was introduced by King David. It begins with the words: "Have mercy, O G-d, our G-d, on Israel Your people, and

[43a] See p. 275 f. above.

on Jerusalem Your city, and on Zion the abode of Your glory, and on the Kingship of the House of David Your anointed. . . ." To this, his son King Solomon, after he built the Beth Hamikdash, added: ". . . and on this great and holy House, on which Your Name is called."

The benediction includes a plea for sustenance—not through the gifts of man, but through "Your full, open, holy, and ample Hand."

It continues with a prayer for the rebuilding of Jerusalem, the Holy City, speedily in our days, and concludes with the blessing: "Blessed are You, O G-d, Who in His mercy rebuilds Jerusalem, Amen."

It is not customary to say "Amen" after one's own blessing. The reason it is included at the end of the third benediction of Grace is to indicate that the first three benedictions are based on the direct authority of the Written Torah, while the fourth that follows rests on Rabbinic authority—the Oral Torah.

On Shabbos a special prayer—*Retzeh* ("Be pleased, O G-d")— is inserted here. In this prayer we ask G-d to graciously accept our observance of His Mitzvoth, especially "the Mitzvah of the seventh day, this great and holy Shabbos," and that no distress or sorrow mar our day of sacred rest and Divine love.

On Rosh Chodesh and Holidays, the prayer *Yaale v'Yavo* is also inserted here. It has been discussed elsewhere.[44]

הטוב והמטיב

FOURTH BENEDICTION

The fourth benediction of Birkath Hamazon is an expression of gratitude to G-d, "The Good, Who does Good." It was intro-

---

44 See p. 179 above.

duced by the Sanhedrin at Yavneh, on the 15th day of Av, the day when permission was finally given by the Roman authorities to bury the martyrs of Bethar. The story of the unsuccessful revolt led by Bar Kochba in a desperate effort to free the country from the oppression of Emperor Hadrian of Rome, is told in the Talmud and Midrash.[45] For a long time the fallen heroes of Bethar could not be buried by order of the cruel Hadrian. When Hadrian died, permission was given to bury them. Miraculously, the bodies had no bad odor after all those years. To commemorate that event, and to remind us that G-d is good, "has done good, does good, and will do good" to us always, the Rabbis introduced this fourth benediction into Birkath Hamazon.

A number of requests were later added to this benediction, each beginning with the word *Harachaman,* "The Merciful One." Included among them are: "The Merciful One break the yoke of the Galuth from off our neck, and lead us upright to our land." "The Merciful One send abundant blessing upon this house, and upon the table at which we have eaten." There is also a request for a blessing for one's parents and family. Also a request that the Merciful One help us be worthy of the days of Mashiach and everlasting life.

On Shabbos, Rosh Chodesh, Yom Tov, Rosh Hashanah, and Succoth, an additional *Harachaman* is included.

Birkath Hamazon concludes with several appropriate verses selected from T'NaCh.

Because of the importance of Birkath Hamazon, and also because it has to be recited several times during the day, a special handy pocket "Bentcherl" is often published. It is very useful to have one, and easy to carry in one's pocket.

---

[45] Berachoth 48b; Taanith 31a; Midrash Eichah Rabba.

קריאת שמע שעל המטה

•

PRAYER BEFORE RETIRING TO BED

קריאת שמע שעל המיטה
PRAYER BEFORE RETIRING TO BED

רבונו של עולם
MASTER OF THE WORLD

Although we usually speak of "three daily prayers," we actually have a fourth daily prayer—the prayer before retiring for the night. It is called *Keriath Shema she'al ha-Mittah*—the "Reading of the Shema before Going to Bed."

According to Nusach Ari (Chabad) it begins with a short prayer, the opening words of which are:

> *Master of the Universe, I forgive all who have angered me . . . and may no one be punished on my account. . . .*

This is, indeed, a beautiful prayer. Here we are ready to retire to bed for the night. In the course of the day that is now behind us, we may have been offended by other people. But we do not want to go to bed with a grudge in our heart against anybody. We want to go to bed with a peaceful mind, and with love in our heart for all of G-d's creatures. So we declare that we forgive everybody. It helps us enjoy a restful sleep, and it will also bring us G-d's forgiveness. For G-d's reward is in kind. When we fulfill the commandment of the Torah, "You shall not hate your brother

301

in your heart,"[1] and "you shall not take vengeance, nor bear a grudge against the children of your people,"[2] and, above all, "you shall love your fellow as yourself"[3]—we may rest assured that G-d will also forgive us and love us. Needless to say, if we offended anybody in the course of the day. we must make amends and obtain the personal forgiveness of the offended party, and no amount of prayer to G-d can bring us forgiveness until we have first obtained forgiveness from the person we offended.[3a]

Having said the prayer "Master of the Universe," we continue with the prayer of *Hashkivenu*:

> *Grant us, O our Father, to lie down in peace, and enable us, O our King, to rise up to a good and peaceful life....*

This prayer is also said during the Evening Service (*Maariv*), and we discussed it at some length in that connection.[4]

Then comes the familiar prayer of the *Shema*.[5] We say all three portions of it. It is the central prayer, and it gives the prayer of *Keriath Shema she'al ha-Mittah* its name.

It is particularly important to recite all three sections of the Shema before going to bed, if there is a doubt as to whether the Shema of the Evening Prayer had been recited at the proper time —after nightfall. For sometimes, especially in the long summer days, some people recite the Evening Prayer before dark, in which case they have to recite the Shema over again after nightfall. But, in any case, it is customary to recite *all* the Shema in the prayer before retiring to bed.[6]

---

1 Lev. 19:17.
2 Lev. 19:18.
3 Ibid.
3a This prayer is omitted on Shabbos and on Yom Tov.
4 See p. 269.
5 See pp. 152 ff.
6 Berachoth 4b.

Several selected passages from the Holy Scriptures follow, beginning with "Let the pious exult in glory, let them chant upon their beds; the high praises of G-d in their mouth, and a double-edged sword in their hand."[7]

Our Sages, referring to this passage, declared that "he who reads the Shema before retiring to bed is as though he were protected by a 'double-edged sword.' "[8]
In the same spirit follow the next verses:

> Behold Solomon's bed—three-score valiant men surround it, of the valiant men of Israel. They all hold swords, they are expert in war; every man with his sword at his hip, because of the fear in the night."[9]

According to our Sages, the "valiant men" referred to above are the Sanhedrin and Torah scholars, all expert in the battle for Torah, and thoroughly familiar with all the sixty (three-score) tractates of the Talmud. These are the true protectors of Israel with whom King Solomon surrounded himself.[10]

The two verses quoted above are repeated three times, emphasizing their significance. They are followed by the familiar Priestly blessing, "G-d bless you and keep you," etc,[11] also repeated three times.

Next comes Psalm 91—"He that dwells in the shelter of the Most High," of which the first nine verses are recited.

Our Sages tell us that the great Rabbi Joshua ben Levi, who was one of the outstanding Sages of his time, used to recite this Psalm for protection.[12] This Psalm speaks of great faith in G-d,

---

7 Ps. 149:5-6.
8 Berachoth 5a.
9 Shir Hashirim 3:7-8.
10 Yahel Or, p. 584.
11 See p. 56 f.
12 Shavuoth 15b.

as we find in the verse "He is my refuge and my fortress; my G-d, in Whom I trust."[13] It speaks of the protection and care which G-d shows to the faithful, as "He shall cover you with His pinion (wing), and under His wings shall you take refuge; you shall not be afraid of the terror of the night. . . ."[14] Of course, people who are fortunate enough to live in a free country, such as ours, know nothing of "the terrors of the night." But in olden days, and even nowadays in some countries where Jews are enslaved and persecuted, the night was full of terror and danger. Some people are troubled by another kind of "night terror"—bad dreams and nightmares.

During the day, when a bad thought comes to the mind, it could be more easily pushed aside, for we can get busy with doing something good instead. But resting in bed at night, and especially dreaming, the bad thoughts may come back. All sorts of fancy, strange thoughts and dreams begin to play tricks with our imagination, and as our mind and good sense are asleep, there is nothing to say, "This is silly!" That is why the most fanciful and ridiculous things may appear so real in a dream.[15] But bad thoughts and bad dreams are not good for the soul, which must be pure and holy. The best way to avoid bad thoughts is to think of, and concentrate on, good thoughts just before getting into bed and falling asleep, and this is one of the reasons why we say the Prayer before going to bed, especially the *Shema.* If we think for a moment what a wonderful prayer the *Shema* is, we can see why it is so good for us to say it before going to bed. For, in the *Shema* we declare that G-d is one, that He is the Master of the world. We declare our love for G-d, and we can be certain of G-d's love for us, and feel secure under His protection.[16]

---

[13] Ps. 91:2.
[14] Ps. 91:4-5.
[15] See p. 285 f.
[16] Bamidbar Rabba 12:3.

On days when *Tachnun* is said, the confessional prayer *Ashamnu*[17] is said here. Next follows the famous prayer composed by Rabbi Nehunia ben Hakaneh, who was one of the Sages of the Talmud.[18] It is a holy and mystical prayer composed of seven verses, each containing six words. The initial letters of each three words form a Divine Name, so that there are fourteen such Names in all. It is a prayer that G-d redeem us from Exile, and that He accept the prayer of His people and protect them while they are still in Exile. For the Jewish people are those who declare the Unity of the One G-d; therefore we pray that G-d protect us "as the apple of the eye," and bless and purify us. It is concluded with the additional verse, "Blessed be the name of His glorious kingdom for ever and ever."

Next comes Psalm 51, in which King David expresses in very moving words the feelings of a repentant and remorseful soul.

> *Be gracious unto me, O G-d, in Your kindness; in the abundance of Your mercies wipe away my transgressions. . . . A pure heart create in me, O G-d, and a right spirit renew within me. . . . I will teach transgressors Your ways, and sinners will return unto You. . . . O G-d, open You my lips, and my mouth shall declare Your praise. . . .[18a]*

This Psalm is omitted on Shabbos and on Yom Tov.

Psalm 121 follows next:

> *I lift up mine eyes unto the mountains: From where shall my help come? My help comes from G-d, Who made heaven and earth. . . . Behold, the Guardian of*

---

[17] See p. 186 f.
[18] See also p. 93 f.
[18a] Ps. 51:3, 12, 15, 17.

Israel does neither slumber nor sleep. . . . G-d shall
guard your going out and your coming in, from this
time and for ever.[18b]

A number of selected verses from Scriptures follow, and finally
comes the prayer of "Hammappil"[19]:

Blessed are You . . . Who makes the bands of sleep to
fall upon mine eyes and slumber upon my eyelids. . . .
May it be Your will, O G-d and G-d of my fathers, to
let me lie down in peace and to let me rise up again
unto good life and peace. Let not my thoughts trouble
me, nor evil dreams, nor evil fancies, but let my rest
be perfect before You. . . .

The prayer of *Hammappil* gives us in a few chosen and beautiful words the meaning of this prayer before going to bed. It
begins with blessing G-d for the great gift of sleep. Our Sages say
that nightly sleep is one of the most precious acts of kindness of
G-d to man, from the day He created the first human being.
Rabbi Shimon ben Elazar, for instance, says that the words, "And
behold it was good," refer to sleep, which is a very good thing that
G-d created.[20] It enables us to rest our body and our mind after a
tiring day, so that we get up in the morning refreshed and fully
rested, and can start the new day with new life and strength.
This depends on having a good and restful sleep. That is why we
continue with the prayer that we have a restful night.

The prayer concludes with the blessing:

Blessed are You, O G-d, Who gives light to the whole
world in His glory.

18b Ps. 121:1, 2, 4, 8.
19 Berachoth 60b.
20 Ber. Rabba 9:8.

INDEXES

I. QUOTATIONS AND REFERENCES

II. GENERAL INDEX

INDEX I

QUOTATIONS AND REFERENCES

309

2. MIDRASHIM

GENERAL INDEX

A

Aaron, 55, 122, 191

Abaye, 89

Abba Shaul, 89

Abigail, 45

Abraham, 8, 9, 43, 45, 64-69, 72, 74, 83, 110, 131, 133, 141, 150, 154, 168, 173, 174, 177, 178, 250, 251, 252

Abudraham, 37, 38, 113, 194, 199, 253, 258

Adam (& Eve), 32, 222, 223, 228, 253

Aharon — see *Aaron*

Ahavath HaShem, 65, 68, 151, 152, 156-8, 204, 205, 208, 209, 269, 270, 286

Akedah, 64-70, 72

Akiba, Rabbi, 126, 262

Albo, Rabbi Joseph, 286

Aleinu, 14, 42, 228, 235, 239-248, 254, 256, 257, 271

Aleph-Beth, 126, 127, 145, 169, 192, 201, 235, 305

Al Netilath Yadayim, 18-21, 290

Alshich, Rabbi Mosheh, 284

Altar, 86, 88, 90, 91, 278-280, 282

Amalek, 266

Amen, 47, 235, 297

Amittai, Rabbi, 195

Am Yisrael, 120, 150, 151, 164, 265

Amidah — see *Shemone Esrei*

Amram Gaon, Rav, 11, 12

Amora(im), 97

Angels, 3, 80, 93, 144-148, 184, 185, 188, 205, 217, 251

Animal Soul — see *Soul*

Anshe Knesseth Hagedolah — see *Men of the Great Assembly*

Antiochus, 159

Aramaic, 137, 147, 202-204

Ari, 93, 113, 170, 186, 189, 192, 201, 207, 253

Ark, 111, 112, 215

Arunah The Jebusite, 215

Arvith — see *Ma'ariv*

Asaph, 111, 218, 220

Asham, 95, 96, 106

Ashamnu, 186-188, 305

Asher-Ben-Yechiel (Rosh), 26

Ashrei, 125-7, 254

Attributes, Divine, 4, 9, 19, 20, 63, 66, 76-80, 82, 94, 112, 115, 118, 124, 125, 127, 142, 144, 147, 150, 156, 170, 184, 188-91, 197, 207, 218-220, 222, 223, 226, 228, 236, 242, 250-253, 258, 259, 264, 267

Avishai Ben Tzeruyah, 200

Avodah, 4-6, 8, 9, 84-86, 89-92, 109, 116, 123, 205, 241, 276, 280

B

Baal Shem Tov, 5, 36, 78, 79

Babylon, 10, 11, 130, 137, 173, 282, 283

Bahya, Rabbi, 191, 289

Balaam, 61, 62

Balak, 62

Barcelona, Jews of, 11

Barechu, 63, 136-139, 257

Bar Kochba, 298

Bechor, 95, 96, 102

Belt, Symbolic Meaning of — see *Gartle*

Ben Zoma, 268

316

Jeremiah, 69, 196, 265, 283
Jerusalem, 10, 42, 54, 69, 89, 109,
   111, 178-81, 211, 218, 231, 283,
   297
Jezdegerd II, 70
Joab, 200
Job, 292
Joel, 196
Jose, Rabbi, 125
Joseph, 177, 178, 221
Joseph, Benjamin & Samuel (Com-
   posers of VehuRachum), 195
Joseph Ha-Cohen, Rabbi, 242
Josephia, Rabbi, 195
Joshua, 97, 240, 242, 295
Joshua Ben Levi, Rabbi, 83, 303
Joy, 287, 288
Judah, 89, 177
Judah Halevi, Rabbi, 55
Judah The Prince, Rabbi, 11, 50, 97

K

Kabbalah, 13, 85, 93, 94, 170
Kabbalath Ol, 147, 152-6, 247, 267,
   270
Kaddish, 63, 109, 114, 136, 239, 246,
   254, 256, 257, 271
Kapporeth, 107, 108
Karaites, 108
Kavanah, 3, 8, 84, 153-6, 275-81
Kedushah, 63, 70, 94, 145, 146, 202-
   204, 254, 271. See also *Holy*
Keriath Shema — see *Shema*
Kiddush, 168
Kiddush HaShem, 80, 137, 191, 198,
   207, 241
Kings I, 210, 211
Kodashim Kalim — see *Korban*
Kodshei Kodashim — see *Korban*
Kohanim, 20, 56, 57, 59, 91, 96, 99,
   100, 190, 280
Koheleth, 76
Kohen Gadol, 86, 91, 241
Korah, 87, 216
Korban (oth), 82-85, 88, 90, 94,
   109, 254. See also *Altar*
Kosher, 279, 280

Ketoreth, 82, 85-90, 94, 235, 254
Kuzari, 55
K'zayith, 295

L

Lag B'Omer, 198
Lashon Ha-Kodesh, 213
Lashon-Hara — see *Evil Tongue*
Lechem Hapanim, 91
Leviim, 11, 91, 134, 190, 205, 213
Levush—see *Jaffe, Rabbi Mordechai*
Light and Darkness (Good and
   Bad), 26, 141, 142, 149
Limbs (248 in Body), 170
Loaves' Offering, 95, 121
Lot, 67, 292
Love, 9, 149-153, 156-158, 265, 266,
   301, 302
Lulav, 19, 227
Luria, Rabbi Yitzchak, 12, 13

M

Ma'ariv, 8, 70, 228, 240, 250, 256-
   272, 302
Maaser, 95, 96
Machzor, 11
Machzor Vitri, 12
Maggid of Mezeritch, 12
Maimonides — see *Rambam*
Majesty, Divine — see *Attributes,
   Divine*
Malachi, Prophet, 89
Malchuyoth, 215
Manasseh Ben Israel, Rabbi, 242
Manna, 222, 294, 296
Mar Bar Ravina, 182
Mashiach, 92, 109, 114, 116, 133,
   137, 138, 181, 200, 210, 211, 215,
   217, 218, 223, 225, 245, 284, 286,
   287, 298
Masorah — see *Tradition*
Matzah, 121
Mayim Achronim, 290-293
Melach Sedomith, 290, 291-293
Menachem Mendel of Lubavitch, 284
Men of the Great Assembly, 10, 97,
   117, 137, 173, 179

Poor, 206
Posture, Human, 30, 31
Prague, 13
Prayer — see *Tefilah*
Priestly Blessing, 56, 57. See also
 Kohanim
Prophetesses, 45
Prophets, 97, 120, 223
Psalms — see *Tehillim*
Psalm of the Day, 91, 205-228
Purim, 45, 296.
     Kattan, 198

R

Rabbanan Seburai, 97
Rambam, 2, 12, 60, 279, 286
Rashi, 12, 98, 118, 216, 217, 267,
 284
Rav, 241, 242, 267, 282
ROSH — see *Asher Ben Yechiel*
Redemption, 92, 138, 171, 175, 178,
 200, 225, 267, 268, 284, 285, 295,
 305
Red Sea, 131-133, 171, 178, 204
Re'iyah, 59, 95
Resurrection, 18, 25, 174, 177
Retzeh, 297
Reuben, 177
Reward, 58-60
"Right Hand," 182, 184
River of Fire, 146
Rokeach, 201
Rosh Chodesh, 10, 11, 83, 91, 95,
 179-181, 198, 201, 284, 297, 298
Rosh Hashanah, 11, 180, 181, 186,
 193, 198, 215, 221, 228, 230, 241,
 242, 298

S

Saadia Gaon, Rav, 12, 109
Sabbatical Year — see *Shemittah*
Safra, Rav, 73
Sanctification of G-d's Name — see
 Kiddush HaShem
Sanctuary, 45, 63, 90, 107, 108, 134.
 See also *Beth Hamikdash*

Sanctuary, Inner, 90, 216
Sanhedrin, 298, 303
Sarah, 45
Schneur Zalman of Liadi, Rabbi, 13,
 207, 212, 216, 217, 228
Seder Rav Amram Gaon, 12
Sefer Hachinuch, 281
Sefer Torah, 5
Self-Sacrifice, 153, 158, 159, 241, 242
Selichoth, 186, 189
Selim, Sultan, 242
Semichah (on Korban), 84
Service of Awe,
     Love,
     Mercy — see *Avodah*
Sfardic (Siddur), 113, 186
Shaatnes, 165
Shabbos, 10, 11, 56, 69, 71, 83, 91,
 95, 103, 108, 121, 161, 165, 198,
 201, 213, 223-8, 231, 235, 259,
 284, 297, 298
Shacharith, 8, 186, 189, 191, 240,
 250-3
Shaloh, 133, 282
Shalosh Regalim, 11
Shamash, 166
Shavuoth, 11, 59, 95, 121, 180
Shechinah, 92, 179, 184, 191, 201,
 216, 232, 233, 237
Shefatiah, Rabbi, 195
Shelamim, 95, 96
Shema, 11, 13, 52, 61, 70, 71, 80, 94,
 139, 140, 152-168, 256, 257, 260,
 262, 263, 265.
     She'al Hamittah, 301-306
Shem Hameyuchad — see *Divine
 Name*
Shemini Atzereth, 180, 228
Shemittah, 44
Shemone Esrei, 10, 11, 13, 14, 18,
 122, 139, 172-185, 254, 257, 271,
 296
Shemuel, 241
Sherirah Gaon, Rav, 64
Shevach, 120
Shevat, 198
Shimon Ben Elazar, 306